1 MONTH OF FREE READING

at

www.ForgottenBooks.com

By purchasing this book you are eligible for one month membership to ForgottenBooks.com, giving you unlimited access to our entire collection of over 1,000,000 titles via our web site and mobile apps.

To claim your free month visit:
www.forgottenbooks.com/free620790

* Offer is valid for 45 days from date of purchase. Terms and conditions apply.

ISBN 978-0-267-75352-9
PIBN 10620790

This book is a reproduction of an important historical work. Forgotten Books uses state-of-the-art technology to digitally reconstruct the work, preserving the original format whilst repairing imperfections present in the aged copy. In rare cases, an imperfection in the original, such as a blemish or missing page, may be replicated in our edition. We do, however, repair the vast majority of imperfections successfully; any imperfections that remain are intentionally left to preserve the state of such historical works.

Forgotten Books is a registered trademark of FB &c Ltd.
Copyright © 2018 FB &c Ltd.
FB &c Ltd, Dalton House, 60 Windsor Avenue, London, SW19 2RR.
Company number 08720141. Registered in England and Wales.

For support please visit www.forgottenbooks.com

THE FATHERS OF THE DESERT

TRANSLATED FROM THE GERMAN OF
THE COUNTESS HAHN-HAHN

By

EMILY F. BOWDEN

*With a Chapter on The Spiritual Life of
the first Six Centuries*

By

JOHN BERNARD DALGAIRNS
(Priest of the Oratory)

In Two Volumes: Volume II

BURNS AND OATES
28 ORCHARD STREET
LONDON W

SERAPION THE SINDONITE

"He who is joined to the Lord, is one spirit."—1 Cor. vi, 17

THIS wonderful anchorite had no other hermitage for many years but his love of God. His body was the cell in which his soul dwelt, and wherever the body went the soul remained undisturbed, and suffered nothing to interrupt its spiritual recollection and its union with God. Serapion was an Egyptian, and the ascetic tastes which early developed themselves in him led him to the great and holy men of the desert, with whom he underwent a severe probation. He brought his body and soul into subjection by austere mortification of the senses and the practice of obedience. He became thereby so docile to the inspirations of the Holy Ghost, that he was moved by grace as easily and surely as a boat is guided by the rudder. His penances were so great that they appeared superhuman, and gained for him the name of "the impassible," because no one could conceive that a man who was capable of suffering could undergo so much. He was also called the Sindonite, from the piece of linen which formed his only garment. Unbroken contemplation of the Holy Scriptures, together with his spiritual and bodily mortifications, grounded him securely in humility and in the spirit of penance. Therefore, the guides of his interior life made no opposition when he formed the resolution of exchanging his cell for the world, and of living the life of an anchorite in the midst of other men.

Serapion in his desire of attempting to save souls from the world's abyss, came to the voluptuous city of Corinth, where the people were still frivolous, notwithstanding the Epistles of St Paul to them, and where there were singers and actors in abundance. A heathen juggler who with his whole family lived on the boards of the theatre filled Serapion's heart with the deepest compassion. He had no means of getting near these unhappy people but by selling himself to them as a slave, and so entering their service, and seeking by his life and his love to win them to the Gospel. He sealed up and kept the twenty florins which he received as his price. He paid no attention to the dissolute, unbridled life, which was led in this house, and which would have been a mortal grief to one less perfect than he. A noble-hearted man who sees other men drowning in a muddy pond and longs to save them, does not consider the filthiness of the water, but precipitates himself into it; in like manner did Serapion act for the sake of these souls in danger. He punctually fulfilled the lowest offices, carried water, washed his master's feet, and was never discontented nor weary of the most repulsive labour, but slept little and fasted much. Absorbed in the contemplation of heavenly things, he kept almost continual silence; and when he did speak, there flowed from his lips celestial wisdom, which filled the poor juggler, first with amazement, then with admiration, and finally with love. He treated his wonderful servant with respect, listened more and more to his admonitions, asked his advice, and at length renounced his miserable profession, and was converted to Christianity. His family followed his example. Then they all looked upon their slave with very different eyes, and the more pious they became the more highly they prized him. After some time Serapion's master said to him, " My brother, because thou hast delivered us from the disgraceful slavery of heathenism, and hast redeemed us from the world and from sin, I will free thee from my service, and let thee live where and how thou pleasest." Serapion answered, "Now that God has given you the grace to recognise the truth and to enter upon the right road to salvation, I can leave you with comfort, and go in search of other souls to save." And he related to them how he was an Egyptian monk, and a free man; and how, after the example of the Son of God, who took upon Himself the form of a servant to free the world from the bondage of sin, he had of his own will become their slave out of love for their souls. Then they burst into tears, and implored him to remain with them as their lord and father But Serapion could be detained no longer, and gave them back the price they had paid for him. "Oh! keep this money which has helped to save us," exclaimed they, weeping, "or distribute it amongst the poor." "It belongs to you and not to me," said Serapion, "for I am a poor monk, who can neither possess nor give away anything." And he took an affectionate leave of them.

Divine Providence guided him to Lacedæmon to a childless widow, who was ill, and in extreme want. He knew not how to help her, yet he could not leave her in such misery. He heard that a distinguished man of that town, who was infected by the Manichean heresy, but otherwise upright, was in want of an active servant. He went immediately to him, sold himself to him, gave the proceeds to the poor widow, and managed so that within the course of two years, his master's family and whole household returned to the Catholic faith. This master also gave his holy slave his liberty out of gratitude, clothed him in a good coat and cloak, and gave him a book of the Gospels as well. Serapion joyfully departed; he had never before been so well provided for. He had indeed never been in such want of it before, for the winter was cold in the mountains of Lacedæmon. As he was wandering on, peacefully awaiting God's guidance, he met a poor half-naked man. Quickly Serapion pulled off his cloak and gave it to the beggar, who wrapped himself comfortably in it. He went a little farther, and found an old man lying in the road nearly frozen with cold. He did not hesitate to take off his coat and cover him with it, and went his way in his linen garment only. In the evening he met some compassionate people who gave him shelter; and when they asked him, who could have so robbed him, Serapion pointed to the book of the Gospels, and said, "It was this book that did it." But even that book did not long remain in his possession. In the neighbouring town he sold it for the benefit of a family who had fallen into great distress. It was bought by an ecclesiastic, who gently rebuked Serapion for parting with such a treasure. He answered humbly, "You will hardly believe it, my father, but it seemed to me as if the Gospel was constantly crying out to me, 'Go, sell all that thou hast and give to the poor.' Now, this very book was all that I had, and therefore I sold it."

In Athens there were many philosophers, but very few charitable people. Serapion was there three days without receiving a mouthful of bread. Then he joined some people who were assembled in a public place, and told them that since he had left his native country of Egypt, he had fallen into the hands of a hard usurer, who tormented him without ceasing. Every one was willing to help him if he would only name the usurer. "It is hunger," said Serapion. A philosopher who was passing by contemptuously threw him a piece of silver. Serapion humbly picked up the money and took it to the nearest baker's shop, where he received a single loaf, and then contentedly left the city. The money was brought back to the philosopher, with the exception of the halfpenny the loaf had cost, and he then confessed that the poor stranger was further advanced in contempt of the world than he.

From Greece Serapion sailed to Rome. As he ate nothing whatever in the first days of the voyage, the other passengers thought he suffered from seasickness, and did not trouble themselves at all about him. At last on the fifth day, some one said to him, "Why dost thou not take any nourishment?" Serapion answered, "Because I have none, nor have I any money wherewith to buy even a bit of bread." The people were all amazed at such mortification. One of the sailors alone exclaimed, "You rogue! if you have no money, how can you pay for your passage?" "I cannot pay for it, it is true," replied Serapion, gently, "but if you positively will not give me a free passage, make for the nearest coast and set me ashore there." "No," said the captain, "I will not do that, for it would delay us, and wind and weather have never before been so favourable to us as they are this voyage." The passengers then vied with each other in supplying Serapion with food and drink, which he received with the greatest gratitude, and thus arrived safely at Rome.

His first care was to visit with great devotion the tombs of the holy Apostles Peter and Paul, and those of the holy martyrs. His second was to serve his neighbour, and that in his own peculiar manner, which he had learnt from his Divine Redeemer Himself—he made himself a servant in order to save souls. Twice more he practised this heroic deed of love, twice more he became the slave of men, who by their conduct would have been repulsive to his natural feelings, but whom he loved because he looked upon them with the eye of faith, and saw a trace of the divine image still remaining in them. And God, who made Himself the slave of sinful men for their redemption, assisted Serapion by His grace, so that twice men were converted and saved who seemed ready to fall into everlasting perdition. They could not withstand such self-sacrifice and humility, such obedience, and such love. For thirty years Serapion fulfilled his task, which was to imitate this feature in the life of the Incarnate God. Then he returned to the desert, his home, where he soon found death, and through death eternal and blessed liberty in return for a short slavery. When the Patriarch of Alexandria, St John the Almoner, read the history of Serapion's life, he called his steward, and said, with many tears,—" How miserable it would be in us to pride ourselves on giving our goods to the poor! This holy Serapion found means to give himself to them, and that not once but many times."

ST. ARSENIUS.

"He retired into the desert and prayed."—St. Luke v. 16.

It created no surprise in those days, although it now appears strange to us, to see men follow the frequent injunction of the Apostle St. Paul, and break all worldly ties in order to be more perfectly united to Christ. The great and important business of sanctification was not then one among a thousand affairs, but it was the chief occupation of the Christian's life. Christians in name and appearance only, Arians and other heretics whose false doctrine of the Incarnation of God swept away the whole of Christianity; and heathens whose philosophy knew nothing of the fall, of redemption, or of the sanctification of man born again in Christ; these indeed were all inclined to gainsay a life of Christian asceticism, because in the former the spirit of Christianity was too feeble, and in the latter materialism was too strong for them to accept in the light of faith the doctrine of renunciation.

But the genuine Christians were then in the fervour of their first love; and as love exacts a complete renouncement, they kept before their eyes the example of this renouncement and of the holiness inseparably bound up with it; namely, the Saviour dying on the Cross for the love of sinners, between Mary and John on Calvary. This was done by men of the most opposite characters, by great and small, learned and simple, sinners and saints, old men, and tender youths alike. Whomsoever Christ called, the same followed Him, no matter whither; in the bloody circus, in the peaceful cloister, on the top of pillars, in the palace of the emperors, in the barren desert, they broke all ties which were inconsistent with the call of Christ.

The Emperor Theodosius the Great sought a tutor for his sons Arcadius and Honorius, and begged the Emperor Gratian in Rome to send to Constantinople a person to whom he could intrust the youths. At that time Arsenins was deacon of the Roman Church, a man of prayer, of profound study, and of holy works. Although he was related to the most noble families of Rome, he and his pious sister lived in the greatest retirement. Pope Damasus, to whom the Emperor Gratian had referred the weighty matter, cast his eyes upon Arsenius, for in him was found faith and learning, wisdom and prudence, all that could qualify him to be the tutor of the youthful Cæsars. Arsenius obeyed the successor of the Prince of the Apostles, and leaving his solitude, he renounced his desire of total separation from the world and its dangers, and went to Constantinople. Theodosius knew his worth; he gave him the rank of senator, with a magnificent residence, and a numerous retinue, and made him not only the teacher of his sons, but also their godfather, desiring that they should honour him as their second father. Arsenius remained always humble, even outwardly. When he gave instructions to the young emperors, he stood while they sat down. Theodosius once visited them during their lesson hours, and blamed his sons for this as being extremely disrespectful, and pressed Arsenius to take a seat also. Arsenius was supremely indifferent to all these honours, for his mind was too securely fixed on heaven to be drawn aside by gold or purple. He performed his laborious and unthankful task with the greatest zeal and love. Whilst he was using all his endeavours to train his pupils to be worthy to wear a crown, he could not but see how they listened to the courtly flatterers that surrounded them, and how they gave themselves up to that indolence and effeminacy which made them so unlike their noble father, and which afterwards rendered their reign so pernicious. Nevertheless, Arsenius did not lose courage, but spared neither instructions nor warnings, neither the gentleness nor the severity of love. Arcadius once committed such a great fault that Arsenius judged a severe chastisement necessary. Instead of entering into himself, the young prince was furious with anger, and began to hate and persecute his tutor, being spurred on and encouraged by those who were envious of Arsenius; and, finally, he charged an officer of his body-guard to deliver him, at all costs, from this rigid supervision. Fortunately the officer did not consider in Arcadius, as so many others did, the future emperor, into whose favour he might have wished to ingratiate himself, but he feared Theodosius, and respected Arsenius. Therefore he disclosed the affair to the latter, and advised him to withdraw secretly from Constantinople, as his life was in danger, and all hope of his influencing Arcadius for good was at an end on account of the hatred which he bore him. Arsenius betook himself to prayer to obtain light to discern the will of God, and he heard a voice which said to him, " Fly from all men, Arsenius, be silent, and at peace, and thou shalt save thy soul." These words were in such perfect accordance with the longing for complete solitude which he had long perceived and struggled with in his soul, that he believed the time had come which God in His mercy had appointed for him to dedicate himself henceforward to a severe and ascetic life. He left the imperial palace, went on board a ship bound for Alexandria, which lay in the harbour, and sailed from thence, not so much to save his life as to sacrifice it. All the grandeur of the luxurious and populous city of Alexandria was to him as nothing. He passed on to the desert of Scete. There, in a cavern, he once more prayed with great fervour to know the will of God ; and again he heard a voice in prayer which said: " Arsenius, fly from men, keep silence, be at peace, and thou shalt save thy soul."

Whoever wished to join a community of anchorites or monks had first to present himself to the superior, and beg for his permission to be allowed to serve God under the direction of the experienced and aged, who were called out of respect the fathers, or the ancient fathers. This act of submission was particularly necessary amongst the anchorites. If each one had settled in the desert at his own pleasure, without spiritual direction and supervision, it would soon have been peopled by savage and independent hordes. But humility and obedience united the individuals into one holy family of brethren. In compliance with this rule, Arsenius also presented himself at once before the abbot Pastor who had, at that time, the spiritual direction of those who dwelt in the desert of Scete. Arsenius was already forty years old, and he came from a most brilliant position in the world; from the imperial court of Byzantium. The abbot Pastor intrusted him to the care of a brother called John the Dwarf, who was remarkably pious and spiritual, although he was still very young. His office was to put the novices to the proof by various mortifications, and to discover how much they were inclined to penance; and above all, whether they were capable of the ascetic life. John therefore added Arsenius to the number of his disciples. In the evening, when they assembled to take their scanty meal, and the brethren all took their wonted places, John did not show Arsenius to any place at all, but left him standing in their midst without noticing his presence. This slight was followed by another. John contemptuously took up a piece of bread, threw it at the feet of Arsenius, and sharply said, "Eat if thou hast a mind." Arsenius knelt down and ate the bread upon his knees. The brethren gazed upon him with admiration, and John, transported with joy, exclaimed, "This man is fit for the hermit's life. Oh, my brethren, pray that the blessing of God may be upon him and upon us!" From that moment, till his last hour, Arsenius buried himself in solitude with God. He often asked himself these questions: "Arsenius, wherefore hast thou left the world? wherefore hast thou come hither?"

A great ascetic of later times, St. Bernard, put before himself over and over again the same question, in order, like Arsenius, to excite himself to perseverance. He asserted that the chief duty of a monk consists in detaching himself from the earth and from all temporal concerns without exception; in weeping in the spirit of contrition over all his faults and infirmities, and in waiting with desire for a glorious eternity. Therefore Arsenius sought to bury himself with all his talents and learning in his mountain cell, striving to put to death the earthly man, and thereby to attain to union with God. The Emperor Theodosius was sorely grieved at the disappearance of Arsenius. He caused him to be sought for everywhere, in the cloisters and deserts. But the great emperor died in the year 395, and his sons divided the crown, which he had worn, but which was, nevertheless, too heavy for them both.

The search for Arsenius was not, however, fruitless. Arcadius, who now sat on the throne of Constantinople, learnt the abode of his holy tutor, and wrote to him by a special messenger to beg pardon for his former offences, and to recommend himself to his prayers, and offered to make over to him all the revenue of the Egyptian taxes, that he might spend them as he thought fit, in favour of the poor, the hermits, the churches, and the monasteries, because the care of the poor would be safest in his hands. Arsenius did not accept this magnificent alms, but only wrote in answer: "May God forgive us all our sins! I cannot have anything to do with the distribution of the money, because I look upon myself as one already dead." He remembered the warning of that heavenly voice which had so clearly pointed out his path to him. He was firmly resolved to follow it, and to remove all occasions of distraction however good they might seem. In his eyes no worldly affair was worth a single thought. He occupied himself solely with death, and in preparing his soul for the judgment of God. At first he retained unwittingly many little habits he had brought with him out of the world; for example, he crossed his legs one over another when he sat down, or he placed one foot on his knee. But in the assemblies of the monks, position, movements, and demeanour were all regulated in order to accustom them, even exteriorly, to a certain discipline. Yet all were unwilling to draw his attention to this little fault, because they were filled with the greatest respect for his sublime penance. The wise abbot Pastor adopted the expedient of once sitting himself in an assembly with his foot upon his knee, and thereby drawing upon himself a rebuke from an aged solitary. Arsenius understood the admonition, and took pains thenceforward to combat little worldly habits no less than greater ones. In the world he had been splendidly clothed, now he wore the coarsest and most inconvenient habit. In the world he had taken great pleasure in intellectual conversation; here he observed silence more rigidly than any, and for that reason he chose a cell which was an hour's journey more distant than any of the others. In the world his keen and penetrating intellect found joy in all sciences, and he studied even the profane ones with deep interest; now he denied his mind all recreation, and studied nothing but the knowledge, alas! too sadly neglected, of the Four Last Things. In the world he was very fond of perfumes, which it was then the custom to burn in rooms, and to place among garments; but now he kept the water in which he soaked palm-leaves for a whole year without changing it, only adding a little fresh water to it when required. When some of the fathers asked him why he did not throw away such offensive water, he replied, "To mortify my sense of smell, which was formerly so much indulged." He accustomed himself with difficulty to the universal occupation of the Egyptian hermits, that of weaving mats. The more laborious he found this work the more earnestly did he devote himself to it, but not so much as to let it disturb his heavenly contemplation. Through this latter the merciful love of God, and the sinful ingratitude of men, were so deeply impressed upon his soul that his eyes were always bathed in tears of love and sorrow, and this holy contrition lasted to the end of his long life, and established him securely in humility, the foundation of perfection. The hermits of Scete once received a small present of figs, but they were so few that the abbot did not like to send so contemptible a gift to Arsenius. He learnt this from some of the solitaries, who supplied him with his scanty necessaries because of his extreme unwillingness to leave his cell for the sake of earthly things. But after that he left off attending the Offices of the church, and when the brethren came to visit him, supposing him to be ill, he said to them; "You have expelled me from your community by considering me unworthy to share in the blessing which the good God sent to you." Extremely edified by the humility which esteemed the gifts of God so highly, and himself so lightly, the priest of the community hurried to him, brought him a few figs, and conducted him to the church. In church he always sought a place behind a column, where he could see no one, and be out of sight of all, so greatly did he fear every occasion of distraction. The abbot Marcus once asked him, "Wherefore dost thou avoid thy brethren?" "God knows how I love them," answered Arsenius, "but I cannot be with God and men at the same time, and it is not lawful for me to leave Him in order to join myself to them. I must endeavour to keep myself in company with the heavenly hosts, in constant and unremitting application of my will to God, and amongst men it is always divided."

Intercourse with mankind always filled him with fear, and he was in the habit of saying, "Silence has never given me any regret; conversation always a little." Hence he could never be persuaded to answer letters in writing, nor even to explain the Holy Scriptures, for which he was so admirably fitted by talent, prayer, and enlightenment, for he feared not only distractions, but also vanity and self-complacency. He often repeated, "All our mental culture does not help us Romans in the progress of virtue, for the glory of knowledge easil fills the heart with pride. On the other hand, ythese unlearned Egyptians have advanced along the road to perfection by labour and simplicity." Once he asked advice from a very simple and aged Egyptian solitary, and another who was listening said, in amazement, "Father Arsenius, thou art versed in all the knowledge of the Greeks and Romans, and dost thou ask counsel from this uneducated old man?" "Yes," answered the holy man; "it is true that I know the sciences of the Greeks and Romans, but, unfortunately, I have not yet learnt this old man's alphabet." Theophilus, archbishop of Alexandria, once visited him with an eminent magistrate, and begged him to say something edifying to them. Arsenius replied that he was much too sinful. After a short silence, he added: "However, if you will promise to take my advice, I will willingly say a few words." The two visitors joyfully consented, and he said: "If you hear that the poor sinner Arsenius is here or is there, do not go to see him." The same archbishop wished on another occasion to speak with him, but knowing already by experience his exceeding love for solitude, he sent first to ask him if entrance into his cell was permitted. Arsenius gave this answer to the messenger: "If the archbishop comes I will certainly open my cell to him; and not only to him, but to all the world; and then I will depart from it myself." When this declaration was reported to the archbishop, he said: "It is better not to go than to drive him away."

The younger solitaries, Daniel, Zoylas, and Alexander, who rendered him their services, were thus brought into intimate connexion with him, and they rejoiced in observing his holy demeanour, and in the teachings which he gave them at times. One of the youths complained that although he knew the Holy Scriptures by heart, and would like to contemplate them, he did not properly understand their deep meaning, and therefore remained lukewarm. "Continue, nevertheless, your holy contemplation, my son," said Arsenius. "The holy abbot Pastor used to say: The snake-charmers understand not the force of the words with which they capture the snakes; but the snakes understand and obey them. Even if we ourselves do not understand the full meaning of the holy writings, the ancient serpent acknowledges their power when we occupy ourselves therewith, and the divine words which the Holy Ghost has spoken to us through the prophets and apostles drive him far from us." He said once to Daniel, "An ancient father gave me this piece of good advice: Be diligent in directing thy interior works by the will of God, and they will help thee to conquer the evil desires of the exterior man." Another time he said, "If we seek the Lord God we shall find Him, and if we keep Him He will remain with us." Arsenius attained to this union with God by the direction of all his powers to this sublime end, and he found strength for his fifty years of struggle in fervent, constant, and humble prayer, joined with mortification of the senses. His disciples often heard him in his cell weeping and exclaiming, "O Lord, forsake me not, although I have hitherto been so faithless. Give me the grace at length to begin to serve thee." He said that one hour's sleep should suffice for a monk, and he allowed himself still less. When he had spent the night in prayer, and was overpowered by fatigue towards morning, he said to sleep, "Come hither, thou bad fellow," and after sleeping a little while went quickly back to his work. Every Saturday evening, as the sun sank behind him, he began to pray with his hands lifted up towards heaven, and he never arose from his prayer till the rising sun shone upon his face early on Sunday morning.

The example he set of sanctity and humility gained him unlimited obedience on the part of his disciples. Arsenius said one day to Alexander— "As soon as thou hast finished thy palm-weaving to-morrow, come to me, and we will take our meal together. But if strangers visit thee, eat with them, and do not come at all to me." At that time Alexander was quite unpractised in weaving palms, though he tried to do his work as well as he could. He was not nearly ready, therefore, at the time for eating, and Arsenius ate alone, in the supposition that some strangers had required Alexander's hospitality. When the latter came to him late in the evening, he immediately asked if such had not been the case. Alexander said no. "Why, then, didst thou not come sooner?" said Arsenius. "My father," replied Alexander, "thou toldest me to come when I had finished my palms. My store was large. I have only just now finished it, therefore I did not dare to come sooner." Arsenius was delighted with such perfect obedience, but instead of expressing his joy, he said, "Learn to work quicker, and then thou wilt have time to recite psalms, to worship God in other ways, and to eat, otherwise thou wilt be starved in body and soul." But reproofs and severity only bound the pious youth more firmly to Arsenius, for by them he measured the holy love of his teacher and his own imperfection.

Arsenius also practised perfect obedience in a way that was most painful to him. He once became so seriously ill that the priest who had charge of the spiritual necessities of the hermits of Scete thought good to cause him to be brought into the vicinity of the church, and into a dwelling which could afford a few comforts. The sufferer was laid upon some skins of wild beasts, with a small pillow, and these little indulgences were to him more unbearable than his dreadful pains, but he submitted himself with resignation to the arrangement. An aged solitary visited him, and angrily exclaimed, "Is it really Father Arsenius that I see in this comfortable bed?" The sick man was silent, but the priest took up the discourse, and said, "What was your rank in the world?" "I was a shepherd," answered the solitary. "And how did you gain your livelihood?" "With the greatest difficulty." "And how do you live now?" "Much better and more easily." "See, then," said the priest, "it is exactly the reverse with Arsenius. In the world he was, as it were, the father of the Cæsars. He had a hundred servants, clad in silk, and magnificent apartments with carpets and sofas. Here he renounces all that luxury to be poor and suffering, while you are now better off than you were in the world. And yet you take scandal at his couch." The aged anchorite threw himself on his knees, and exclaimed, "Forgive me, my father; for I have sinned. Arsenius is on the right road to humility." He who was formerly so richly clothed, was now so poor that his only possession was his monastic habit. During his illness he had to wear a linen shirt. He did not possess one, and having money given him to buy one, he said, ' My God, I thank Thee for the grace of being permitted to receive an alms in Thy Name.'. At that time a messenger was sent to him from Rome, to bring him the will of one of his relations, a rich senator, who had made him heir to all his property. He asked when his cousin had died, and the messenger said it was three months ago. " Then I cannot inherit

anything from him," said Arsenius, "because I died long before him;" and nothing could induce him to accept the inheritance. After his recovery ne returned with joy to his poor cell, which was dearer to him than a paradise, and he left it still more seldom than before. He also advised all the other anchorites to keep as much as possible at a distance from him, and he repeated to them the words he had once heard in prayer, which were so deeply impressed upon his heart, " Fly, remain silent and in peace, and thou shalt save thy soul."
' But, my father," said a young monk, " wherefore dost thou avoid the conversation of thy brethren? It would all be of God." " I had rather listen to what God says in the interior of my heart than to what others say of Him," was the answer of Arsenius.

When he was advanced in age, God sent him a trial which was the hardest to him of all. The torrent of the migration of nations continued to spread ever wider desolation over the ancient Roman empire. The northern barbarians poured irresistibly across the frontiers, first into the provinces, then to Rome, and beyond Rome to the shores of the Mediterranean Sea. Their devastating scourge fell also upon the Roman provinces of Africa. Genseric, king of the Vandals, conquered Carthage, and founded a kingdom there. During these tribulations St. Augustine, bishop of Hippo, departed from the earth. The African deserts no longer offered a safe refuge from the hardy barbarian tribes of the north, who everywhere drove away the inhabitants. They fled into the deserts, and the savage Mazices followed them, carrying fire and sword even into the solitude of Scete, and scared away the peaceful anchorites. Arsenius departed weeping, and exclaimed, " Woe unto us! the world has lost the city of Rome, and we monks the desert of Scete." He directed his steps to a distant region between the Egyptian Babylon (now Cairo) and the ancient royal city of Memphis, and lived there ten years. But the neighbourhood of the great cities brought disturbance and molestation, and he therefore fled into Lower Egypt to a marshy wilderness, where he increased still more all the austerities he had practised for fifty years; and, as if he were a young beginner in asceticism, he daily asked himself the same question, "Arsenius, wherefore didst thou come hither?"

About this time a noble Roman lady left her home, and travelled to Egypt to refresh and strengthen her soul in the spirit of Christianity, which there brought forth such glorious blossoms of perfection that their perfume filled all the lands of the East and the West. The sublime holiness of her countryman, Arsenius, attracted the noble Roman lady above all others. She rejoiced to learn from the patriarch of Alexandria that he was living in the neighbourhood, and she begged the archbishop to obtain her an interview. But Arsenius, who had been unwilling formerly to receive the patriarch himself, flatly refused this request, and the astonished lady thought it advisable to visit him without any more ceremony. She went into the desert, and waited there a long time, till he returned from a visit to a sick brother. He came at last, a thin, tall man, somewhat bent with the weight of his ninety-two years, but majestic in his walk and carriage, with a long snow-white beard, with beautiful and attractive eyes bathed in tears, and with that sweetness of countenance which betokens victory over the earthly man. She thought she beheld an angel, or one of the prophets of olden time. The celestial beauty of his exterior sprang from the peace of his soul, which reposed in unbroken union with God by means of prayer; and this beauty can never be shared by the sensual man. She hurried to meet him; and, falling at his feet, sought to express her veneration for him. Arsenius raised her up immediately, and said, with great gravity, "If you insist on seeing me, look at me as much as you like, only send no more Roman ladies across the sea to look upon the aged Arsenius. I wonder, moreover, very much at your leaving your home and your family to come to Egypt to annoy the solitaries." The lady, in the greatest confusion, said that she would certainly dissuade all Roman ladies from undertaking this journey, but she entreated Arsenius to remember her in prayer before God. "I will, indeed, pray God to blot out the recollection of you from my memory," Arsenius answered, and retreated to his cell. The lady returned in haste to Alexandria. Consternation, fear, and sorrow threw her into a violent fever, and the patriarch had the greatest difficulty in consoling her, and making her perceive that Arsenius had shown in his answer greater severity to himself than to her.

Arsenius, on his part, was full of fear because Lower Egypt was directly in the line of the pilgrimage from Rome to the Oriental ascetics. These journeys were becoming more and more common amongst devout people, and Arsenius fled once more to his cell at Memphis. On the road thither he met a Moorish maiden, who out of curiosity seized hold of his coarse habit. He refused to allow it, and said that it was not proper to touch the garment of a monk, whereupon the Moorish girl, nothing daunted, said to him, "Wherefore dost thou not remain in thy cloister, as thou art a monk?" These words went to his heart. He made still more haste to reach his solitude, and said to his disciples, "The dove found no branch whereon to rest, and returned to Noe's ark." At length, at the age of ninety-five, the strength of this giant in spirit was exhausted, and he felt his last hour approach. He made only one request to his disciples, that they would pay him no honour after his death; but on the contrary, that they would remember him in their prayers as the greatest of poor sinners. Then exceeding fear fell upon him. "Is it possible, my father, that thou dost fear death?" asked his sorrowful disciples. "Certainly, I fear death," said the holy old man, "and I can truly say that this fear has not left me for a single instant as long as I have been a monk." But this fear diminished as his end drew near. At last it gave place to a deep and holy calm, and he fell asleep in the peace of the Lord. When the patriarch Theophilus was informed of his decease, he exclaimed, "O happy Arsenius, who hast always had thy last end before thine eyes!" And the ancient father, Pœmen, said with tears, "O blessed Arsenius, who didst weep over thyself as long as thou wert upon earth! Whoso does not weep here, will weep for ever in the next life."

THE BLESSED MOSES.

"The sins of my youth do not remember, O Lord."—Ps. xxiv.

THE wild and depraved life which Moses led until his fortieth year, made his conversion a miracle of grace. The history of it was related to Palladius by all the anchorites of Scete. His native country was Abyssinia, or, as it was then called, Ethiopia. His skin was black, and his passions burnt as hotly as the sun of those lands. In condition he was a slave, and he belonged to a master who filled some public office. He was guilty of so many thefts and infidelities, that he often brought severe punishments upon himself. But instead of improving, his wickedness and insubordination increased. H killed another slave in a quarrel, and partly because he feared for his life, partly because slavery was wearisome to him, he fled from his home, collected other bad characters about him, and with their aid lived by highway robbery for fifteen years. His immense bodily strength and his boldness gained for him the distinction of becoming captain of this band. They roved about in all directions, robbing and plundering, carrying terror everywhere, and were yet so ingenious in concealing themselves in various and scattered lurking-places that they escaped every search that was made for them. Moses was once deterred from committing a robbery by the barking of a shepherd's dog. He determined to revenge himself for this upon the dog's master, and learned that he was a shepherd who watched his flocks on the opposite b of the Nile. He therefore stripped off his clothes, wrapp them round his head like a turban, stuck hisedpear through them and swam across the Nile, as the Nubians do at the present day. But the poor shepherd having had timely warning of the threatened vengeance, had hidden himself, and in lieu of the shepherd, Moses revenged himself upon the flock, by killing all the sheep except four of the strongest rams, which he bound together, and swimming back with them, sold them in the nearest village. No one dared to lay hands upon him, and he escaped safely to his companions.

We know not how it happened that a ray of grace penetrated into this nature, darkened as it was by the fiercest passions, or how a soul so remote from God's kingdom determined upon winning it. God, who wills not the death of a sinner but his conversion, did not permit Moses to perish in his sins. He suddenly glanced over his profligate life, shuddered at himself, and began upon the spot the arduous task of converting himself to God. It was inexpressibly difficult to him, for his untamed passions and his long habits of sin kept him, as it seemed to him, insuperably chained to evil. In order to avoid, at least, all dangerous occasions of sin, Moses fled to a mountain on the Lybian boundary of the desert of Scete, begged the ancient father Isidore, who was the priest of those anchorites, to have pity upon his soul, and then began his combat, which was difficult beyond all belief. How long had an Antony, a Pachomius, a Hilarion, had to struggle, who from their childhood upwards had aimed at higher things, and had never known the desire to sin! But Moses had been young and grown old in sin, and had been wholly given up to it. But he was not to be deterred, for he had now learned to know God, in Whom the Apostle St. Paul trusted, when he said, "I can do all things in Him who strengtheneth me." A hundred times Moses was strongly tempted to abandon the penitential life of the desert and return to the world, and each time he overcame the temptation. But he hastened to the abbot Isidore, and complained to him of his trial. The old man comforted him thus: "Fear not, my brother, these attacks of the enemy; he knows that thou art a beginner, and he therefore seeks to inspire thee with disgust towards the desert. Listen not to him, stay peacefully in thy cell, and the enemy will depart." Working, fasting, and praying he remained in the narrow cavern which served him for a cell. He divided his day into fifty parts, and at the close of each part he recited a certain number of psalms, while he also wove mats and twisted ropes. His daily nourishment consisted of twelve ounces of dry bread and one draught of water. He hoped in this way to subdue his fondness for eating and drinking, and his roving disposition, and, by reciting psalms, to occupy his memory and curb his imagination. But the wicked one would not surrender his prey so easily. He attacked the penitent with alluring images and deceptive representations, and plunged him into fearful anguish, for it was only with his higher will that he could close his mind against these seductive delusions. The earthly man was in compact with them against his better will, and in spite of prayer, labour, and fasting he could not entirely overcome them. His wearing restlessness drove him once more to Isidore, and the holy old man gave this answer to his complaints, "Thou hast not defended thy mind with all thy strength against these picturings of thy sinful past, my brother. From long habit thou hast allowed them to enter, and therefore they have mastered thy thoughts. Combat them more vigorously than heretofore. They give thee no rest; very well: pay like with like, never give them rest enough to find footing in thee. Watch and pray night and day." Moses followed literally the advice of the experienced and holy man. For six years he was never content with devoting the whole day to uninterrupted prayer, but when night set in, he placed himself in the middle of his cell, and with uplifted hands he continued to call on God and to praise Him. For fear of falling asleep from fatigue, he never once ventured to kneel down at his prayers. Sometimes he slept a little towards morning, leaning against the wall. Many nights he never closed his eyes. He was determined to overcome his earthly nature, which sought to enslave him and separate him from God. But he did not as yet always succeed. He made known all his struggles and sufferings to St. Isidore, who felt great pity and sympathy for him, and who once said to him, "Thou dost fight thy wicked enemy too violently; that enrages him. Observe moderation, my brother. The spiritual combat must not be carried on too eagerly." Moses replied, " My father, let me fight as best I may ; for I shall never find any rest till I have conquered all that keeps me back from union with God."

Instead, therefore, of abating his austerities, he invented new ones. In the night time he went to the cells of the sick and aged anchorites, and, secretly taking their empty water-jars, drew water to fill them, and brought them back again. This was an immense exertion for a man nearly worn out with fasting, watching, labour, and mental torture, for the only drinkable water was 5000 paces distant from many of the cells. But Moses rigorously pursued his end, for he was not afraid of succumbing to bodily, but to spiritual weakness. When he was one evening carrying a jar full of water to the cell of an aged solitary, he felt himself suddenly thrown to the ground, and a violent pain deprived him of consciousness. A brother found him thus, called others to help him, and they bore him, still insensible, to Isidore, who lived near the church. Moses lay there for a whole year extremely ill. When he had recovered, and Isidore called upon him to return to Petra, the rock in which his cave was, he objected, for he feared to find again in solitude his former foes. " Thou art not alone in thy struggles, my brother, although thy cell seems to thee so solitary," said Isidore; "look up." He pointed towards the east, and Moses saw legions of angels, who shone so brightly with supernatural light that the sun seemed dark in comparison with them. Then he looked towards the west, and perceived a swarm of hideous forms, who, gloomy and sad, seemed to be retreating in confusion. " See, my brother," said Isidore, " this dark array fights indeed against us, but Almighty God sends to our aid that bright host which is much more numerous, and is always with thee in thy solitary cell."

Greatly consoled, Moses received Holy Communion, and returned to his cell.

Three months later, Isidore visited his beloved disciple, and asked him if the ancient enemy had tormented him as before. "Oh no, my father," replied Moses, humbly; "all the temptations have ceased since thou, a friend of God, didst open my eyes to the help of His grace." "God has so ordained it, that thou mightest not glorify thyself for having overcome Satan and his temptations by the austerities of thy life. Be comforted now in the Name of Jesus Christ; the assaults are over." These combats had brought forth in Moses the saving fruits of courage and humility. He was then for the first time called to the assembly of the fathers of the desert of Scete, who were holding council over some important matter. When Moses appeared, some of them exclaimed aloud, on purpose to try him, "What business has a negro here?" But he kept silence, with a serene countenance. They who had treated him so contemptuously asked him afterwards what he had thought about it. Moses made answer, "I thought of this, 'But Jesus held his peace.'" He was sent for at another time to an assembly which was to judge a guilty brother. But Moses came not. Then Isidore sent to tell him that all the fathers were waiting for him, and to ask wherefore he did not come. Moses filled a basket with sand, took it upon his back, and thus entered the assembly. Being asked the meaning of this, he answered, "I have to bear the heavy burden of my own sins, and shall I make bold to judge the sins of others?" Then no one spoke a word against the guilty brother.

The evil spirits who for so many years had tormented the valiant Moses, now acknowledged themselves to be overcome. A holy hermit heard them say to Moses, "We can do thee no harm, for when we try to cast thee into despair by setting before thine eyes the sins of thy past life, thou dost raise thyself full of confidence to the mercy of God; and whenever we seek to make thee proud, thou dost humble thyself before the justice of God. We have nothing to do with such men."

The anchorites were always wishing to hear his good advice and instructions, and he likewise desired theirs. Thus all were satisfied, each one learnt and taught with humility. "There are four things which are before all else necessary to a monk," said Moses, drawing from the store of his experience, "keeping the commandments, humility, poverty, and silence. And there are three things which he must especially lay to heart, because they are very difficult to him as well as to all men, he must always carry his cross cheerfully, he must always remember his sins, and always have the hour of his death before his eyes." He often repeated to the brethren, "If a man does not truly in his heart look upon himself as a sinner, the Lord God will not hear his prayer." "And who is there who really in his heart considers himself a sinner?" asked a young solitary. "He who always looks at his own sins, and never at those of his neighbour," replied Moses. He then proceeded to say, "If a man's works are not in conformity with his prayers, all his trouble and labour is in vain." "In what does this conformity consist?" said the young solitary. "In not committing any more the sins for which we ask God's forgiveness. If a man has renounced with his will in the inmost depths of his heart each and every sin, then he is reconciled to God, and his prayers may be heard." "But how can we bear so much labour and trouble?" asked the curious youth. "By the help of God," said Moses. The young solitary found the spiritual combat very hard, and mortification very burdensome; so he exclaimed with some impatience, "Oh, my father! what is the use of all this fasting and watching? the evil inclinations and temptations always wake up again." "But mortifications send them to sleep again," said Moses. "How can a man best die to himself?" asked another brother. "My son," said Moses, "unless a man imagines to himself that he has been lying for three years in the grave and under the earth, he will never die to himself."

An anchorite of the name of Zacharias was then living in the desert of Soete, of whom the holy abbot Serapion used to say, "Although I surpass him in bodily mortification, he is far beyond me in humility and silence." This Zacharias was with Moses when some of the brethren visited the latter, and begged him to give them some salutary instructions. "I beg of thee, my brother, to tell me what I am to do, and what to say to our brethren," said Moses to Zacharias. The latter fell at his feet, and said, with tears, "Wherefore dost thou put me to shame by such a question?" "I saw the Holy Ghost descend upon thee," answered Moses, "and that impelled me to ask thee." Then Brother Zacharias took off his mantle, threw it on the ground, and trampled it under foot. All looked at him in silence and amazement. Then he said, "A man who does not let himself be trampled under foot in this way will never be a true monk." This has been the teaching of the ascetics through all ages. A thousand years later the sweet and thoughtful ascetic of the fourteenth century, Henry Suso the holy Dominican monk, saw a little dog playing with a cloth, and understood thereby that he was to let himself be dragged about in the dirt, no matter by whom. Humility is love of God carried to the most complete contempt of self. The last hour of Brother Zacharias was nigh. As he lay between life and death, Moses said to him, "Seest thou heavenly things, my brother?" "I see that nothing is better than silence," answered Zacharias humbly. "Keep silence then to the end, my brother," said Moses. And silently, in perfect peace, Zacharias gave up his soul to God. Abbot Isidore looked up joyfully at the same hour, and said, "O thou blissful Zacharias, the gates of heaven open to thee, for humility is the road to God."

The contrast between what Moses had been and what he had now become gave him in the eyes of the world a celebrity which deeply pained him. He feared that the glory of his conversion would not be given to God alone, but that he himself might be admired and praised; and he said with St. Ignatius of Antioch, and with all the saints, "He who praises me scourges me." Whenever he was able to do so, he fled from his admirers, and no one could render him a greater service than that of warning him of these visits; then he hurried away, and only his empty cell was found. Once a great dignitary set out to go to Seete to make the acquaintance of this Moses, who had begun as a highway robber and ended as a saint. Moses was informed of his coming, and hid himself in a swamp, where he was safe. But the stranger, with all his followers, lost their way amidst the sandhills and rocks of the desert, and Moses came unexpectedly upon those from whom he was flying. The stranger was thankful to see a guide, and said to Moses, "My father, I beg of thee to tell me where lies the cell of the renowned Moses the holy solitary?" He peacefully answered, "What desirest thou of that man? and wherefore dost thou call him holy? We know him better here. He is a fool and a heretic. If thou dost wish for edification, go and visit the other brethren, but not him." Then he went away and left the visitor greatly amazed that Moses should be so much thought of at a distance, and so little esteemed in the desert. In the meantime he followed the advice given him, and visited some of the fathers, who received him with distinction, and by whom he was greatly edified. He told them afterwards how he had originally intended to visit Moses, and how he had been dissuaded therefrom. The pious fathers were exceedingly troubled to hear of such a calumny, and asked him to describe the monk who had uttered it. The stranger answered, "He was old, tall, and thin, clothed in a worn-out monk's habit, and his skin was quite black." "That was Moses himself!" exclaimed the fathers joyfully; and the stranger left the desert more edified by this behaviour of Moses than he could have been by the most holy discourse from his lips.

When Moses had not to do with admirers and flatterers, he was extremely affable and accessible. A youth who wished to devote himself to the ascetic life, begged an anchorite of the desert of Scete to conduct him to one of the most holy fathers that he might receive advice and instruction from him. The anchorite took him to Arsenius. He was sitting in his cell weaving a mat, and was so immersed in contemplation that he did not observe their entrance, and did not greet them or say a single syllable to them. After some time they went away as silently as they had sat there, and the anchorite took the youth to Moses. He received them so lovingly, spoke of the youth's intention with such fatherly benevolence, and showed him such hearty sympathy, that he said to his companion after they had taken leave, " Oh, how much holier and better the former robber is than the former courtier." This saying reached the ancient fathers, and one of them, who was extremely holy, and who had a high opinion of Arsenius, begged God to enlighten him upon the interior state of these two men. " The one, O Lord, avoids for Thy Name's sake all intercourse with men, whilst the other, for the same reason, is kind to them.

Which of the two is in the right?" And he fell into extasy, and saw two boats floating on one stream. Arsenius sat in one, peaceful and still, and the Holy Ghost hovered above his head. Moses was in the other, and angels travelled with him and were dropping honey upon his lips. Then the father understood that both these holy men, although outwardly different, lived in perfect love, which guided all their actions and made them pleasing to God.

Another time Moses had visitors of a very different kind. Four bad men, who lived by robbery and plunder, were vexed with him for having left the ways of sin, and adopted a penitential life. Their evil conscience saw in his repentance a secret reproach. They wished to revenge themselves on him, to illtreat him, and perhaps to kill him. They fell upon him in the night. But the old giant within him was dead only to sin. He overpowered his four adversaries, bound them, and dragged them to the church. He said to the priest, " I am not allowed to punish these men who have fallen upon me in my cell with violence. Tell me what I am to do with them." This childlike simplicity made so much impression upon the robbers that they humbly craved forgiveness and were converted to God. " For," said they, " if this strong man has found One stronger than he, why should we strive any longer against Him!"

The holy anchorites were most anxious to avoid every honour, and above all that of the priesthood. They were kept back from it not by cowardice or earthly-mindedness but by humility, and the high sanctity of the priestly office. They very seldom received holy orders without the express command of the bishops. Moses had to submit in his old age to this loving constraint, for the patriarch of Alexandria bestowed holy orders upon him. " Now thou art become white, Moses," said the patriarch playfully to him, after he had made him a deacon, and laid the white stole upon his shoulder. " Have I become white inwardly or outwardly?" asked Moses. Then the patriarch secretly told the sacristans not to suffer Moses to approach the altar on the following day to fulfil his office as deacon, and to observe his conduct closely. The sacristans accordingly drove away the old man as if he had been an impudent intruder, and called after him, " A negro has no business at the altar." He withdrew gently and patiently, and said, " The negro is rightly served. He is hardly a man, and he wishes to serve at the altar amongst the angels!"

Moses was sixty-five years old when the desert of Scete was overrun by the barbarian race of the Mazices. Shortly before this, seven hermits came to him to be edified by his heavenly wisdom, and to cleanse their souls in the holy sacrament of penance. After he had performed this office as the representative of God, he said to them in the spirit of prophecy, " To day, my brethren, I have served souls for the last time. Fly now in haste, for the barbarians are already near." " Wilt not thou take flight also?" they asked. " No," said Moses; " in looking back upon my early life I have long expected this day, that the words of my Saviour might be fulfilled in me, ' All that take the sword shall perish with the sword.'"[1] Then the anchorites said with one voice, " If thou wilt not fly we will remain too, and die with thee." Moses said, " There is no reason why I should fly. But do you consider well what you should do. You can still escape, but it will soon be too late." They were, however, determined to stay with him, and he did not forbid it. The night passed in holy prayer and pious discourse. When morning dawned, Moses said, " The hour is come." Imme-

[1] Matt. xxvi. 56.

diately after, bands of savages broke in from all sides upon the stillness of the desert. One troop ran to the rocky cell of Moses, who was kneeling in prayer. A spear transfixed his breast, and he fell lifeless to the ground. Six of the brethren followed him in the same way to eternity. The seventh, trembling with fear of death, had hidden himself under a heap of palm-leaves and mats, and he saw seven crowns descending from heaven upon the seven brave warriors of Christ. But he himself went away destitute.

BROTHER VALENS, BROTHER ERO, AND BROTHER PTOLEMY.

WHEN Palladins had finished writing the life of Moses and other saintly hermits, he said, "The tree of the knowledge of good and evil stood in paradise in the midst of fair and pleasant trees and plants. It will not, therefore, be useless to give an account of some of those who fell because they prided themselves upon their own excellence. If virtue is not practised for the pure intention of pleasing God, it easily becomes the source of falls, because man trusts to his own strength and makes shipwreck from his feebleness. For it is written: I have seen the just man perish in his justice."

Valens was born in Palestine, and went to the desert of Soete, where he lived for many years an extremely rigorous and austere life. But unfortunately, he pursued it without humility, and more with the object of seeking his own glory than that of God. Holy souls, in measure as they advance in perfection, ascribe their virtue to the grace of God, and keep their faults in mind that they may despise themselves for their sinfulness. Valens, on the contrary, overestimated himself so much that he imagined he had become a friend of God by his own exertions, and was therefore entitled to especial privileges. He entirely forgot the teaching which was handed down by all the ascetics from the mouth of St. Antony. That patriarch of the spiritual life saw in a vision the whole earth overspread with a thick net, and he understood that this signified the snares the devil lays for all men. "Alas!" said he, "will no one then escape from them?" A voice answered, "Yes, he that is humble." For the humble man is prudent, knowing the frailty of the soul and the deceitfulness of human nature. Brother Valens was far indeed from such humility and circumspection. He thought he had risen so high that the angels were ready to serve him. The anchorites related to Palladius that Brother Valens was once sitting at his work by night, and dropped the needle that he used for fastening his baskets together; then a strange light illuminated his cell, and he found his needle by it. From that hour he became so inflated with pride that he despised all the other anchorites. Macarins the Great, the priest of Scete, received a cake as a present from some guests. He blessed it and sent a share of it to every brother in the whole desert, a loving custom of those times, typifying the community of faith and grace which proceeds from the Holy Eucharist. But Valens received in a very unfriendly manner the messenger from Macarius who brought him the Eulogia, as the blessed bread was called. "Away with thee!" he called out, "and say to Macarius that I am every bit as good as he, and have no need to receive his blessing." When Macarius received this answer he saw how badly it must be faring with the soul of Brother Valens, and he set out at once to go to him, and lovingly showed him the danger in which he stood. "Turn to God, my brother," implored the aged priest, "call upon His mercy! Thou forsakest Him because thou art deceived." But the deluded monk would not listen to him, and sad at heart, Macarius was constrained to leave him to himself.

Soon after Valens had thought it beneath his dignity to accept the token of fellowship with his brethren, he went a step further, and despised even that fellowship with our loving Saviour which He Himself deigns to enter into with men in holy communion. When the brethren perceived that Valens kept away from the holy sacraments they were inexpressibly troubled, for they knew that he could never overcome pride if he scorned to receive within himself its true Conqueror. But the wicked enemy triumphed; he well knew that he had Valens in his power. He showed the foolish man a deceitful illusion which, in the extreme heedlessness of his pride, he accepted without proof as a veritable heavenly vision. A bright angel appeared before him, and said, "Christ loves thy doings, thy firm confidence, thy liberty of spirit. He is coming to thee, go forth and meet Him, and fall upon thy face to worship Him." Valens hastened out of his cell. The dark night was as bright as day with innumerable torches and lamps, and in the midst of all these lights, he saw a shining form. He prostrated himself on the ground and adored—the spirit of falsehood. The following Sunday, after the Office, he spoke thus to the assembled brethren: "Communion is henceforward useless to me, for Christ the Lord visits me in my cell." He had hardly uttered these words before he became insane. The brethren were obliged to put him in bonds, and he remained out of his mind for a whole year.

When the saints had heavenly visions, they

always mistrusted them, and considered them self-deceptions or temptations of the evil one endeavouring to flatter their pride. But if the vision truly came from God, the Eternal Truth and Wisdom, and brought them supernatural light about divine mysteries, this light so brightly illuminated their souls that they not only perceived every spot upon them, even in their most hidden depths, but also every spot, however small, appeared so hateful in comparison to that unspeakable beauty, that they were inspired with a profound contempt of themselves. They always walked in fear along the dangerous and narrow path of supernatural light and revelations. They ever bore in mind that the enemies of salvation were only watching for a weak moment of self-complacency in which to lay snares for them. They kept constantly before their eyes the inscrutable decree of God by which it pleased Him to choose them, in this way, for the instruments of His designs. And therefore, the unusual gifts of grace which fell to their share, produced the still more unusual one of humility, and where that is, neither God's glory nor the salvation of souls can suffer loss.

The prayers of the brethren, and a severe spiritual discipline, gradually restored Valens to his senses, and finally to the perception of his fault. After having wished to pass for a companion of the blessed spirits, and having instead of that lost even his reason, he saw the misery of all human excellence which is not grounded in God, and led ever after a simple penitential life, blessing God who puts down the mighty from their seat, and exalts the humble.[1]

Brother Ero came from Alexandria, a noble and beautiful youth of clear understanding and pure morals. The ascetic life singularly attracted him, and he dedicated himself to it in Scete with a

[1] Luke i. 52.

vigour and perseverance which excited the admiration of the most experienced fathers. He studied the Holy Scriptures day and night. He so accustomed his body to fasting, that his chief nourishment in the course of three months often consisted of holy communion, with only a few wild herbs now and then. When Palladius wished to journey from Alexandria to the desert of Scete, the patriarch directed him for that purpose to the two hermits Albin and Ero, who had just then brought the work done by the anchorites to S. Isidore, the master of the hospital at Alexandria, that he might sell it for the benefit of his pilgrims and sick poor. Palladius, accordingly, set out with them. He says: "We had forty leagues to go. Brother Albin and I took food twice on this journey, and a draught of water three times. But Brother Ero took nothing the whole way, and went, nevertheless, so fast that he seemed to fly over the sand, and we could not keep up with him. At the same time he recited from memory, to our great edification, the Prophet Isaias, and a portion of Jeremias, the Gospel of St. Luke, the Epistle to the Hebrews, the Proverbs of Solomon, and a number of psalms." Ero lived thus for many years in peace, until the tempter suggested the thought to him that he was living an angelic rather than a human life. Instead of thanking God for the assistance of His grace, Brother Ero indulged in self-complacent reflections. It soon came to pass that he despised the other solitaries and the admonitions of the fathers, nourishing, on the other hand, a great desire to be admired by the world for his angelic demeanour. As he despised the warnings of the ancient fathers, and the holy sacrament of penance, his soul lost at length the power of struggling against these violent temptations to vanity, and even the will to struggle. He fell into spiritual idleness, lukewarmness, and weariness, and at last into disgust with the ascetic life. His cell becoming unbearable to him, he cast off his anchorite's habit, and hastened to Alexandria. But there were none there to admire him, or even to look at him. He roamed idly about, with a desolate heart and an unbridled mind, sought distraction in wine, and sank deeper and deeper, so that he who had lived upon the Bread of angels as long as he was in union with God, now in his separation from God, sought to satisfy himself as though with the husks of the unclean beasts. Nevertheless God was merciful to him, and sent him a severe illness, which afflicted him with indescribable pains, and entirely destroyed his health. Then he thought with regret of his lost peace, and hurried back into the desert. The good fathers received their prodigal son with kindness, and nursed him tenderly. But he had only time enough to confess his guilt, with innumerable tears, before God called him into eternity to give an account of the talent intrusted to him.

Pride and vanity are powerful antagonists to perfection; but its mortal enemy is self-will. When a young man of the name of Ptolemy began the ascetic life, the holy anchorites of Scete were anxious and concerned about him, for he did not follow the way which was good for beginners. Our Blessed Lord says that those who wish to win heaven must become like little children. The chief virtue of a child consists in obedience. By obedience it is led and practised in all good; without obedience it may have good inclinations and impulses, but the lasting foundation of virtue is wanting. Those who left the world for the sake of the kingdom of heaven, and who renounced all joys and pleasures the more surely to enjoy the delights of eternity, had also to make themselves like little children and to enter the school of obedience, as Paul the Simple had done under St. Antony.

This was the first rule both for monks and solitaries. Furthermore, it was not exactly a precept, but a wholesome custom, that beginners should ask for counsel and consolation from the experienced. Hence the many beautiful teachings and maxims which the ancient fathers gave to the younger brethren when they disclosed to them their temptations. Thus a young hermit said once in distress to a father, "What am I to do to keep myself from despair ? This thought is constantly in my head, that I have left the world in vain, and that I shall never be saved." " My brother," answered the old man, " even if we are not worthy to enter the promised land, still it is better for us to die in the desert than to turn back to the fleshpots of Egypt. Lay that to heart." Another brother said to his spiritual father, " How comes it, my father, that I am overcome by idleness and disgust ?" " It is a sign that thou dost not duly set before thine eyes either the glory of heaven or the pains of hell," was the answer ; "for if thou didst, the desire of eternal bliss and the fear of everlasting punishment would be sufficient motives to excite zeal and contrition, with which we may bravely combat laxity and lukewarmness." And even if all the young anchorites did not hear such words of encouragement in their struggles, yet experience taught them that it was always very useful to speak freely about the state of their souls ; because childlike openness is often sufficient to drive away the strongest temptations.

But Ptolemy disdained all advice. He asserted that he need learn the spiritual life from none save the Holy Ghost, of whose inspirations any man of good will could be certain. He was told, on the contrary, that an inspiration of the Holy Ghost and the understanding of the same are two distinct things, and that this understanding is disclosed only to him whose will has been purified by the long practice of obedience and humility. Thereupon Ptolemy alleged the example of Paul of Thebes, the patriarch of all the anchorites, without considering that this holy man had not by any means separated himself from others out of obstinacy, but had rather been obliged by the pressure of circumstances to fly into the desert, and had there, by the extraordinary purity of his heart, attained to that union with God which became to him a heavenly bond. Neither Paul nor any of the ancient fathers ever laid claim to a special inspiration or guidance of the Holy Ghost, it was only granted to them as a favour. But these representations did not produce any effect upon Ptolemy. He separated himself entirely from the brethren, and made his dwelling in a cave on the other side of the desert of Scete, in a completely uninhabited spot, from whence the only drinkable water was eighteen leagues distant. However, in the winter months the nightly dew was tolerably heavy, and Ptolemy collected it in sponges, which he squeezed into earthen vessels for his use. He lived there for fifteen years. But what did he gain by his bodily mortification, when he was thereby nourishing and pampering his self-will? Alas, nothing whatever. Absent by his own fault from the holy sacraments of penance and of the altar, from the hearing and the exposition of the Gospel, from the converse and teaching of the ancient fathers, wilfully confined to his own thoughts, he soon followed as wrong a path inwardly as outwardly. Error took more and more possession of him, he strayed further and further from the truth, the doctrine of salvation was veiled before him, and he fell into misbelief and infidelity. He imagined that the world was governed by chance, and not by Divine Providence, and therefore that there were no eternal rewards or punishments; that man had no judgment of God to fear after death, and that the menaces of Holy Writ were vain fables. In spite of all his fasting, Ptolemy was powerless to make a stand alone against this storm of wild thoughts. Even yet he could have saved his soul, if he had fled to the fathers and placed himself under their guidance, but his stubbornness would not suffer it. He preferred going to Alexandria. His long habit of an austere and mortified life had inspired him with a great dislike to every sort of immorality, and he proposed to himself to lead a most virtuous life, partly because he considered it more becoming, and partly because he wished to show the anchorites to what heights of virtue he had attained in his solitude, and how far he had surpassed them. Idle and aimless, he wandered about the voluptuous Alexandria, visited the theatres and the public baths, mixed everywhere with the crowd, and saw and heard a thousand things of which he had never dreamt in the desert, and which were very dangerous for him. Then it happened that a very holy and aged solitary of Scete came to Alexandria to sell the handiwork of the brethren, and to buy materials for their clothing. He saw Brother Ptolemy going into a wine-shop. This grieved the holy old man beyond measure. He waited outside the door of the house till Ptolemy came out again, took him affectionately by the hand, and led him away with him, saying mournfully, "My lord and brother, thou dost wear an ecclesiastical, yea, an angelic habit; thou art still very young, dost thou never think then of the manifold snares of Satan? Dost thou not know that the wicked enemy enters into the heart through the eyes and ears, and that nothing is more prejudicial to the hermit than the motley and infatuating throng of men in a great city. How, therefore, canst thou dare to enter a wine-shop, where so much that is unholy must be seen and heard?

Oh, I beg of thee, do so no more! Fly rather once more to Scete, where, with the help of God, thou mayest save thy soul. I am going back there this very day;[1] O my brother, come with me." Here again was a moment in which Divine grace was seeking admission into Ptolemy's heart, but he would not suffer it to enter. On the contrary, he said very contemptuously to the holy man, "Go back alone, old man, and do not chatter so much. Thou knowest well that God regards nothing but a pure heart." Then the old man lifted up his eyes and hands to heaven, and humbly said, "Praise and glory be to thee, my God! Behold, I have lived now for five and fifty years in the desert of Scete, and I have not yet a pure heart. But this young brother, who frequents the wine-shops of Alexandria, says that he already possesses a pure heart." Thereupon he turned to Ptolemy, and lovingly said to him, "May God keep thee, my brother, but may He also not suffer me or my hope to be confounded." They parted thus, each to follow the way he had freely chosen, the one the way of salvation, the other that of perdition.

Ptolemy could not maintain himself upon his imaginary heights. Darkness and unbelief, which are ever in league with all bad passions, were no protection to him when these latter were powerfully excited by bad example and evil company. It is enough to say that he sank down into a wretched and despicable way of life, associated with the lowest of the rabble, and wandered forlorn over the whole of Egypt, a sorrow and a shame to Christian hearts, and a mockery to the heathen. How and where he perished is not known; one thing only is certain, that the desert saw him no more, for contact with the world had been his ruin. Recollection of spirit,—a recollection which gives strength to aim at holiness by the mortification of sinful nature and discipline of the passions, by meditation and prayer—finds its safest home in the ascetic cell. If his vocation calls the ascetic forth, if the priest, the missionary, the teacher of the faith, must have intercourse with the world, then the grace of his state is the shield which preserves him from distraction and pollution, and in his heart he always remains, by longing desire, an inhabitant of his cell. But voluntarily to choose dissipation out of levity or from weariness of the ascetic life, is to cast a poisonous blight upon those graces and gifts which only come to perfection in recollection and elevation of mind.

ST. EPHREM THE SYRIAN.

"The voice of the turtle is heard in our land."—CANT. ii. 12.

EGYPT, the Babylon of polytheism, the land of dark problems before which the sphinx keeps guard, had thus become a clear and bright fountain from which flowed forth in plenitude the "waters of everlasting life." The enigma of the world, unread by the polytheistic ages which bowed before the dumb sphinx of stone, was solved by the sons of Egypt at the foot of the Cross, when by asceticism and mysticism they restored man to his state in paradise, and turned caverns and cloisters into nurseries of the highest Christian virtue. From thence this new life poured forth over the world in two vast streams full of rich germs of untold fertility. The one flowed towards the east, the other towards the west and north. The channel for this latter stream was prepared by Athanasius, the great and saintly Patriarch of Alexandria, the spiritual hero of the century, the champion and representative of the Church in the battle of faith for the Divinity of Christ against Arianism. During his banishments to Trèves and Rome, at once a disciple and a master in asceticism, he became a leader in this holy and mysterious realm by his example, his exhortations, and his writings. We have no certain account of how the ascetic life, under its two forms, made its way into the east. St. Basil the Great found flourishing and well-regulated monasteries in Coele-Syria and Mesopotamia as early as the year 357, and a very perfect form of monastic life flourished also in Palestine and Persia at that time. Therefore we may infer that the spirit and life of the cloister develope themselves as naturally from a lively Christian faith, as a flower unfolds from the bud. Man learnt by faith to know the God of infinite love, and as the simple consequence received Him into his heart with a corresponding love, and dedicated himself entirely to His service. The greatest and most distinguished men in the Church were disciples of the ascetics, and spread and encouraged this disposition in their own disciples.

Near Nisibis, the ancient capital of Mesopotamia, there dwelt a married couple of worthy peasants, who brought up their son in the fear of the Lord. This boy was Ephrem. His gentle and thoughtful disposition was developed by continual contemplation of Holy Writ, with whose treasures his parents had early made him acquainted. It shed such light upon his soul that a high degree of virtue was ever before him as his only aim. Little bursts of anger, and passing doubts of the Providence of God seemed to him afterwards grave sins, and he deplored some boyish tricks as bitterly as though they had been serious crimes; so pure did his heart remain from youth up to extreme old age. An indescribable peacefulness and invincible meekness, together with perfect firmness of faith, rendered his virtue unusually attractive. Some visions in sleep, and an unjust imprisonment which endangered his life, but was followed by his release, inspired him with the liveliest gratitude for the dispositions of God's mercy; and about the age of eighteen he received holy baptism, and formed the resolution of dedicating himself in peaceful contemplation to the service of God. There were then in Syria and Mesopotamia, as in Egypt and Palestine, very many who devoted themselves to the ascetic life, and who practised spiritual exercises with great mortification of the senses, and were at the same time diligent in manual labour. There were three forms of this life. Some were solitaries in the strictest sense of the word, and each of these lived in complete solitude in his cell, hut, or cavern; others lived so far in community that they united together daily in prayer and praise, dwelling without shelter upon the mountains of the great Syrian desert, chiefly upon Mount Sigoron, between Nisibis and Edessa. They slept in fissures in the rocks, and ate no bread; each one had a small sickle with which he gathered at mealtime some wild herbs for his nourishment. This appalling austerity of life was practised only by a few; most of them joined some community where they had their dwelling, their meals and prayer in common. Here also severe mortification prevailed, and the body was allowed the least possible quantity of sleep and food. Labour was one of the chief conditions of the ascetic life, under every form. The anchorites in their cells, or on the mountains, the monks in their cloisters, all worked that they might supply their own wants and give alms. This last duty was considered so holy that the most extreme poverty gave no exemption from it, and hence their great zeal in labour. They plaited baskets, mats, and ropes, prepared paper, wove sails and cloths, ground corn, worked in the fields and gardens, and copied books; some, like Ephrem, wrote books themselves, but he also wove sails. Their labours, except that of writing, did not hinder either prayer, or the singing of psalms, or reading the Holy Scriptures, or contemplation.

Ephrem went to the holy hermit James, who afterwards became Bishop of Nisibis, but who was then leading the life of an anchorite in his cell at the foot of a mountain, and made the confession to him of all the wicked and evil deeds of his life, for such did his little faults appear to him when weighed by heavenly measures and compared to the infinite perfection of God. He received permission from James to dedicate himself thenceforward under his guidance to penance and mortification. Here Ephrem went through the purifying discipline of obedience, and laid the foundation of his holiness and of his spiritual enlightenment. He is said to have been ignorant of the Greek language and of worldly science, and to have received only an ordinary school education, but to have acquired by incessant study of the Holy Scriptures the supernatural wisdom which he expressed in his writings. The most learned fathers of the Church honoured Ephrem as an enlightened teacher. The clear vision of his soul being devoted to heavenly things alone, he contemplated untroubled and undazzled that light which had illumined first the Prophets and then the Apostles. And in prayer Ephrem spoke so uninterruptedly, so simply, so lovingly, and so humbly to the Eternal Word, that at length the Word spoke to him in return, and bestowed knowledge upon him which he could never have learnt from books or from the lips of men. He was violent and passionate by nature and prone to anger; but he so completely subdued this passion that he was never known to dispute or to be angry with any one, and he gained for himself the surname of " the peaceable man of God." In his later intercourse with hardened sinners and evildoers, with heretics and heathen, prayers and tears were his sole weapons. He despised himself beyond measure, and his greatest desire was that others should hold him in equal contempt.

With indescribable humility he wept and mourned over his spiritual misery. " I should fear to be like those," he writes in his *Confessions*, " who were consumed by flames from heaven, because they presumed to offer an unholy fire upon the altar, if I were to appear before God without the consecrated fire of love in my heart, and so to deserve that punishment." He declared that he could never shed tears enough to wash away all the stains upon his soul, which he alone perceived; and to this contrition was joined an earnest desire to establish the kingdom of God perfectly in his heart. Because pride is the declared enemy of this kingdom, he feared nothing so much as its snares. " There is no more dangerous sin," he writes ; " it destroys even the gifts of God, makes virtues sources of pride, and changes them into abominations. Oh! if we would only constantly remember that in the day of judgment all our virtues will be tried by fire, and that none can bear the trial save that of humility." Praises terrified him. Whilst he was being praised he stood in spirit before the judgment-seat of God, trembling lest by his hypocritical simulation of holiness he had deceived those who praised him. He insisted strongly and earnestly on the necessity of this penitential and humble contrition in presence of the infinite love of God, and the awful strictness of His judgments, for himself first, but also for others. He writes, " Contrition is the daily bread of all spiritual men. By it they obtain mercy, and acquire for themselves everlasting graces which are more precious than all treasures." St. Gregory of Nyssa says of Ephrem,

"Weeping was as natural to him as breathing is to other men. By day and by night his eyes shed floods of tears."

From his hermitage Ephrem went to live for some time in a religious order, to exercise himself in the various mortifications which a community life imposes. There he joined himself to a holy monk of the name of Julian, who had been driven out of the West by severe misfortunes, and had taken shelter in that haven of repose. Julian was by birth a Visigoth, and had fallen into slavery through the fortune of war, and suffered incredible hardships at the hand of his heathen master on account of his faith. For the Christian faith with its purity and holiness was no welcome guest at Heliopolis in Cœle-Syria. Heliopolis, (the city of the sun,) is the Greek name for Baalbec. Baal, the god of the sun, and his sister Astarte, goddess of the moon, were the principal and favourite deities of Syria, and no idolatry was more strikingly opposed to Christianity than the worship which was paid to these idols.

Cœle-Syria is the strip of land lying between the two mountain ranges of Lebanon and Anti-Lebanon, a wide, level, and fruitful valley. There was situated the voluptuous Baalbec, the head-quarters of the worship of Baal, rich, effeminate, and adorned with temples; there even now lie its gigantic and beautiful ruins, in whose vast extent the amazed and admiring traveller may easily lose himself. The contiguous quarries of Anti-Lebanon readily supplied the splendid materials for these colossal structures. Enormous blocks still lie there, from twenty to thirty feet long, such as were used for the foundations and the surrounding walls. They are left half finished; before the workmen could complete them Baal was no more. The bare and wild peaks of Anti-Lebanon look frowningly down upon its devastated loveliness, and near it we now find only a little Maronite village, and a couple of walnut-trees by a small stream.

Here Julian had to bear much cruelty and disgrace before he obtained his freedom, of which his first use was to take upon himself the sweet yoke of the Saviour by practical imitation of Him. His spirit had been purified by his severe trials and inflamed with a burning love of God. He could not hear or read the Name of God without bursting into tears and imploring pardon of his sins. Julian and Ephrem were alike in this, and strengthened each other in the holy love which is inseparable from holy sorrow for offences against God by sin. The two friends were parted by the holy death of Julian, and Ephrem went to Nisibis, where the Episcopal throne was then occupied by the saintly anchorite James. It was in the year 350, and Sapor, king of Persia, was besieging the city with innumerable forces, for it was the bulwark of the Roman empire against the East, and against the kings and nations of the rest of Asia. For this reason it was as strenuously and indefatigably defended as it was attacked. But after the fearful exertions of a seventy days' siege Nisibis was exhausted, while Sapor, on the contrary, received assistance and fresh troops from the kings of India. The fall of Nisibis seemed inevitable; the men of action gave it up for lost. Then the men of prayer, James and Ephrem, arose at the request of the people to beseech God to deliver the city. They mounted the walls of the town, and James looked over the camp, the army and the warlike array, and King Sapor's ramparts, trenches, and redoubts; he then knelt down and begged Almighty God to show forth His omnipotence. Then cloud after cloud rose up from the horizon, and spread over the earth, darkening the light of day, for they were formed of myriads of flies which entered the trunks of the elephants, and the nostrils, eyes, and ears of the horses, camels, and other beasts of burden. This so maddened them that they broke their harness, tore away from the ranks, trampled the men under foot, and fled in every direction, spreading destruction in the camp. The soldiers were utterly powerless to prevent it, because they were themselves blinded by the innumerable flies. The disorder of the camp was so great and so complete that King Sapor in his rage shot an arrow towards heaven and raised the siege.

The holy Bishop James was soon after called out of this life, and Ephrem went to the province of Osroene, where, in peaceful solitude, he led an extremely austere life in the neighbourhood of Edessa, the capital. Here he began to compose his writings. An aged anchorite who visited him now and then to gladden himself with the sight of his growth in holiness, once found him having just finished his commentary on the First Book of Moses, the history of the creation. The old man read the writing, kept it, and taking it to Edessa showed it to the ecclesiastics and most learned men of the city. They admired the book, and congratulated the old man on having written so excellent a treatise. He then said that he was not the author of it, but that it was the work of a stranger hermit who lived very piously in a miserable cavern. From that time Ephrem's hidden life ceased. He was frequently visited, some requiring his advice, others his teaching, all, his prayers. The Bishop of Edessa heard of the great influence which Ephrem's words exercised upon the people, and of the great love they felt for him on account of his meekness and piety. Therefore he resolved to put this bright light upon a candlestick in the church, and ordained Ephrem deacon. Ephrem submitted with fear and trembling to this command; but even the bishop could not induce him to receive priest's orders. He remained all his life a humble deacon of the church of Edessa, fulfilling the duties of that office to their utmost extent, preaching the Gospel and tending the poor. The more deeply penetrated he felt by his unworthiness and sinfulness the more did his humility affect all with whom he came in contact. When he preached and censured the sins of others he was always careful to condemn himself, placing himself on the same footing as his hearers, or indeed beneath them. At the end of a sermon which he preached to enkindle a desire for martyrdom when there were fears of a persecution of the Christians by the Emperor Julian, he exclaimed, " I desire to die for this faith! Assemble, O ye Jews and heretics, unite with the pagans and barbarians! Let me die for Jesus Christ! Your cruelty will, indeed, grieve me for your own sakes, but I should esteem myself most fortunate to be allowed to die for my faith. It is true that I fear death if I consider myself alone, but Jesus Christ is my hope and my trust. In my own weakness I fly; in His strength I persevere. If I look at myself I tremble, if I cast my eyes upon Him I am full of courage. O my God! I tremble because Thou hatest sin, but nevertheless I am filled with joy, for Thou hast died for sinners."

The spirit of penance which animated Ephrem made him an irresistible preacher of penance. His appearance was also very striking; he was tall and thin, his bright eyes were always overflowing with tears, and his face had a serene and wonderful expression, which betokened the highest sanctity. He was so overcome by the saving truths which he announced, that he was continually obliged to pause to recover himself. If he then gave free course to his tears, his hearers wept and sobbed with him. St. Gregory of Nyssa asserts that it was impossible to read his sermon on the Last Judgment, and still more so to hear it, without tears. "My dear brethren," he said, "you are listening to the words which I am going to speak concerning the fearful coming of the Lord. But who can relate such terrible things? If I think of that dreadful moment I am entranced with fear. The King of kings will descend from heaven, from the throne of glory, to take His seat as Judge, and will call all the inhabitants of earth before His judgment-seat. Alas! a clap of thunder makes us tremble now; how then shall we bear the clang of those trumpets which shall wake the dead? As soon as the sleeping bodies in the bosom of the grave shall hear this sound, life will animate them once more. All will rise again in one and the same moment, without a single hair being wanting to them; they will collect together and stream towards the place of judgment; for the heavenly King issues His commands, and the stricken earth and the agitated depths of ocean give back their dead." Then he described the fire which enkindles the whole world; the angels who separate the sheep from the goats; the sign of the Cross shining with light, which is carried before the King; mankind in fear and confusion; the just overflowing with joy, and the wicked a prey to despair; the heavenly hosts glorifying the thrice holy God with their songs of praise; heaven opened, and the Lord surrounded by such glory that neither heaven nor earth can support it. Ephrem was so affected that his voice melted into tears, and he was unable to proceed. But the congregation cried aloud to him, "Continue to instruct us in these fearful things, say further, O thou servant of God, what will happen after that." Ephrem then unfolded before their eyes the Book of Life in which all our thoughts, words, and works are written. "Then each man will be called up to undergo a severe examination, and will not dare to lift up his eyes to the Eternal Judge, whose divinely just decree awards to each one life or death, heaven or hell. O my dearest brethren! how many tears ought we not to shed day and night in expectation of this fearful judgment. At the mere thought of such things my limbs stiffen."—" We conjure thee," exclaimed his hearers, " continue to speak to us for our welfare and the salvation of our souls."—" O my dearest brethren!" continued Ephrem, "then will each Christian be examined whether he has the seal of holy baptism and the treasure of the faith; each Christian will be asked whether he has lived according to his renunciation of Satan and his works, not only one or two of his works, but all in general. Oh, blessed is he who has faithfully kept his promise! Then is announced that woeful sentence which parts men for ever from one another: bishops from bishops, priests from priests, deacons and lectors from their companions in orders; children from their parents, brothers from their sisters, friends from their friends. After the separation has taken place, the reprobate will call upon the elect with unspeakable lamentation, and will say: " Farewell ye saints and servants of God! farewell ye prophets, apostles, and martyrs! farewell ye parents, children, and friends! farewell for ever O thou most Blessed Virgin, Mother of God! All ye have prayed for the salvation of our souls but we would not be saved. Farewell O saving Cross! farewell Paradise, thou field of delights, thou everlasting kingdom, thou heavenly Jerusalem! Farewell ye blessed! Farewell to bliss! We shall see you no more! We are sinking into an abyss of pain and torments, we have no more hope of salvation for ever." Ephrem continued to speak in this way for a long time to the breathlessly attentive congregation, and wept and sobbed, and struck his breast in penitence. He did not do this with the motive of affecting his hearers, but the sinfulness of men, and the justice of God, represented themselves so forcibly to his mind, that his interior agitation made him lose his self-command.

He once, with two companions, left Edessa before sunrise, when the whole sky was sprinkled with thousands of sparkling stars. His pure heart was flooded with joy, and he exclaimed, " Oh, if the beauty of these created things is so inexpressibly lovely, how great must be that glory which will proceed from the Uncreated Light at the coming of the Saviour of the world, and which will shine around the blessed!" Then he directly turned his thoughts humbly towards himself and added, "Alas! what a direful day! Oh, woe is me!" And he fell down fainting. When he recovered his consciousness his companions asked him what had befallen him. "O my brethren," Ephrem answered, "I thought of the state in which I should appear before my Judge, I so miserable amongst so many perfections, I a withered tree without fruit. The martyrs will show their wounds, the religious their virtues, but I——, alas! I shall have nothing to show in my vain and proud soul but idleness and lukewarmness." At night when he was going to allow himself a little rest he was hindered by the recollection of his sins. He found it impossible to sleep, and like King David, he watered his couch with his tears. Or he thought of the infinite love of God for men, and throwing himself upon his knees, he sought, in the fervour of his love, to pour forth his gratitude. "But," he said, "the remembrance of my sins deters me, and I can do nothing but dissolve in tears. I feel clearly that the anguish the day of judgment causes in me would be insupportable if I were not sustained and encouraged by examples of the mercy of God, such as those of the publican, the Good Shepherd, the Canaanite woman, the Magdalen, and the Samaritan." Ephrem advised his disciples, above all things, to banish tepidity from their souls, and he said, "What a man builds up today with one hand by mortification, he pulls down tomorrow with the other by lukewarmness. And when Satan is overcome by fervent souls, he says, 'I will go to the lukewarm, they are my friends! I hold them fast without any difficulty by the bonds which they love.'" He taught his disciples to encourage themselves with the thought that this earthly life is a time of usury, and a very short time in which to acquire everlasting profits. He said, "Repeat often to yourselves; I have only a very little more of the way left, and I am near to the haven of repose, therefore I will not delay upon the road." Although Ephrem was very gentle, yet he thought that obedience promoted virtue only when it commanded difficult, or even harsh things. "For," said he, "wild beasts are never tamed by gentleness."

Ephrem was accustomed to call Edessa the "city of benediction." It had very early received the teaching of the Gospel, and kept it pure. When Arianism overspread those parts Edessa remained unstained by it, and eighty priests with their holy Bishop Barses were banished for their fidelity to the Catholic faith. The Emperor Julian avoided it in his Persian campaign, because of the piety of its inhabitants. Nevertheless, the heretical teaching of a certain Bardesanus, denying, amongst other things, the resurrection of the body, was propagated from mouth to mouth in this pious city of Edessa. In order to gain admittance for these doctrines where their falsehood would otherwise have caused them to be rejected, and to secure their greatest possible diffusion, Harmonius, the son of Bardesanus, clothed them in verse and set them to music, and by means of the attractive melodies, the heretical poison entered the ears, and flowed from the lips of the unwitting people. What a grief for Ephrem! But this holy sorrow made him a poet, like many earlier divinely inspired minstrels. He wrote Catholic songs, partly in the same metre, to be sung to the well-known tunes, and partly in new and still pleasanter rhymes. To make them known, he assembled the consecrated virgins, the "daughters of the covenant," as they were called in the Syrian language, and instructed them to sing these hymns at the gatherings of the faithful and in pious family circles. Ephrem's praises of the most Holy Virgin Mary are inexhaustible. Perhaps no other poet has worshipped her with such fervent and glowing devotion. He opens the whole treasury of Oriental fancy, and calls upon heaven and earth to bring their best and sweetest to form an adornment that shall be worthy of its object. These songs, hymns, and prayers in honour of Mary have come down to us from the most ancient times of the Church, from the fourth century, and the universal consent which they express gives them their childlike and confident tone. They issue forth from Ephrem's fervent devotion like a silver stream; he can set no bounds to their flowing. As the waves of the sea rise and fall, and ever rise again, so does the fulness of his love ever break forth anew in praise and admiration. One of the prayers is as follows:—" Most Holy Mother of God, all unspotted, perfectly inviolate! Throne of the heavenly King, Gate of Heaven, incomprehensible Miracle, Revelation of the hidden Mystery of God, life-giving Fountain, unfathomable Sea of unspeakable divine grace; after the Most Holy Trinity, Queen of all things; after the Mediator, Mediatrix of the whole world; spotless Robe of Him who is clothed with light as with a garment; Bridge of the entire world, which leads us to heaven. Mother and Servant of the never-setting Star; True Vine, bearing the fruit of life; Safety of those who stand, Resurrection of those who fall, Arouser of the slothful, Dispenser of all good, Haven of the tempest-tossed, Staff of the blind, Guide of the wandering, Deliverer of the imprisoned, incorruptible Flower dispersing sweet odour throughout all the world, most glorious Lily, Rose full of the most fragrant perfume; my salvation, my consolation, my light, my life, my joy, my glory, bright lamp of my darkened soul, oh look down upon my faith and my desire! Receive my soul, and make me, by thy help and intercession, worthy to stand one day at the Right Hand of thy Son, and to enter into the rest of the saints and the elect. Neither the will nor the power are wanting to thee. Thy Son honours thee as His Mother, and willingly grants thy prayers. Therefore I trust in thee, O true Mother of God, to whom honour and glory are due, with the Father and the Holy Ghost, now and always and for ever. Amen."

In a penitential prayer, he thus addresses Mary: "O Virginal Mother, arouse my soul to penance and guide me to the way of salvation. When I shall have found it, be thou still my leader, that under thy guidance I may attain to eternal bliss. O Mother of the God who loves men, melt and humble my heart, fill mine eyes with tears of repentance, and enlighten them by the light of thy intercession, that I may not die the death of the soul! Sprinkle me with the hyssop of thy pity, that I may become clean and whiter than snow! O Mother of my Lord Jesus Christ, accept my humble confession and prayer, and during the life that yet remains to me, keep me without stumbling on the path of penance! But when my poor soul must leave this body, then, O my Lady, appear to me with thy merciful eyes, and deliver me from the terrible accusations of my enemies and of the prince of this world. Be thou my defender, cancel my debt of sin, and lead me saved and fearless before the judgment-seat of thy Son."

Ephrem made another prayer a veritable garland of loving and honourable appellations:—

"O all pure, all inviolate, all spotless, all stainless, all blameless, all praiseworthy, all untouched, all undefiled, most holy, most venerable, most estimable, most commendable, most desirable! O holy Ark, in which we are saved from the deluge of sin; unconsumed Bush, seen by Moses the prophet of God; golden Censer, in which the Word, by putting on flesh, filled the world with sweet savour; seven-branched Candlestick, whose light exceeded that of the sun; holy Tabernacle, built by the spiritual Beseleel;[1] Vessel that preservest the manna; holy blossoming Staff of Aaron, dew-bearing Fleece of Gideon, Book written by God, by which the penalty of Adam's sin is blotted out; Mountain of God, holy Mountain in which the Lord was well pleased to dwell; holy Root of Jesse, City of God, of which David speaks,[2] Glorious things are said of thee. Most beautiful by thy very nature, and incapable of receiving any stain. Paradise, holier than that of Eden; life-giving Tree, bearing sweetest and most lovely fruit; beautiful Apple, fragrant Rose, whitest Lily, Sealed Book which none can read, inviolate Pattern of virginity, highly-treasured Vision of the Prophets; Purple woven by God, eloquent Mouth of the Apostles, unconquerable Trust of the combatants, Support of kings, Glory of the priesthood, Appeaser of the just Judge, my Hope, my Refreshment, my heart's Joy, my Delight, my Glory, my never-sleeping Helper with God! inexhaustible Sea of divine and unspeakable graces and gifts; Height exalted above the heavenly powers; unfathomable Depth of sublime thoughts, Pride of all Nature, Ornament of the Angels, incomparably more glorious and sublime than the Cherubim and

---

[1] The builder of the tabernacle of the testimony in the Old Testament. [2] Ps. lxxxvi. 3.

Seraphim, Key that admits us into heaven; Glory of the true and mystical day, illuminating Light of believing souls, Morning cloud that bringest heavenly dew to the inhabitants of earth. . . ." And so on for pages and pages. How cold, how short, how poor, are our songs in honour of the most Blessed Virgin Mary, in contrast with those of Ephrem. And how simply and completely he expresses the ground of his love and his trust; "Thou, who art above all praise, and canst gain what thou wilt from God whom thou hast borne." "Mighty Mother of the mighty and living God, thou canst and wilt, because thou hast brought forth in an unspeakable manner One of the Trinity in Unity." "O Bride of God! great confidence hast thou in Him who is born of thee! As Mother of God thou canst do all things; as exalted above all creatures, thou art all powerful. Nothing is impossible to thee that thou willest, O thou good Mother of Christ our God."

Ephrem wrote hymns upon the whole life of Christ, His birth, His baptism, His fasting, His passion, His resurrection and ascension, upon the martyrs, the dead, and the cleansing of the soul in the sacrament of penance; and the aged but loving anchorite stood in the midst of the sweet choirs of the "daughters of the covenant" like a teacher of the melodies of a supernatural world. But since he could not always win heretics and heathen by hymns and songs, he went forth to do them battle as an ardent missioner, and brought faith and conviction to their hearts. He won over numbers to the fold of Christ,—Manichees, who denied the Divinity of the Holy Ghost; Arians, who disbelieved the Godhead of the Only-begotten Son; Novatians who rejected the power of penance and condemned second marriages; Ophites, who worshipped Jesus under the form of a serpent; and Bardesanes, who would not credit the resurrection of the body. The East was full of these and other heresies, each of which had more or less numerous followers, to the deep sorrow of the Catholic Church, whose doctrine and teaching were never in the smallest degree influenced or modified by them.

With regard to the future life, Ephrem taught that souls immediately after their separation from the body undergo a particular judgment, and that the just who die in venial sin, or who have not sufficiently expiated their former sins by works of satisfaction, must still suffer in the flames of purgatory before they attain to the vision of God; but that the faithful who are still upon this earth can mitigate and shorten these pains of the holy suffering souls, by sacrifices, prayers, and other good works. The doctrine of the Catholic Church was then exactly what it is now, and this testimony of the Syrian father of the Church in the fourth century proves that neither the worship of Mary nor the doctrine of purgatory were the invention of the Middle Ages. Ephrem nourished also an especial veneration for the symbol of our redemption, and said, "All nations honour the saving emblem of the Cross, and we sign therewith our doors, our foreheads, our eyes, our mouths, our breasts, our whole selves." Notwithstanding the fervour of his faith, which impelled him to use the greatest severity towards himself, he was very gentle and considerate to others. He never allowed recent converts to follow the impulses of their first fervours indiscreetly, and to begin severe mortifications; he advised them rather to adopt such practices as they could persevere in, and could gradually increase, according to the advice of experienced spiritual persons.

Ephrem lived for some time with St. Basil, in Cesarea, to rejoice and to bask in the rays of this spiritual sun, and the great archbishop esteemed no less the humble deacon. Once when Basil was preaching, Ephrem saw a dove hovering over his head, a beautiful emblem of the Holy Ghost, Who spoke by the mouth of the archbishop, and revealed Himself to the deacon. In one of Ephrem's discourses about Basil, the accents of admiring friendship flowed from his lips in figurative eloquence, and he could not find words enough to express his veneration. He says, " Basil is in truth, the life of miracles, the path of virtue, the book of praise. He walks in the flesh, but lives in the spirit. He lives upon the earth like other men, but is immersed in the contemplation of heaven. He is the magic wand that strikes mysterious chords whose melody ravishes the angels. He is the protecting wall encircling the doctrine of the faith and the goodly grapes of the Divine vineyard. He is the rich harvest-field of the kingdom of heaven, that brings forth precious fruits of justice; the valley adorned with a thousand blossoms of spiritual roses, that send up a grateful odour to heaven. As the holy writings are his constant study, and the apostolic precepts his rule, and as he lives amid them as if amongst imperishable flowers, his speech flows forth like a stream, and his justice like the waves of the sea."

But we must return to Ephrem himself. In the midst of all his labours as preacher, missionary, poet, teacher, and father of the poor, he still retained in his soul the attraction to solitude which he shared with all the saints; for the Holy Ghost, speaking to the soul by the mouth of the prophet, says, "I will lead you into the wilderness; and there I will plead with you face to face." In the times of solitude, which he devoted to penance and heavenly contemplation, he made still greater progress in purity of heart by his indefatigable watchfulness over all his inclinations. As often as was possible, without offence against charity,

Ephrem withdrew from Edessa into the cavern not far distant, which he had formerly inhabited as a hermit, and there he plunged into the joys of intercourse with God and the depths of holy contemplations. Shortly before his death, Edessa was visited by a terrific famine, and its usual consequences, poverty and disease. Then he joyfully left his beloved cell, and entered the excited and terror-stricken city. He addressed himself to the rich and the opulent, by turns begging and threatening, praying and reproving, to prevail upon them to relieve the necessities of their poorer fellow-citizens. In such public calamities as these, self-love always reigns supreme, each one thinking only of himself and of his own in the most restricted sense, and thus it was at Edessa. But in Ephrem's eyes all were his who suffered, and he never ceased appealing to the consciences of the rich, until they announced that they were willing to give alms if they only knew who would distribute them properly. For the holy Bishop Barses and eighty Catholic priests had just been sent into exile for the faith by the Arian Emperor Valens, and people had grown so accustomed to intrust the distribution of alms to the Bishop, that in his absence some were truly at a loss, whilst others found therein a welcome excuse for their parsimony. But Ephrem had been consecrated deacon in order to impart sacramental grace to the care of the poor, according to the apostolic custom, and to combine with it the dispensing of higher graces. The Church so highly prized her poor and needy, that she bestowed an especial blessing on their care, and made the future priest, who was destined to the holiest intercourse with God in the sacrifice of the mass, undergo a sanctifying preparation of intercourse with God in the person of the poor. Therefore Ephrem said, " What think you of me?" and immediately alms and gifts flowed in plentifully upon him, and he displayed an activity equally circumspect and universal. He provided for all the wants of the poor of the town and the neighbourhood, and converted public buildings into hospitals, for such of the sick as had no other shelter. He spent a whole year in feeding the hungry, nursing the sick, burying the dead, converting and consoling the dying, moving the rich to love their neighbour; edifying the whole population of Edessa and inviting them to imitate his example. When the pestilence had passed away he returned to his cell, where he soon fell sick. Nevertheless, or perhaps for that very reason, he then wrote his exhortations to penance. Till his very last breath he continued to remind himself and others of the one thing necessary, a penitential conversion to God. He also made his will, that is to say, he wrote down his profession of faith for his disciples, testifying that he had ever remained without wavering in the pure faith and communion of the Church, abhorred heresy and avoided all intercourse with its sectaries, and exhorting his followers to do the same. He forbade that any one should praise him after his death, or give him stately burial, and still more stringently that any one should ask his intercession, "as we do that of the saints who have died in the Lord." He urgently implored them, on the contrary, to pray much for his soul, and to have the Holy Sacrifice often offered up for it. At the end, he gave his blessing to his disciples, with the exception of Paulonas and Aranad, although they seemed very fervent and gifted, because he foresaw, in the spirit of prophecy, that they would fall away from the true faith. He entered into the peace of the Lord in the year 378. He was mourned by the whole of Edessa. The Church, however, does not fulfil his wish, but

keeps his memory holy; and St. Gregory of Nyssa, who wrote his life, thus addresses him:—
"O thou, who standest now on the steps of the Divine Altar, before the King of life, where with the angels thou dost worship the Most Holy Trinity, be mindful of us all, and obtain for us the remission of our sins."

ST. MACRINA.

"Mind the things that are above, not the things that are upon the earth."—Col. iii. 2.

THE great influence exercised by the example of parents and by a good education, was strikingly shown in the family of saints to which the two Macrinas belonged. The elder Macrina, the ancestress of the highly favoured race, was of Neo-Cesarea in Pontus, where the holy Bishop Gregory Thaumaturgus had worked his miracles, and had blessed in tender childhood this lamb of the flock he had won for Christ. She espoused a husband who was her equa in rank and disposition, and in treasures of happiness and virtue. The persecution of the Christians by the Emperor Diocletian, which was continued with still greater fury by the Emperor Maximin, fell heavily on this couple. They were robbed of their lands, deprived of their property, and forced to fly into the wooded hills, where they wandered so long without any shelter, bore so many tribulations with joyful courage, and encouraged such numbers in the faith by their example, that they were honoured as holy confessors, and Macrina was looked upon as a saint. In later times, more favourable to Christianity, when the persecuted recovered their possessions,

Macrina and her husband arranged their worldly affairs, and lived thenceforward in Pontus, where they enjoyed all the consideration which virtuous behaviour united to great riches generally commands. These enlightened parents gave their only son Basil such an education as was to be expected from them, and it produced so much fruit that even in his youth he was admired throughout the country for his talent, his virtue, and his learning. Basil ripened into so great excellence, that not only does the Church reckon him amongst her saints, but God also gave him a saint for his wife, and a gar-
.and of saints for his children. The maiden whom Basil espoused was called Emmelia. Her inclinations were towards the cloister, but circumstances, or rather the Providence of God, ruled it otherwise. She early became an orphan, for her father succumbed to the cruelty of the Emperor Licinius, and her mother died of grief. Her rare beauty and immense wealth gained for her many suitors, who would sooner have carried her off by force than left her in the peace of the cloister. The unsettled state of the times afforded her no protection, so she chose Basil for her spouse, and bestowed on him her large possessions in Cappadocia. This union was blessed with ten children, of whom three sons were saints and bishops of the Church, namely, St. Basil the Great, Archbishop of Cesarea; St. Gregory, Bishop of Nyssa; and St. Peter, Bishop of Sebaste. The eldest of all the children was a daughter, who received her grandmother's name, Macrina. The fulness of the choicest gifts was bestowed upon her; a mind so powerful, penetrating, and lofty, that her brothers, those pillars of the Church, were edified by it; a heart so loving and courageous that the whole family leant upon it; a spirit so completely devoted to heavenly things that it overflowed with light; a beauty of form and grace of demeanour that added the charms of loveliness

to her higher prerogatives. Emmelia loved this daughter with boundless tenderness, and hardly ever let her leave her own arms and bosom. She was herself her nurse and afterwards her teacher. She never suffered the child's intellectual faculties to be occupied with the fantastic creations of the poets, nor her memory to be filled with verses as was then customary. She gave her mind strong and healthy food in those parts of the Holy Scriptures which are suited to the capacity of a child. Macrina learnt the Book of Wisdom and the Psalms easily and joyfully by heart, and found so much pleasure in the singing of psalms that she continued it during all her labours and occupations. This song arose with her in the morning, and went to rest with her in the evening; and in all her needlework, in which she was a great proficient, it was ever on her lips. Her mind was early and richly developed in this pure atmosphere of piety, and at the age of twelve her father betrothed her to a noble youth, who strove to emulate her perfection. But he died shortly after the betrothal. Macrina considered this circumstance as a dispensation of God, to show that she should remain in a state of virginity. She refused all other offers, for she said that death was only a journey, and not a lasting separation, and that she should one day see again the husband to whom her father had betrothed her, and could not therefore join herself to any other. Henceforward she lived as it were with her soul in heaven, whilst she fulfilled all her duties as fully and punctually as if her thoughts were wholly devoted to her family.

Her father died in the year 342, and at the same time her youngest brother Peter came into the world. Emmelia was overwhelmed with grief for the loss of her husband, who left her ten children to bring up and provide for, the eldest, Macrina, being thirteen years old. She would have allen a victim to these burdensome cares had not Macrina assisted her with wisdom and strength far beyond her years, and with exceeding love and tenderness. She undertook the entire charge of her little brother, who grew up in her arms as she herself had done in those of Emmelia. She undertook also the difficult management of a considerable estate, which consisted of lands scattered over the three provinces of Pontus, Cappadocia, and Lesser Armenia. She took such care of her delicate and tender mother, that she even dressed her herself, and prepared with her own hands a kind of bread that she liked. Her mother was only allowed to occupy herself with the children and the business of the house, enough to give her pleasure; the cares and the troubles Macrina kept for herself. In her inexhaustible love and power of consolation, this great soul became the spiritual sister of her mother, and the spiritual mother of her brothers and sisters. She presided over the education of the little Peter, and became his instructress, after having been his nurse. She would not allow the pure mind of the little boy to occupy itself with the profane sciences. He profoundly studied the Holy Scriptures and divine things, both for their doctrine and example, and early exercised himself in prayer, contemplation, mortification of his awakening passions, and the subjection of his will.

Her eldest brother Basil returned in the year 355 from Athens to Pontus, with that profound and haughty contempt of the world, which often ensnares a great genius that has acquired in early youth vast treasures of intelligence and of learning, without having exercised itself in the virtue of evangelical humility. Basil was only twenty-six years old, and yet the fame of his wisdom and his rare talent was so great, that the people of Neo-Cesarea offered to place him at the head of all their educational colleges,—indeed the entire population came to him with this request as soon as he arrived in the city. Basil refused the offer, for he was above that ambition which desires offices and dignities. He felt himself called to higher things, and thirsted for glory, for the renown of an imperishable name, for the admiration of the noblest minds of the present and future world. Macrina saw with pain that the noble soul of her brother was clouded by a disposition opposed to that of the Gospel, which teaches contempt of the world for love of God, and not out of self-esteem. Gently and softly she made him aware of the danger of such subtle self-complacency; and Basil awakened, as he himself expressed it, as out of a deep sleep, to the true light of the Gospel. He abandoned his haughty philosophy, and made a journey through Egypt, Palestine, Syria, and Mesopotamia, to study the divine wisdom of the great ascetics, and after their example to raise himself truly above the world. In the meantime, Macrina began on her part to practise with austerity this wise abnegation.

Her sisters being now all married, her brothers at school, or in a career where they were no longer in need of woman's care, Macrina proposed to her mother to form a religious community, and to dedicate themselves without distraction to the service of God in solitude. Emmelia was rejoiced to acquiesce, for she beheld the wish of her youth about to be fulfilled. Macrina established the monastery on one of their estates in Pontus. It lay on the river Iris in a wooded and solitary district in the diocese of the Bishop of Ibora. Barely a quarter of an hour from the convent was a church dedicated to the Forty Martyrs, those warriors who, in the reign of the Emperor Licinius, suffered death for the Christian faith at Sebaste in Armenia. Emmelia had caused the relics of these champions of Christ to be brought to this church; and God having given miraculous testimony to their holiness during their translation, the Forty Martyrs were held in great veneration by all the family. Macrina was superioress of the monastery and the soul of the entire community, which consisted partly of holy virgins and widows, partly of her own and Emmelia's friends and relations, and partly of their maid-servants. All their property was in common, and the dress, food, and beds were alike for all. Mortification was their delight, the renunciation of all earthly goods their riches, and to be forgotten by the world their glory. At the appointed ecclesiastical hours of the day and night their chanting arose, and their time sped in labour, prayer, spiritual reading, and contemplation.

In the year 358 Emmelia's motherly heart was deeply wounded by the death of her second son. He was called Naucrates, and was Macrina's favourite brother, a promising youth, handsome, intelligent, refined, learned, certain of success in every career. And behold! at the age of twenty-two, he, the first of the family, was seized with the spirit of asceticism. He took his paternal inheritance, divided it amongst the poor, renounced everything he possessed, and with only a bow and arrows retired to a wood on the river Iris, where he built himself a hermitage. His companion in this hard and rough life was his poor and holy slave called Chrysaph, who would let no tribulation separate him from his beloved master. Not satisfied with the austerities of such a life, Naucrates took two sick old men into his hermitage, tended their infirmities, and supplied them with food by his bow. After five years of these labours he and Chrysaph were found dead in the wood. Emmelia's heart was nearly broken, but Macrina's heavenly mind rejoiced in the bliss of her brother's early-ripened perfection, and she encouraged her mother in unconditional resignation to the will of God.

They had built a second monastery not far from their own for pious men who wished to dedicate themselves to holy contemplation in peaceful retirement. Peter was brought up and educated in this monastery; and when Basil returned from his travels and settled in a hermitage in a neighbouring wood, he undertook the government of it according to a rule which he himself composed. Then Macrina enjoyed the holy pleasure of seeing her noble brother tread the paths of perfection, for which his soul was in the highest degree adapted. He was soon called to the priesthood, and to do battle for the faith by word, deed, and pen, and was afterwards made archbishop of Cesarea; and though in every position he practised all the virtues of his state, yet holy solitude ever remained the object of his desires, and holy asceticism the means whereby he kept his soul in peaceful recollection in the midst of the activity of a stormy world.

At length Macrina was visited by a severe affliction; a cancer began to consume her life. Emmelia consulted all the doctors, and Macrina punctually used their remedies, but in vain; the fearful disease continued to increase. She remained as calm, as joyful, as active in labour, and as fervent in prayer, as she had ever been, but Emmelia was deeply afflicted. She could not believe that God would require from her the sacrifice of this child. She no longer placed her confidence in medical skill, but rather in the mercy of God; and she began to implore God night and day that this chalice of unspeakable bitterness might pass from her. And when she had stormed Heaven with her prayers, and was completely filled with confidence in Him who desires to be besought with glowing fervour and perseverance, she made the holy sign of redemption over her sick daughter, and the virtue of the Cross healed the disease and restored Macrina to health.

But Emmelia's last hour came. Too soon indeed for Macrina's loving heart, but just in time to spare the tender mother the pain of surviving Basil. On the first of January 379, the great St. Basil passed into eternity. Macrina followed him and her beloved mother in mind and in desire. All that she inherited from them she immediately gave to the poor. She treated her body with extreme contempt as the prison of her soul, which was thirsting more ardently than ever for eternal liberty. Prayer was her only solace. Her youngest brother Peter was superior of the neighbouring monastery, and comforted her by his brotherly love, which was heightened and sanctified by his priestly dignity. But she had not seen her third brother Gregory, the saintly Bishop of Nyssa, for eight years, because the tempest of Arianism had driven him from his bishopric into exile. The heretics were violent persecutors of all who would not join their heresy, but more especially of the bishops. Towards the end of the year 379 Macrina fell grievously ill. At the same time the council at Antioch came to a close, at which Gregory had been present, and he was at length able to hasten to Pontus and visit the two monasteries that were so dear to him. The monks came to meet him solemnly according to custom, and led him to Macrina's monastery, where the nuns were waiting for him in the church; they received his blessing with humility, and silently withdrew. Gregory understood from this that the superioress was no longer amongst them. He caused himself to be taken to her, and found her very ill in her miserable little cell. Her bed was a board, her pillow a hollowed block, her covering a penitential garment of hair. This poor couch was turned to the east, that she might pray in a decorous attitude.

He remained the whole day with her, and they spoke first of the death of Basil; Gregory with deep sorrow, Macrina as a parting soul, whose wings were already bearing her to glory. She spoke so beautifully of the worshipful will of God, of His love in sending us sorrows, of the dignity and destiny of the soul, and of the joys of everlasting life, that Gregory composed a treatise from her words, called, "The Soul and the Resurrection." Towards evening, when "the prayer of the lamps" as vespers were then called, began, Macrina sent her brother into the church, and prayed alone on her bed of suffering. Early on the following day he hastened to her, and saw at once that she was dying. She could not speak any more, except in low tones of prayer. She signed her heart and mouth with the Cross, and so gave up her beautiful soul. There was not found in the whole cloister any garment or mantle in which to clothe the holy corpse. Vestiana, a noble widow who governed the community during Macrina's illness, said with tears, "She had nothing but her poor religious habit." Then Gregory threw his episcopal mantle over the lifeless body, and took for himself the iron ring, containing a particle of the True Cross, which Macrina had always worn on her heart. Her cross, also of iron, he gave to Vestiana. Assisted by the Bishop of Ihora, he gave her solemn burial. Monks and nuns divided into two choirs, bearing candles in their hands, sang psalms in turn, whilst they accompanied the body which Gregory and the bishop themselves helped to carry to the Church of the Forty Martyrs. This church was only twenty minutes distant, but on account of the thronging crowd of people, it was not reached till near evening. Here Gregory, with the usual prayers and ceremonies, had the grave of his family opened, and laid Macrina's corpse next to that of her beloved mother Emmelia. Then he knelt down by the grave and kissed its earth. This happened in December of the year 379, and St. Gregory of Nyssa himself wrote the history of the life and death of his holy sister.

THE BLESSED MARANA AND THE BLESSED CYRA.

"Thy name and thy remembrance are the desire of the soul."—
ISAIAS xxvi. 8.

THE holy and learned Theodoret, Bishop of Cyrus in Syria, who died in the year 457 speaks in his "Lives of the Saints," of many holy persons whom he had himself known and sought out, or about whom he had certain information, and who lived, moreover, so near his own time that their lives and virtues were known to all. He visited many ascetics who lived as solitaries or in community in Syria, Cilicia, and Palestine; and he describes two courageous women, who had, when he saw them, led together for twenty-two years so penitential a life, that its severity was appalling even to him, although he had seen much austerity of like kind. "From the time," he writes, "in which Christ honoured virginal purity by willing to be born of a Virgin, the everblooming garden of virginity brings forth for the Creator alone thousands of undecaying flowers. Woman can practise this virtue, and attain to spiritual perfection as well as man. The difference between the sexes is not in matters regarding the faith and the soul, but in those of the natural order. Women have striven no less, perhaps even more boldly for heaven than men, and they are the more praiseworthy, in that they have borne the battle in their more tender bodies as bravely as men, and wiped out the infirmity and disgrace inherited from Eve. The Apostle St. Paul writes: 'There is neither male nor female, for you are all one in Christ Jesus.' And therefore our good God has only one heaven for His faithful servants."

Marana and Cyra were the daughters of wealthy and noble families of Berea, in Syria. They were friends from their youth, and the link that bound them together was not their distinguished birth, the riches of their parents, or the consideration they enjoyed in city and country,—not their brilliant education, their splendid dress, or other worldly frivolities,—it was their glowing love for Him who had first "loved them with an everlasting love." They not only regarded with indifference, but even with dislike, all the joys of youth, the pleasures of the world, and the luxuries of riches, because the Divine Bridegroom of their souls had lived in poverty and want, in suffering and abnegation, and whatever He did not share with them was in their eyes only false good and deceitful happiness. His Holy Passion was so deeply imprinted on their hearts, and stood so vividly before their eyes, that they desired nothing else but constantly to suffer out of love. Suffering borne for the perfect love of God is the highest step in the spiritual life, from which the soul takes flight to behold God in eternal glory. Their favourite contemplation in the Holy Scriptures was the parable of Dives and Lazarus, from which they learnt how much God loves poverty and suffering. For what had Lazarus done? What works of mercy, of piety, or of religion did he practise? We know not. We only learn that he suffered poverty, sickness, and scorn, and then that the angels carried him to Abraham's bosom. Marana and Cyra therefore loved sufferings, and would not lead upon earth the life of the rich man, lest they should have one day to languish in everlasting fire, banished from the sight of God. They soon perceived that marriage was not the state in which they could unreservedly satisfy their love for suffering, and also that it would be impossible for them to practise in their parents' house those works of penance for which they so longed, for there they were surrounded by comfort and luxury on every side. Therefore they left the city, and withdrew to a garden which Cyra's father gave to them; but they had no intention of living in the magnificent country house that stood therein. They had a little hut, without any roof, built in the garden, or rather a wall round a small open space. And this place, which afforded them no shelter from the heat of the sun or the cold of winter, from storm, rain, or dew, nor the smallest protection from insects or reptiles, became their dwelling-place, sleeping-room, eating-room, and oratory— a palace of holy love. They had the entrance built up, and two little windows opened in the wall, which they could close with shutters from the inside at pleasure. One window looked into the garden, and through it their scanty supply of bread and water was passed to them. The other looked into the little monastery against which one side of their wall leant. It was then the custom for people of rank to have an immense number of servants, consisting of slaves they had bought or inherited, who belonged to the family. When one of these families became Christian, their entire household frequently followed their example, and then the relations between masters and servants were arranged in a Christian manner. Sometimes newly converted rich people gave to all their slaves, numbering hundreds and even thousands, their liberty and a provision for their maintenance. When the masters dedicated themselves to an ascetic life, it always happened that some at least of their retainers wished in some manner to follow their example. This was the case with the servants of Marana and Cyra, and a small cloister, which joined the dwelling-place of their former mistresses, was built for them. They led there a completely secluded life, dividing their time between manual labour and spiritual exercises, and they received instruction and encouragement from Marana and Cyra, through the little window adjoining.

These two heroic virgins were not content with the penance which their dwelling and the want of the shelter of a roof caused them. The joy they felt in their hearts at having taken upon themselves the sweet and gentle yoke of the Lord was so great that it constrained them to undertake yet greater austerities as proofs of their love. They took iron chains, so heavy that a man could hardly carry them, and hung one upon their necks, and wound the other round their waists, both being so long that they hung down to the ground. Then they loaded their hands and feet with similar heavy chains, and over all these trinkets they threw long and broad veils, which in front hung down to their girdles, and behind down to the ground, covering their whole figures. In this bridal adornment they waited with unspeakable joy for the Spouse of their souls. And who was this Spouse? It was Christ in prison, Christ in bonds, Christ in the power of a savage populace. His imprisonment, first in the flesh, and then in His Passion, was the solution of this enigma of love, which the natural man will never be able to solve. Cyra, who was an extremely delicate person, could hardly bear up under the weight of her beloved chains. She was always immersed in holy contemplation, and no stranger ever heard her speak. Marana spoke at the window to the women who had recourse to these heroines of Christ in their various necessities and asked their prayers, but she did so only at the time of Pentecost, that the Holy Ghost might grant her to say what would be for the salvation of souls. With this exception, they kept unbroken silence. Notwithstanding the scantiness and poverty of their food, they observed a forty days' fast three times a year, and three times besides, one of twenty-one days.

The spirit of mortification also inspired them to visit the Holy Places in Jerusalem, and in silence and prayer, they made the long pilgrimage of twenty days' journey fasting, to gather on the actual scene of the Passion, fresh joy and love of suffering. In like manner they made, at another time, a pilgrimage to the tomb of St. Thecla at Seleucia, in Isauria. Each time they returned to their austere cell inflamed with renewed desire of penance. But they never gave a thought to all their pains. They lived in one almost continual extasy of prayer. Theodoret says: "I have many times visited and spoken with these servants of God and even seen them, for they opened the walled up entrance for me, to express their reverence for the priesthood. For the same reason, at my earnest request, they took off their heavy iron chains as long as I was with them; for I feared they would give way under their burdens before my eyes. They had then lived forty-two years in this terrific austerity, and in spite of the long and painful combat, they felt as much joy and fervour in it as if they had only just begun. They have ever before their eyes, on the one hand the Love and Passion of their Divine Spouse, and on the other His beauty and glory; and, in expectation of the reward He has promised them, they run their career without difficulty, regarding neither heat nor cold, hunger nor thirst, rain nor sun, pain nor fatigue; for at the end of their race stands their

Beloved, with the heavenly bridal crown. And, enchanted as it were by a holy love-potion, the desire of their soul soars above the earth to God."

If the Marys did these things, what should the Magdalens do?

ST. THAIS.

"At the voice of thy cry, as soon as he shall hear, he will answer thee."—ISAIAS xxx. 19.

THAIS was a Magdalen before her conversion. She was the child of Christian parents, and she had heard in her earliest years of God and the Christian faith. But her parents died, and Thais came to Alexandria very young, inexperienced, and beautiful. The passions of sinful nature were in league with the allurements of the world, and she trod the path of perdition. As she was not only very beautiful, but also clever and sensible, she won some by her grace, and others by her talent. The fame of her personal charms, and of her miserable way of life, rang through all Egypt, and penetrated even to the ears of the holy and enlightened abbot Paphnutius. What he heard of her did not awaken in him the curiosity of the worldly, or the scorn of the Pharisee, but an unspeakable sorrow that a creature so richly endowed and beautifully made after His image by the Creator, should be faithless to all His graces, and should precipitate herself headlong into hell. Like a good disciple of the merciful Saviour, who sat down by the Samaritan woman at the well, Paphnutius longed that she should acknowledge the gifts of God, and God enlightened and guided His holy servant. He put on worldly attire, took some money with him, and travelled to Alexandria, where he easily found the magnificent house of the beautiful Thais. Paphnutius caused himself to be introduced to her, and she received him in a splendidly furnished apartment. He then begged her to take him to a room more remote. She did so, but he asked her again if there was not a still more solitary room in her house. "Yes," answered Thais, surprised; "but what dost thou fear here? No man can see thee, and there is no place in the whole world where thou canst hide thyself from the all-searching Eye of God." "Thou knowest, then, that there is a God?" asked Paphnutius. "Certainly," replied Thais; "and I know also that there is a paradise of eternal bliss for the good, and a hell of everlasting torture for the wicked." "O miserable one," exclaimed Paphnutius, "if thou knowest this, how canst thou then condemn thyself to eternal torments, to which thou art sending, not thine own soul alone, but the souls of others also?" Never in all her life, had poor Thais heard such words. They penetrated her heart like a thunderbolt, and a shower of grace followed them. At one glance she saw the guilt of her whole life. Overcome by the horror of the sight, she fell upon her face, and with many tears, exclaimed: "O my venerable father, impose upon me a salutary penance, and by thy prayers obtain for me from God the pardon of my sins! What shall I do? Whither shall I go?" The holy abbot described to her the gate of a monastery of nuns at which he should wait for her. "I will come," she said; "give me first three hours time, and then I will come without fail." Paphnutius left her, for he saw that the grace of God was powerfully working in her. It was the age of great conversions, and great penances,—the age of great souls, in which grace abounded, as sin had done before. When sinners were converted, they were so grieved for their offences against God, that public humiliation was eagerly welcomed by them. These dispositions rendered possible the public penances of the Church, which consoled the deep sorrow of the sinner, and made satisfaction for his sins, and afforded to the rest of the faithful great edification, and a wholesome example of humility.

Thais collcoted together all her valuables, jewels, pearls, gold-embroidered garments, all that she possessed of trinkets and rich ornaments, and had them made into a heap in the public market-place, and then set fire to it with her own hand, in the sight of all the people. She did not leave the spot till the costly pile was consumed; the gold melted, the jewels blackened, and the purple and silks reduced to ashes. Then she went away and sought the holy abbot at the appointed place. Paphnutius received her, led her into the nuns' cloister, and into the cell which he had ordered to be prepared for her. It was a very small room, with a little opening in the door. "Here," said he, "thou shalt do penance, and through this little window thou shalt receive daily a small quantity of bread and water. The religious will bring it to thee, but thou shalt never speak to them." "And how shall I pray?" asked Thais, humbly. "Thou art not worthy to speak with thy impure lips the Name of God, nor to lift up thy sin-stained hands to heaven, so thou shalt content thyself with turning towards the rising of the sun, and saying: "Thou who formedst me, have mercy on me." Thereupon he left her, shutting the door, and securing it with a leaden seal.

Thais was alone. So she remained for three years. No human voice encouraged her, no human eye beheld her, no human consolation refreshed her. She felt that one who was unworthy to associate with mankind was still more unworthy to approach God. Without once lifting up her eyes to heaven, she prayed with a truly contrite heart, using no other words but those which Paphnutius had prescribed to her. After three years, the holy abbot thought that Thais had sufficiently purified herself by penance to be instructed in the faith and received into Holy Church. But lest he should be moved by untimely pity, and do her soul harm rather than good, he went to the great St. Antony in the desert and besought his advice. The saints so highly esteem the concerns of a single soul, that Paphnutius did not hesitate to make this long and wearisome journey on her account, and Antony bade all his disciples betake themselves to prayer to obtain light in this matter, and then impart to him their opinion upon it. They all obeyed and amongst them Paul the Simple, who had a beautiful vision. He saw a magnificent couch in heaven, and three august virgins watching it. When Paul rejoiced, and with childlike simplicity exclaimed, "That must be for my father Antony," he heard a voice which said: "By no means, it is for Thais the penitent." Paul related this in the assembly of the brethren to the great edification of all, and Paphnutius, enlightened in spirit by this vision, repaired to Alexandria to the captive of God, and taking off the seal from the door, said to her, "Come forth and tell me how thou hast spent these three years." Thais answered, "I have prayed as thou didst bid me, and have contemplated day and night the number and grievousness of my sins, and have wept. "See," said Paphnutius, "God forgives thy sins, not because of thy penances, but on account of thy contrition." As Paphnutius desired it, Thais left her cell, although she would rather have remained in it. But at the end of a fortnight God called her to Himself in heaven.

ST. PELAGIA.

"Deep calleth on deep."—Ps. xli. 8.

Mount Olivet and all the hills of Palestine were favourite abodes of the ascetics. Those who preferred the contemplation of eternal goods to the enjoyment of perishable ones, withdrew into hermitages, cells, and convents; and they felt themselves more impelled to suffer for love of God on the very spots where the Son of God had suffered for the love of men. All the hills between Jerusalem, Jericho, the Dead Sea, and Bethlehem were pierced by caverns and clefts formed by nature in the soft limestone, and easily multiplied by the hand of man. The village of Siloe, near Jerusalem, is a complete village of caves. Several of these caves are closed in front by a mud wall with a door in it, some have a kind of penthouse, but others are merely rough caverns. Perhaps Siloe was once a monk's laura. On no place did the monks better love to raise their cells than on "the holy Mount Olivet," as ancient pious books call it, for there began what they term "God's distress," the bitter Passion of the Lord; and there, with the Ascension began His eternal joys. There is no place in the whole world where souls who desire to associate themselves to His sufferings here below in order to share His glory above, can better or more easily make their *via crucis* than on Mount Olivet. It is a long hill, with three peaks, lying to the east of Jerusalem. The southern peak is called the Mount of Offence, (*Mons Offensionis*,) because King Solomon, deprived of his wisdom, caused sacrifice and incense to be offered there to Moloch, Astaroth, and other idols, when amongst his strange women he forgot the Lord. The northern summit is called "the Mountain of the men of Galilee," because the Galileans were in the habit of dwelling there when they came up to Jerusalem for the prescribed feasts of the law. The centre hill is the site of the Ascension of Christ. From thence there is a view of Jerusalem, the deicide, curse-laden city, trodden under foot by the infidels, and no part of it is so conspicuous as the Turkish mosque of Sakarab on Mount Moria. From Mount Olivet there is also an extensive prospect over the country, which looks like a petrified sea, desolate, barren, and stony. Far away in the east, between the clefts of the tawny hills, is seen the sparkling blue of the Dead Sea, eight leagues distant. And beyond it rise the mountains across the Jordan, one of which is Nebo, from whence Moses wistfully gazed into the land of promise, which he was never to tread. In the western distance, if the day is clear and the light favourable, the Mediterranean Sea is visible, near Jaffa and Ascalon, where the old crusaders landed to drive the Mussulman, the jaokal of the desert, out of the kingdom of the " lion of the race of Juda."

The road from Jerusalem to Mount Olivet leads first along the *via dolorosa* (the way of sorrows,) the way along which Christ, bearing his Cross, passed from the judgment-hall to Golgotha, but in the opposite direction. Golgotha is now enclosed in the church of the Holy Sepulchre. The *via dolorosa* leads past all those Stations of the Cross,—so many thousand times accurately measured, copied, and illustrated by art,—and ends at St. Stephen's Gate, which received its name from the holy deacon who was stoned outside of it. Here a slope of Mount Moria falls steeply away, and with Mount Olivet which rises opposite, forms a dell which is called the valley of Josaphat. Through this valley flows the brook Cedron. The whole character of this landscape is of an appalling severity. The walls and houses of the city, Mount Moria, Mount Olivet, the ruins, the ground, the bed of the river Cedron, are all of the same yellowish stone. Not even a blade of grass is visible between the loose stones which cover the ground, nothing but thinly scattered olive-trees, whose silvery grey leaves are in perfect harmony with the colouring of the whole landscape. It seems as if the earth, like the ancient penitents, had strewn its head with dust and ashes, because the King of Life, its Creator and Preserver, had here died. A bridge crosses the Cedron, and then the road passes by the ever adorable Garden of Gethsemane, lying at the foot of Mount Olivet. Eight of its ancient olive-trees witnessed the Agony of God. Their mighty stems are completely hollow, and are filled with stones, to enable them to afford resistance to the wind. Gethsemane lies on the right of the road; on the left is the grave of the "Blessed among women," over which rises a little church, so greatly honoured and frequented, that even the Turk, who drinks coffee and smokes in the church of the Holy Sepulchre, has here made a praying place; for, as she said in her prophetical song of triumph, "from henceforth all generations shall call me blessed." The Turk honours Mary, although Christ is not his God; and yet Christians are to be found who will not honour Mary, the Mother of their God! The road leads between this grave and Gethsemane, round the foot of Mount Olivet to Bethany, to the rocky desert of Quarantana, where Jesus kept the forty days' fast, and then to Jericho and Ghor, the second valley through which the Jordan flows before it empties itself into the Dead Sea. But if, instead of taking the road to Bethany, we begin to ascend Mount Olivet at Gethsemane, in a short half-hour we shall reach the middle summit, that of the Ascension. Here, in former ages, stood the church of

St. Pelagia, the great penitent, whose soul was first like Jerusalem in its desolation, and afterwards became a city of peace.

In the middle of the fifth century, when many anchorites had established themselves on Mount Olivet and in the valley of Josaphat, there was one of them distinguished above the rest by his extreme austerity. He had come one day, no one knew whence, and had visited the Holy Places of Jerusalem with such devotion and contrition and such floods of tears, that all were moved who saw him, particularly as he seemed of weak frame, refined countenance, and delicate complexion. He was taken for a pilgrim, and it created no little surprise when this delicate youth entered a cavern on Mount Olivet, shut himself up therein by a door with a hole in it to admit light and air, and only left this cell once a week to draw water and gather a few herbs, upon which he lived. Otherwise he never showed himself, and spoke to no one. If he met a hermit on the way to the well, he greeted him with exceeding humility. He lived for prayer and penance alone. Besides the ecclesiastical office which he recited at the appointed hours, he occupied himself in singing psalms, which were interrupted only by his sobs and tears. Even in the stillness of night, when all the monks and solitaries were reposing for a short time, in order to gain the necessary strength for body and soul, this hermit began to sing hymns so wondrous and so sweet, that the brother who lived next to him thought, the first time he heard him, that he was listening to the angelic choirs. He arose and went out of his cell to enjoy the beautiful song, and then he perceived that it came from the cell of Brother Pelagius, as the young penitent was called. He cautiously approached; but, upon his making some unexpected noise, the music immediately ceased, and the hermit therefore concluded that the singer was no angel but Brother Pelagius himself. If a brother kept watch later than usual for any especial work of penance, he always heard the beautiful singing of Brother Pelagius. This penitent lived thus for four years, his face growing paler and paler, his form more shrunk, his walk more feeble. This was remarked by the brothers when he went to the well, or to pluck herbs. But it was nothing unusual that the bodily strength should be consumed; the strongest penitents, as Hilarion and Macarius, were so reduced as to resemble mummies, and nevertheless lived to a very great age, because it pleased God to prolong their earthly life by supernatural means. When such was not the case, and the hermit was permitted early to accomplish his course, the brethren rather envied than pitied him for it.

About this time James, deacon of Edessa, had a great desire to visit the Holy Places of the promised land; his bishop gave him permission to make a pilgrimage thither, and at the same time directed him to inquire at Jerusalem for the penitent Brother Pelagius, and to carry him his greeting. The deacon found it very difficult to accomplish this commission, for no one in Jerusalem knew the name of the great penitent, but at last they guessed it must be this Brother Pelagius whom James was seeking, and they showed him his cell on Mount Olivet. James knocked gently at the door. The hermit did not open the door, but only the little window in it, and asked what he wished. James then beheld a deadly pallid and wasted face with tearful sunken eyes, and said, "Nonnus, Bishop of Edessa, sends his greeting to Brother Pelagius." And Pelagius answered, "Bishop Nonnus is a holy man, and I recommend myself to his prayers," and shutting the little window he began reciting Tierce. James was extremely edified by the great mortification of the solitary. who could not be induced, even by the greeting of the bishop, to say a useless word, or to ask a single question. Many things that he heard about the brother in the city, and from the other hermits, increased his admiration; and in the hope, that on a second visit Pelagius might perchance say some word for the good of his soul, James went to him once more before returning to Edessa. When he knocked, neither door nor window were opened. He thought the holy penitent might be buried in prayer, or perhaps ravished in contemplation, and he recited his hours, and knocked again, waiting till the sun began to sink. Then he remembered the deathly pallor of Pelagius's countenance, and tremblingly ventured to peep into the cavern by a chink in the door. Pelagius lay outstretched on the stony floor, whether ill or dead, it was too dark for him to determine. He hastened to the nearest hermit, told him his fears, and they opened the door together. As soon as daylight shone upon the body they perceived that the soul had departed, and they assembled all the hermits to pray by the corpse, and to wash it with myrrh according to the custom of the country. Then they discovered that Pelagius was a woman. The solitaries praised the power of God Who had given such strength to so weak a creature, and immediately despatched messengers to the nuns of Jerusalem, and even to those of Jericho and the valley of the Jordan, with this unwonted news. The consecrated women and virgins hurried to the spot in great numbers, to pay the last honours to this sister in whom God had concealed such vast treasures of grace, and with devout chants and festal torches, the great penitent was transferred from her sepulchre above ground to her grave under ground. The church of St. Pelagia on Mount Olivet, which a more religious age had dedicated to her is now destroyed. And as her cavern was near the "cave of the Agony," so her chapel was erected on the hill of the Ascension. "She had come out of great tribulation, and had washed er robes, and had made them white in the Blood of the Lamb;" therefore she stood with the palm of victory in her hand before the throne of Him who maketh all things new, and who wipeth away all tears.[1]

When the deacon James connected the name Pelagius, the terrific penance, and the greeting of his holy bishop, with the departed, his memory was enlightened. He recollected where and how he had seen her before, and he wrote the history of her wonderful conversion as an encouraging example to all poor sinners, and for the great edification of all pious souls.

About the middle of the fifth century, in the reign of Theodosius the Younger, the Patriarch of Antioch assembled together his fellow bishops at his metropolitan see, on account of the necessities of the Church. Amongst these, Nonnus, Bishop of Edessa, formerly a monk of Tabenna, was distinguished for his holiness of life and his wisdom in spiritual things. When all the bishops, and an immense concourse of people were present in St. Julian's Church in Antioch, the patriarch ordered him to edify them by a pious discourse. The noly bishop willingly obeyed the summons, and all his hearers listened with delight to the teaching of the Gospel which he, being filled with the Holy Ghost, explained to them. The crowd was so great and so anxious to hear him, that St. Julian's Church could not contain them all, and the doors stood wide open, with listeners pressing closely around them. Suddenly there was a great disturbance before one of these doors, all heads and eyes were turned, not towards Bishop Nonnus but away from him, to the beautiful Pelagia, the

[1] Apocalypse vii. 14, xxi. 4.

chief singer and dancer at the theatre of Antioch who was passing. Her appearance was sufficient to excite a great commotion. Amongst a multitude of magnificently clothed attendants, she rode, shining with jewels, upon a mule decked with gold-embroidered trappings. From the diadem which encircled her long flowing hair down to her sandals, around her throat, arms, and hands, nothing was to be seen save diamonds and pearls. But these ornaments were all forgotten at the sight of her marvellous beauty, which no worldling could behold without admiration. People were not content with seeing her as she passed by, but they ran after her, or in front of her by a shorter way, and then stood still to see her pass again and again. A great rush of people followed her to St. Julian's Church, when she stopped before the door and cast her eyes over the pious assembly within. There was nothing there to attract her attention, for she soon rode on again and left the air filled with the sweet perfume of scents and essences which issued from her garments and hair; and it seemed as though her mule had borne away the whole of Arabia, the land of precious stones and balsamic odours. Her passing by caused a great disturbance even inside the church. Unfortunately, curiosity is so universal that pious people themselves do not consider it a vice; therefore, for a few moments, Bishop Nonnus and his sermon were forgotten, and all gazed at Pelagia. Even the holy bishop himself did the same, and whilst the other bishops turned away from the disorder, and bent their eyes on the ground, he looked at Pelagia, followed her with his eyes as long as she was in sight, and then finished preaching. He afterwards asked the other bishops if they had not admired the extraordinary beauty of this person. The reverend fathers were much astonished at this question, and made no reply. But he bent his head down upon the psalter which lay upon his knee, sighed deeply, and said, " I looked upon her wondrous beauty with the greatest attention, for Almighty God will set it before our eyes when He calls us and our flocks to account on the Great Day of Judgment. Oh, my brethren! how many hours must she not have employed in dressing and adorning herself! how carefully must she have chosen all that could enhance her natural beauty! and wherefore all this trouble, attention, and labour? To please mortal men, who are as perishable as vapour! And we, my brethren! has not God given us a soul whose original beauty is infinitely greater than the corporeal beauty of this poor creature? For our souls are made after the image of God. And has not God promised to be the Eternal Bridegroom of our souls, and to bestow upon them a superfluity of joys and delights if they love Him and seek to serve Him? Oh, my brethren! where are the pearls and jewels with which we adorn our souls? where the essences and perfumes with which we embalm them? how are we preparing them to appear before the heavenly Bridegroom in festal array, and with the sweet odour of virtue, that they may not be unpleasing in His sight! Oh woe! woe unto us! instead of adorning them, we let them be laid waste and desolate!" And deeply troubled, with many sighs and tears, the holy bishop took his deacon by the hand, and retired with him to the room which had been assigned to him, in a house belonging to St. Julian's church, and contiguous to it. For the hospitality of the early Christian times prepared shelter and lodging for pilgrims and strangers near the churches, as it were under the protection of the Tabernacle.

Bishop Nonnus no sooner found himself alone in his room than he threw himself on the ground, struck his breast with contrition, and with floods of tears exclaimed, "My Lord and my God, forgive me! That woman takes more pains for her body than I do for my soul. That woman has determined to please mortal men, and carries out her resolution with zeal. But I have resolved to please Thee, and from mere sloth I neglect it! And because I have not kept Thy commandments, nor fulfilled Thy will, therefore am I naked, poor, and hateful, before Thee and before men." Bishop Nonnus spent all that day and night with his deacon, weeping and mourning in the bitterness of his heart over his supposed infidelity.

When he lay down for a little repose, to restore his strength before matins, he had a dream which he related to his deacon the following morning, saying, "I stood at the altar to celebrate the holy mysteries when I was in an almost insupportable manner disturbed and vexed by a terribly stained and soiled dove which kept constantly flying about my head. When the Mass of the Catechumens was finished, and the deacon commanded the unbaptized to leave the church, the dove also disappeared, but returned as I gave the blessing at the end of the holy Mass and flew around me once more. At last I caught it and dipped it in the vase of water that stands at the entrance of the church, and it came out of the water as white as a swan, and flew so high that I was no longer able to see it." The following day was Sunday, and the service in the cathedral at Antioch was performed with all possible solemnity by the assembled bishops in the presence of a great concourse of people. After the reading of the holy Gospel, the patriarch gave the Book of the Gospels to Nonnus, and begged him to edify the people by a discourse. Nonnus began to preach upon the future judgment and the joys and pains of eternity. It was one of those sermons in which God speaks by the mouth of His faithful servants to penetrate the inmost hearts of the hearers. The whole assembly was moved to tears, and many a sinner entered into himself and turned with repentance to God. But none shed such floods of tears, or was so appalled by the terrors of the Great Day of Judgment, none cast so despairing a glance upon their misdeeds as the beautiful, the admired, the richly-decked Pelagia. She had heard of the bishop of the Christians and his renowned sermons; in her early youth, perchance, by pious parents she had been enrolled amongst the Catechumens; but she had never since thought of occupying herself with Christian doctrine; and now she felt impelled by a dispensation of Divine Mercy to attend the Christian service as far as was permissible to the unbaptized. The sermon pierced her heart. She left the church changed in her inmost being, and ordered some of her servants to follow Bishop Nonnus when he should return to his own dwelling. They did so, and as soon as she learnt that he was in the hospice of St. Julian's church, she wrote to him as follows:—

"My Lord,—I have heard that thy God came down from heaven to this earth to save sinners, and that He did not disdain to mix with them. I have also heard from Christians that thou, my lord, dost shine with great holiness, and follow Christ as His true servant and disciple. If this is indeed the case, then despise me not, for I hope, through thee, to attain to the knowledge of God, and one day to be worthy to behold His Face."

Bishop Nonnus wrote in answer:—" Whoever thou mayest be, thou art known to God with thy will and thy works. If thou hast an earnest desire and sincere intention of being instructed in the knowledge of God, in the faith and in virtue, and dost therefore wish to see me and to speak to me,

I am willing to receive thee in the presence of my brethren the other bishops."

Full of joy at this favourable answer, Pelagia hastened to Bishop Nonnus and caused herself to be announced. She had to wait till the other bishops were sent for, and not till they were all assembled was she allowed to enter. They did not fully trust her, for they still feared some theatrical display. But Pelagia entering threw herself upon her knees before Bishop Nonnus, kissed his feet, and said, "Oh, my lord, I beg of thee to be mild and gentle, as thy God Jesus Christ is, and to make me a Christian. I am an abyss of sin, grant me therefore that water which purifies from all sin—holy baptism." Bishop Nonnus bade Pelagia rise, and said to her, "The laws of the Church forbid certain persons to receive the Sacrament of Baptism, except under the condition of giving secure pledges that they will not return to their former life, and this law applies to thee." Pelagia fell at his feet once more, and said with burning tears, "I know not what pledge to give, but thou mayest depend upon my never returning to my old life. As this is quite certain, thou must cleanse my soul, that it may be pure and fitted for a new life. If thou leavest me one moment longer under the burden of my sins which weigh me to the grcund, God will impute it to thee, and thou wilt have to render a strict account of it. If thou wilt not this very day offer up my soul to God, and wilt not this very day make me a bride of Christ by being newly born in baptism; then may God retard for thee in the life to come the vision of His most holy Countenance." She lay upon the ground bathed in tears, and would not be comforted, and all the bishops present agreed that this was the true contrition of a Magdalen at the feet of the Divine Saviour.

Bishop Nonnus sent his deacon James to the

Patriarch of Antioch, with the commission to relate the whole occurrence to him, and to beg him to send some religious woman or deaconess to assist at the baptism of the catechumen. The patriarch was greatly rejoiced, and exclaimed, "Truly this affair has rightly waited for the venerable Nonnus, for he can best carry it out and glorify God exceedingly!" He immediately sent for a worthy woman of the name of Romana, the superioress of the deaconesses, and told her to accompany James to the house of Bishop Nonnus, there to assist at the baptism, and then to take Pelagia under her protection and supervision. The poor sinner was still lying on the floor bathed in tears and crushed by sorrow, when Romana came, and raising her up bade her collect herself and confess her sins. "Ah!" said the sorrowful Pelagia, "that will be very easy, for when I search my heart to the best of my power and knowledge, I find nothing good, but an overabundance of all that is wicked. And although I know that my sins are more numerous than the drops of water in the ocean, and heavier than the sand of the sea-shore, yet I hope that the Lord God Jesus Christ will look upon me in pity, and deliver me from my frightful burden." Bishop Nonnus asked her name. She said, "My parents called me Pelagia. But now, alas! I am known by the name of Margaret, because I loved to be adorned with pearls, and because my miserable beauty, that snare of Satan, was compared to the beauty of pearls."—"Then we will give thee thy real name, Pelagia," said Bishop Nonnus, and he immediately commenced the holy ceremony. First he recited the ecclesiastical exorcisms over Pelagia, then he baptized her by complete immersion three times in a deep basin in the middle of the baptistery, into which the catechumen descended by steps. At that period the Sacrament of Confirmation, which bestows the fulness of the Holy Spirit, was administered immediately after baptism, as being especially necessary to the newly-converted Christians in those early times, when they often had to seal their new faith with immediate martyrdom. Finally, after her confirmation, Pelagia received the Holy Sacrament of the Altar, the Bread of eternal life, and became a member of the mystical Body of Christ. The pious Romana had been the witness of her baptism, and now as her spiritual mother she led her away to see that she received full instruction in the Christian faith. And Bishop Nonnus said to his deacon, with the childlike joy of the saints, "We also will spend today joyfully, like the dear angels in heaven, for there is exultation and rejoicing today over the conversion of this soul. Therefore let us have oil with our food, and wine to drink, as we do on the great feast-days, and let us eat a joyful meal in the Lord."

Pelagia now wore the white garment of a neophyte, the type of a purified soul. But she had great temptations to overcome; for the wicked enemy set before her, in the most alluring manner, the pleasant life she had led in his service, the joys, riches, and admiration which had been her share, and that she was now like Judas, who betrayed and abandoned the Master who had loaded him with favours and love. Bright infatuating visions played around her, representing to her under the most attractive form, all that she must now trample on. To Bishop Nonnus Satan showed by terrific menaces, his rage at Pelagia's salvation. But both calmly opposed him with those weapons before which he is powerless; the holy sign of the Cross, and the lifting up of the soul to God. Pelagia thus addressed the enemy of all good: "The merciful Lord who has snatched me from thee, and chosen me for His spouse, will henceforward combat thee in my stead.' And immediately she was filled with deep and imperturbable peace.

On the third day after her baptism she sent for the slave who superintended her household, and kept all her valuables under lock and key. She ordered him immediately to draw up a correct catalogue of all her possessions; gold, silver, jewels, ornaments, magnificent dresses, and furniture, and to bring the list to her. She gave it to Bishop Nonnus, and said: "My lord, herewith I lay all my riches in thy blessed hands, that thou mayest dispose of them as thou pleasest. I, for my part, desire no other riches than those of my Lord and Saviour Jesus Christ." Bishop Nonnus immediately sent for the chief procurator of St Julian's Church, and said to him, in Pelagia's presence, whilst he handed him the list, "All this property has been made over to me. I conjure thee by the Most Holy Trinity not to use the smallest portion of it for the benefit of the Church or of the Patriarch of Antioch, but rather to divide it all amongst the widows and orphans, the cripples, and the needy, that the riches sinfully acquired may be well spent and converted into treasures of justice." The procurator promised to do so, and the poor of Antioch blessed the goodness of God in their unknown merciful benefactor.

Pelagia had one more arrangement to make, namely, the disposal of her numerous retinue, which consisted entirely of slaves, male and female. She made them all come to see her, and gave them not only their freedom, but also as much of the money and jewels she had kept back for this purpose as would enable them to gain an honest livelihood. They all wept and sorrowed, kissing her hands and the hem of her garment, and would not consent to be separated from her, preferring her service to being free without her, so great was their attachment to her. But she spoke to them sadly and affectionately, saying, "Do not grieve; I am otherwise cared for. You can serve me no longer, and we can never live together again upon this earth. But if you wish to meet me again in the happiness of eternal life, do as I am doing, and bid quickly adieu to the world and its wicked service." Thereupon she left them, and shut herself up again in the poor cell in the house of the widow Romana, where she lived.

Thus passed the eight first days after baptism, during which the neophytes always wore their white baptismal garments; these they afterwards laid aside, to resume their daily occupations in the ordinary homely garb of the faithful. In the last night Pelagia disappeared from Antioch, not however, without having informed Bishop Nonnus of her holy purpose; for he gave her a man's clothing, which she put on over a hair shirt, leaving her baptismal garment behind her. The next morning Romana hastened to Bishop Nonnus, almost beside herself with grief and fear, with the news that Pelagia was not to be found; but he said to her, "Weep not, my daughter, yea, rather rejoice that our Pelagia has chosen the better part, that of the holy penitent Magdalen, who was so pleasing to God that she was allowed to stand by the Cross on Calvary, and to be the first to see Him after His resurrection." As Romana saw Bishop Nonnus so unmoved, she thought that Pelagia was going to enter a convent in some foreign country, and she blessed the Good Shepherd who provided so carefully for His lost sheep. Pelagia, the beautiful, the admired, the renowned, remained lost to Antioch. She made a pilgrimage to Jerusalem, and there, in the most holy of places, ended a life amid the thorns and ashes of penance which had begun in the splendour and brilliancy of sinful worldly pleasure. From the abyss of sin she threw herself into the abyss of penance, and this opened to her the abyss of divine love.

ST. SIMEON STYLITES.

"He that believeth in me, the works that I do, he also shall do, and greater than these shall he do."—St. John xiv. 12.

WHEN Theodoret undertook to write this life in his "History of the Lives of the Saints," he said, "This man was indeed known as a wonder of the world to the whole Roman Empire, both eastern and western, as well as to the Persians, Arabians, Indians, and Africans. The fame of his holy life penetrated even to the extreme borders of Scythia, so that I can call the whole world, and all his contemporaries, as witnesses of the truth of what I relate. Nevertheless, I fear to describe the terrific warfare and the superhuman austerity of his life, lest posterity should mistake a true fact for a poetical fiction. All that has to do with holy men and the friends of God is supernatural, but those who are inexperienced in the spiritual life measure these things by a natural standard, and if the history surpasses nature, these divine mysteries and miracles seem to them nothing but falsehood. Yet the earth is full of holy and faithful men, who are well versed in spiritual things, and fortified by the grace of the Holy Ghost, and these, I believe, will be highly edified by this miraculous life." This introduction is as applicable now as it was fourteen centuries ago, and it will be equally so to the end of time. A St. Simeon Stylites, a Macarius, a Marana, and a Cyra, are to be looked upon as the "magnalia Dei," the wonderful works of God, which the people praised in the Acts of the Apostles. For man cannot do these things by his own power and his own will. He may perhaps begin them, but he perseveres not, or he perseveres only out of obstinacy, and without a blessing; or he gains influence, only to use it for evil and deceit. We must therefore always repeat what the prophet says, "Thou hast wrought all our works for us."[1]

Simeon stood upon his column like an angel. God had placed him there to show heathens, Jews, and heretics the way to heaven. All men flocked to this column; princes and people stood there, and listened to the heavenly eloquence of the poor shepherd, and emperors sent him messages of greeting. But he was not inspired by any worldly wish; what he sought was not of earth. His desire, his longing, his consolation, his good, his all, was to suffer for the love of Jesus.

Theodoret was a contemporary, fellow-countryman, and friend of Simeon, and an eye-witness of the extraordinary things that happened to him and around him. He visited him occasionally and died himself two years before Simeon's death. But he was not the only one who wrote Simeon's life. It was written by one of Simeon's disciples, of the name of Antony, and also by Cosmas, a priest of Phanir in Cœle-Syria.[2] They are not all alike in details, for one relates what the other omits, and Theodoret expressly says that he only gives a little drop of honey to taste. But the principal facts, and the description of this new form of the ascetic life, are the same in all the three.

---

[1] Isaias xxvi. 12.

[2] This last biography was published in Rome in the year 1748, by the learned Maronite Evodius Assemani, Archbishop of Apamea.

The village of Sis, or Sisan, in which Simeon came into the world in the year 388, was situated on the borders of Cilicia, in the mountains of Northern Syria. His parents were wealthy peasants, and good Christians. He received baptism as soon as he was born. He was early distinguished for his natural talents, his beauty, his strength, and his ability, and he was, moreover, of a cheerful and kind disposition, and had such a loving heart that he often deprived himself of his own food to feed the hungry. Like the patriarchs of old, Jacob and David, Simeon was a shepherd boy. His parents intrusted to him their flock of sheep, and he fulfilled all the duties of his state with great care. He loved the solitude of the hills and valleys where he led his sheep to pasture, for it suited and nourished the thoughtful tendency of his mind, whilst the images of nature made pure and peaceful impressions upon his soul. He was completely untouched by worldliness or sin, and was entirely destitute of instruction and education. In the morning he drove his flocks out, and brought them home in the evening, so that he had neither time nor opportunity for learning. But on Sundays he went with his parents to church, and what he there saw and heard was the small seed that brought forth later the blossoms of his enlightened and heavenly wisdom. He took great delight in collecting the sweet-smelling gum storax from the bushes, and when he had gathered a little store of it, he lighted a fire on the hills, and burnt it, for he liked to think that the sweet perfume would ascend to heaven. Perchance this was a foreshadowing of all the prayers which were one day to rise up to God from his soul. There are sometimes wonderfully deep thoughts in the mind of a child.

In the course of one winter there fell so much

snow that Simeon could not take out his sheep to feed, but was obliged to remain at home for some time. He then went oftener to church, and listened with the greatest attention to the reading of the Gospel. Once he heard the Sermon on the Mount, with its blessed promises. It seemed to him so beautiful, and yet so unintelligible that the mourners should be comforted, and the clean of heart see God, that he turned to an old man, and asked him what they were reading. The old man said to him, " It is the Gospel, my son, for the instruction of our souls, that we may learn to serve Almighty God and to fear Him." " What is fearing God?" asked Simeon, who was then thirteen years old. The old man was amazed, and said, " I see that thou art certainly very young; but can it be that thou dost ask me really out of igno rance?" " I ask thee in God's stead," answered Simeon; "for I would fain learn to practise what I hear. But I am ignorant and simple." Then the old man said, " My child, when a man humbles himself before every one, prays to God without ceasing, practises fasting, and all kinds of mortification of the senses, and does not let his heart attach itself either to money or goods, parents or friends, but fulfils the commandments of God faithfully and conscientiously, then he will inherit heaven, and walk in the holy and wholesome fear of God; and whosoever does not do so will one day be cast into outer darkness, in which the devil and his evil spirits dwell. But, my son, the cloister is the place where thou canst best learn and practise all these holy things. Yet weigh this well, thou wouldst there have to suffer hunger and thirst, to bear contempt and injury, to let thyself be slandered and reviled, to suffer much from man, without being consoled by the angels of God, for such is the way of perfection. If thou hast the will to tread it, may the Lord of glory give thee His grace to do so." Then Simeon fell at the feet of the old man, and exclaimed, "Thou art my father and my mother! my teacher in all good, the guide of my soul to heaven! may God reward thee for having saved my soul, which was already inclining to perdition! As for me, I will go where God's grace would have me." "Go, my son," said the old man; "tribulation will not be wanting to thee, but thou wilt afterwards be strengthened, and become a chosen instrument of God." Simeon continned to live as a shepherd for some time longer; but he also prayed diligently in a chapel that was dedicated to the holy martyrs. He often lay prostrate on the ground there, and begged God, with ineffable sighs, for the grace to do penance. When he returned to his peaceful mountain, he diligently collected storax, as had been his custom when a child, kindled a fire, and laying the incense reverently upon it, he said, with interior joy, "Rise up to God, Who is in heaven, thou sweet savour, and be agreeable in His sight." Thus incense was the first gift that Simeon offered to the Incarnate Redeemer. Gold and myrrh came later. Grace flowed down upon this youthful and pure spirit, entirely immersed in God, in a very different measure from what is possible when the heart is chiefly filled with the world and earthly things. In his waking hours Simeon was with God, and spoke with Him; therefore God was with Simeon whilst he slept, and spoke to him in dreams and visions. Once, when he was sleeping at the foot of the mountain, there appeared to him in a dream a heavenly form, that bade him arise and build. Simeon excused himself because he did not know how to build. "Then learn from me," answered the bright figure. He put into his hands a large stone, already cut, and said, "Lay this one to the east, another to the north, a third to the south, and a fourth upon the top of them, and then the building will be finished."

"But what does that mean?" asked Simeon. "It is an altar to God Whom thou willest to serve, and Who desires that His Name should be glorified in thee. Keep thyself, therefore, free from pride and arrogance, persevere with constancy and invincible patience, animate thyself with perfect charity to all men, so shalt thou lead many from error to the knowledge of the truth." And a second bright form, with a countenance of heavenly serenity, and with a golden book on the breast, approached him, and put something pearl-shaped, snowy white, and as sweet as honey, into his mouth, which wonderfully satiated his soul. And the first figure gave him the golden staff which he held, saying, "Herewith feed Christ's flock." And Simeon awoke. His soul was so filled with the impression this vision made, that he remained twenty-one days without eating or drinking, a thing he had never done before, having always received and eaten the meat and wine given him by his parents, who were in good circumstances. His fondness for prayer increased. He remained praying in the church for hours together, then whole days, and at length whole nights also. The other shepherds, his companions, began to remark his conduct with mistrust, wondering what he could be doing in the church all night, if he could really be praying all that time, or whether this was not hypocrisy and a desire of attracting attention. They watched him secretly, relieving each other from hour to hour, but none of them saw anything from evening till morning, save Simeon either on his knees or prostrate on the ground, so absorbed in prayer that his body was as motionless as if it were dead. Even then the power of God, that was to work so many brilliant miracles in him, made its presence known by occasional flashes. After those twenty-one days of entire abstinence from food he was hungry, and went to a fisherman of the neighbourhood, and begged his daughter Martha to sell him a few fishes. The maiden, who wanted to set out immediately to take to market at Sisan the rich produce of the last night's fishing, denied that she had any fish in the house, and added an oath in the Name of God when Simeon did not seem to believe her. He left her, and entered the marketplace, where there were many people assembled. Soon after Martha arrived with her fishes, but in a pitiable condition. Driven by an unseen power, she ran about raving wildly, calling unceasingly on Simeon's name, and the fishes all surrounded her, and angrily attacked her. It was a fearful sight, and the mad woman did not recover her senses till Simeon took her by the hand, and bade her be still.

In the meantime Susocion, Simeon's father, had died, and his elder brother Semses wished to have the management of the household in his own hands, and to divide the property. The brothers loved each other heartily, and Simeon said to Semses, "Divide it according to thine own conscience, and take what pleases thee;" and Semses made the division most justly. But Simeon's thoughts were not set upon the goods of this world, out upon the treasures of heaven, which latter are to be acquired by renouncing the former; and as he was firmly resolved to enter a monastery, he on his side began to distribute his property. It was very considerable, for one of his relations had lately died, and made him her sole heir. He gave the lands to his brother, the ready money and other inheritances he made over to the poor and the monasteries. He had no need of anything himself, for he spent the whole of the next Lent in complete abstinence from food. It was sufficient for the holy youth that he was nourished at Mid-Lent, and again at Easter, by the Body of our

Lord in holy communion, for the Lord of life entered into his life. The harvest time soon followed, which in those hot climates is in the spring. Simeon determined to gather it in once more, not in order to lay up corn, but to give alms for the last time. He admitted gleaners from far and near into the fields, and allowed them not only to glean, but even to take from the sheaves. In the evening when he collected together the reapers, and gave them a goodly repast, his heart smote him to see the gleaners, and the poorest people go hungry away from the field. He called them all kindly to him, and served them himself with food and drink, which God multiplied miraculously in his hands. This was the last act of Simeon's life in the world; that pure, innocent life, in which no thought of selfishness or vanity had ever found a place, because it had been filled with ineffable love of God, which made its presence known by three unmistakable signs, holy zeal for prayer, holy hatred of self, and holy love of his neighbour. Now that he had thrown off all the burden of his possessions, he was able to take up the Cross upon his bare shoulders. He knew what awaited him in the ascetic life—mortification for the body and tribulation for the soul. For this the old man had prepared him. It was this very thing that attracted him, for he had heard that same day the words that opened for him the gates of everlasting life, "Blessed are they that mourn, for they shall be comforted." He knew also that he must suffer; but he could say with the Apostle, "I know whom I have believed."[1]

He now took all that he had remaining, and went to the large and important town of Teleda, which lay between Berea and Antioch. It was a pleasant spot; the summit of Mount Coryphe towered over the place, and two large monas-

[1] 2 Tim. i. 12.

teries stood at its foot. In one of these a very holy cousin of Simeon had lived for thirty-five years, without once again beholding the door by which he had entered. Simeon had richly endowed this monastery with his gifts, and now he offered himself for acceptance. Heliodorus, the abbot, was a venerable old man, sixty-five years of age, not less than sixty-two of which he had spent in the cloister, ever since his parents had brought him there as a child of three years old to be educated. He was a perfect stranger to the world and confessed that he did not even know what cocks and hens or pigs were like. Theodoret says, "I have often seen this man, and admired him for his holy simplicity, and loved him no less for his great uprightness."

When Simeon had spent seven days and nights in prayer, weeping and fasting before God, he went to Heliodorus, and throwing himself at his feet, implored him, saying, "Have pity on a miserable sinner, save my soul, which is in danger of being lost, and would gladly serve God." The abbot thought him rather young, and made inquiries about his extraction. "I am of free birth, and am called Simeon," he answered, "I pray thee save my soul." Heliodorus lifted him up, and said, "If God has led thee hither, He will also keep thee here, and will not suffer thy soul to sink under tribulation. Do thou only be truly humble, and willing to serve all the brethren as becomes thy youth, that thou mayest win their love."

Just at that time Bishop Domnus of Gabula, in Coele-Syria, happened to be in that monastery to give the tonsure and his blessing to several young ascetics. Simeon made a very favourable impression upon the holy bishop, for his countenance was fresh and blooming, and full of holy grace. He was not tall, but his form was strong and supple. His brother Semses had come to Teleda to witness the holy ceremony by which Simeon was to consecrate himself entirely to the service of God. Semses approached with the rest of the faithful to receive the blessing of the bishop, who exhorted him strongly and movingly to follow the example of his younger brother. Semses, although he had intended to return immediately to his own home, was so struck by the majesty of the religious life that he determined to remain in the monastery, and received the tonsure with Simeon and the rest. Filled with the spirit of prophecy, the bishop said to Heliodorus, "If a long life is granted to the young Simeon, he will become a precious vessel in which God will repose with pleasure." Semses went home once more to dispose of all he had in favour of the poor and the religious houses, and then returned and lived very holily all his life in the monastery of Teleda.

But Simeon, who had already freed himself from all worldly ties, thought of nothing from the very first moment but of living with the greatest mortification. He was now fourteen, or at the utmost, fifteen years old. According to the rules of the monastery, the monks took nourishment every other day. But Simeon only tasted food on Sundays, and what he received on the other days he gave to the poor who came to the gates of the monastery. This was no indiscreet zeal, for his love and his desire to serve God kept pace with it; he daily received holy communion, and in the first four months of his monastic life he learnt the entire Psalter by heart. Some of the lukewarm in the community already began to complain of his violation of the rule, and of the pride shown by his singularity, but the abbot did not interfere with him, as he behaved with the greatest humility towards all the brethren, was willing to be employed in every service, and never showed the slightest discontent, but when reproved, was only excited to great gratitude and repentance for his supposed sins. His fasts grew continually more rigorous. He passed two and three weeks without taking any nourishment, and then contented himself with lentils that had been only soaked in water and not cooked. In order still further to crucify his flesh, and to keep his soul in unbroken intercourse with God, he set himself to conquer sleep as far as possible. When at night he became so tired, that his will alone was not strong enough to overcome his great need of rest, he stood on a wooden ball and leant against the wall. When sleep overcame him it rolled away and he fell to the ground. He continued this so long that at last his slumber became like the light repose of a bird, which sleeps as it stands on its branch. Although Simeon lived on the most loving terms with all the monks, and was especially friendly to his opponents, yet the attraction towards unbroken solitude with God was so powerful within him, that one day he yielded to it and disappeared from among them. The lukewarm monks secretly rejoiced to be freed from the living reproach that he had been to their unspiritual dispositions; but the abbot and all the well-disposed were deeply grieved and caused search to be made in the monastery and all the neighbourhood, but in vain. A day, a week, a month passed—Simeon was still absent. Then as the brother who had charge of the kitchen was removing a heap of wood from a distant yard, to bring sticks for the fire, he beheld within this heap of wood Simeon, who had hollowed out space enough to make himself a very small cell, and was engrossed in extatic contemplation of God. This increased the love the abbot cherished for him, and the dislike of his adversaries. They sought in every way to harass him, now pressing the abbot to oblige him to conform to the rules, now treating him with harshness and contempt. The good abbot recognised in Simeon the jewel of his community, and in the monks motives of envy and malice, and therefore he contented himself with gently advising Simeon to keep to the rules and not to tempt the Holy Ghost by excesses. But it was the Holy Ghost Himself that was leading Simeon to perfection by these unwonted ways. The hatred of the brothers once inspired them with a cruel thought. They made a heavy iron poker red-hot in the fire, and then said to Simeon, "If thou hast faith, poke the fire with this poker." In his innocence Simeon answered, "Why not?" and taking hold of the heavy and glowing poker with both his hands he quietly poked the fire with it. The monks were appalled when they saw no mark of burning on his hands, and when the abbot heard of it he determined to banish the authors of such wickedness from the monastery. But Simeon pleaded for them so earnestly that they were allowed to remain. They remained accordingly, but their envious hearts only became the more wicked. Simeon procured for himself all those pains and sufferings which he did not receive from others. Once he took a thick rough rope made of palm fibre and wound it tightly round his body. This fearful girdle soon tore his skin and made deep wounds in his flesh. After ten days the fresh blood ran down whenever he moved, and one of the brethren remarking it, asked what was the meaning of it. "Nothing disagreeable," replied Simeon in his gentle manner. But the brother told the abbot Heliodorus what he had observed, and he examined the affair, and this time gave Simeon a sharp reproof. The rope was taken off his exhausted body with the greatest care, and Simeon patiently bore this, but he could not be induced to let the wounds be **dressed with** salves and such like remedies. He said on the contrary, "Oh! let me have this punishment of my sins and thus let me die!" "But, my son," said the abbot, "thou art not yet eighteen years old, what sins canst thou have committed?" Simeon answered, "David says, Behold I was conceived in iniquities, and in sins did my mother conceive me." The abbot was reverently silent before such deep and holy desires of penance. Simeon bore with equal resignation the trials which God Himself sent him. He became blind in prayer. His eyes that had no desire to see earthly things seemed to be shut for ever to this world. The abbot proposed to him to send for a physician. But Simeon thanked him and refused, begging only to be led to the vault of the dead. They took him there, and he remained in prayer, full of confidence, and humbly uniting his will to the Will of God. After thirty days of patient expectation, his eyes were opened again to the light, and he returned to the other monks as though nothing had happened. He had other trials in the temptations with which he was visited by the enemy, unspeakable anguish of soul, and struggles with the powers of darkness; but he made head against them, strong in faith.

There was a deep dark cavern to the east of the monastery, a place so greatly dreaded because of the mysterious terrors which surrounded it, that no one dared to approach it even in the daytime; for it was said that whole legions of evil spirits haunted it, and it was, moreover, swarming with snakes and other poisonous and horrible reptiles. This was the spot chosen by Simeon in which to spend Lent, driven by the Spirit, like his Saviour, into the desert among the wild beasts. There he was surrounded by fearful apparitions, and tortured by interior pains, without ever losing his recollection in God, or seeking any assistance but prayer and the holy sign of the Cross. Suddenly the wicked spirits disappeared, a bright light filled the cave, and a sweet voice consoled him, saying: "Thy brethren persecute thee, Satan torments thee; but fear not, the Lord is with thee, His grace protects thee, and His right hand sustains thee. Thou wilt become the chief of thy brethren, and wilt tread Satan under thy feet." And Simeon spent the rest of Lent in a blissful extasy without any one in the monastery guessing what had become of him. The abbot had sought and enquired for him in vain, none had ever thought of the ill-famed cave. But as the joyful day of the Resurrection of the Lord was approaching, the abbot became extremely anxious about Simeon. He conferred with some of the monks who were kindly disposed towards him, and they went with torches to the cavern; here, in a corner, they discovered Simeon, feeble in body, but peacefully entranced in prayer. They brought him back with joy to the monastery, and on the holy festival of Easter he, with the brethren, received holy communion, the support of his life. But now the whole community of monks, Simeon's friends and foes together, went to the abbot and unanimously begged him to dismiss this brother who so disturbed the peace and order of the monastery, and who was constantly the occasion either of scandal or of painful anxiety, saying, that if the abbot would not send Simeon away they would all go to some other monastery. The good Heliodorus was exceedingly troubled. He knew too well the genuine spirit of penance that animated Simeon to lose the holy youth out of his flock without great sorrow. On the other hand, this flock consisted of a hundred and twenty brethren, many of whom were very holy and pious. Should he give up all the others for the sake of one? Were they not all, even the worst amongst them, his spiritual children? He had often advised and exhorted Simeon to moderate his zeal for penance, but as he saw that this zeal proceeded from no self-will, but from God's guidance of this extraordinary soul, he had never dared to command him, under obedience, to conform himself to the community rules, and Simeon had, therefore, pursued his path undisturbed. Should he now, against his conscience, give such a command? Should he confine and bind down this noble and aspiring soul, because the others could not keep pace with it, and because some envied its lofty flight? He underwent a painful struggle before he sent for Simeon, and said kindly to him: "My son, thou knowest how much I love thee, how I have never grieved thee nor wished that thou shouldst leave the monastery, how I have always taken thee under my protection, ever believing that thou wert led by the Spirit of God, and not by the spirit of contradiction, or the desire of singularity. But, my son, thou art become a stumbling-block to thy brethren; and as our first fathers have given rules and regulations for the community life of the monks, which it is my duty to keep, I have no other choice but to say to thee, Go wherever the Lord, Whom thou dost sincerely serve, may lead thee. He will fulfil the desire of thy heart. But forget not the monastery wherein thy youth was educated; grant it the help of thy prayers. And if I hear some day that the Lord glorifies thee, I will praise and bless Him, and rejoice therein." Then, as he knew that Simeon was deprived of all means of subsistence, having given a great part of his property to this monastery, he wished, with fatherly care, to give him a small sum of money to protect him from extreme want until he had found some place of habitation; but Simeon humbly thanked him, and said, "Far be it from thy unworthy servant to take even a penny from thee. Instead of useless money, give me rather thy holy blessing upon my way." And the old man prayed over him like Isaac over his son Jacob, and blessing him, said, "Depart in peace, and the Lord be with thee." Thus Simeon left the monastery of Teleda and repaired to a wild and rocky district, where he took up his abode in a dry well, and sang therein joyful songs of praise to God. But Heliodorus had a dream in the night which sorely afflicted him. Men, clothed in white, surrounded the monastery, with burning torches in their hands, and called out to the abbot, "We will burn thee and this house if thou dost not recall Simeon, the servant of God. What has he done? Wherefore hast thou expelled him? On the great Day of Judgment his worth will shine in glory!" Heliodorus awoke in trembling, called the brethren, and said, "I have suffered much to-night on Simeon's account. He is a great friend of God, go forth and seek him, and return not without him." The brethren obeyed, and some shepherds told them the road he had taken. They found him and brought him back. But he did not remain much longer in Teleda. God had given him ten years in which to prove whether he would persevere in love of suffering, whether hatred and persecution would so intimidate him, or gentle representations so affect him that he would be turned aside from his thorny path. As he remained immovable in his resolution, and also in love of his neighbour, and as no tinge of bitterness or of self-complacency ever stained his soul, the Hand of God continued to lead him.

Simeon had now reached his twenty-fourth year. He had entirely forgotten the world, hence he knew not whither to bend his steps when he left the territory of the monastery at Teleda. He prayed God to prepare the way before him, and to lead him whither He wished him to serve Him, and went on his way comforted. When he came near a town called Telanessus (in Syrian Telnesche) in the district of Antioch, he stopped under a tree, and prayed thus: "Most Holy Lord and God! if it be agreeable to Thee that I should spend the forty days' fast of Lent in this place, I beg of Thee to lead me to some monastery, and to make the porter say to me, 'Come in here.'" He remained in prayer under the tree till evening, and then went into the town, where he found a monastery, and knocked at the gate. A pleasant-looking boy opened the gate, and, looking up with childlike reverence to the dignified and attractive stranger, bade him enter. Simeon wished first to be announced to the abbot, but the boy seized his hand with loving haste, drew him over the threshold, and then ran away. The monastery was nearly deserted, the monks had joined other communities, and there were now left only this boy of seven years old and an aged man. The latter soon came up and received Simeon like an old and dear friend, respectfully entertained him, and placed the whole house at his disposal. Simeon begged for a remote cell in which he might spend the approaching Lent in complete solitude, and the old man had one made ready as he desired.

There was in Telanessus, at that time, an ecclesiastic whose duty it was to travel about the provinces and visit the priests in the country, as also the single monasteries that were not under the jurisdiction of an abbot, in order at once to remedy any disorder that might arise. He was a distinguished man, of good family, a native of Edessa. His name was Bassus, and he was himself superior of a community of two hundred monks, whom he guided by a very austere rule. They were not allowed to have a mill, nor any beast of burden; they could not accept any money or go out to make purchases, thus being wholly dependent on the Providence of God. Bassus visited Simeon, and his generous soul was filled with admiration for this youth, who, in his simplicity, ran with such gigantic strides along the path of love of suffering. Simeon esteemed himself extremely fortunate to have found so enlightened a counsellor, and he imparted to him his design of devoting the whole of Lent to uninterrupted prayer, immured in his cell, without tasting food or drink. "Wilt thou then voluntarily run the risk of committing the great crime of suicide?" asked Bassus, with apparent severity. "Well, then, my father," humbly replied Simeon, "let me have ten loaves and a pitcher of water brought to me, and I will promise thee to use them in case of need." Bassus could make no further objection. He blessed the holy youth, sent for the victuals, and had the door walled up in his presence. This wonderful penitent remained alone with God as his Saviour had been in the desert. Bassus could hardly wait for the end of Lent, so great was his anxiety and sympathy. At last the door was opened, and he found Simeon lying on the ground, breathless and weak in body, but spiritually strong, for after he had received holy communion from Bassus he arose and left his cell. Both bread and water had remained untouched.

Daniel, the priest of Telnesche, became a great friend and disciple of Simeon. He was very ascetic himself, and therefore he understood the sublime spirit of penance which animated the youth. He went everywhere with him, and provided him with clothes, and with his scanty necessaries of life. Simeon's wishes were all towards the desert; but Daniel, Bassus, and other friends thought him called to work more directly upon the world than is possible in the depths of solitude, and they proposed to him to lead a hermit's life in a mandra, that is, an open space, surrounded by a stone wall. Whoever lives within it is exposed to all the inclemency of the weather, and cannot be seen from without. The two great penitents, Marana and Cyra, Simeon's contemporaries and countrywomen, lived together in a mandra. This proposal coincided with Simeon's wishes, and Daniel, who possessed some land on a neighbouring mountain, joyfully gave the ground on which the mandra should be built. No king ever took possession of his throne and the glories of his kingdom so joyfully as Simeon did of his mandra, in which nothing but extreme abjection awaited him, which, however, was to be marvellously illumined by the glory of God. It was in the year 412, when he was twenty-four years of age, that he entered the place where, for nearly half a century, he was to shine like a spiritual sun, and to become the teacher and benefactor of the nations. He began by entering the mandra at the beginning of Lent, the entrance being walled up by his friend and protector the venerable Bassus, and by g himself up to unintermitting prayer, under the open sky, unprotected from storm or frost, rain or hail; and, moreover, entirely deprived of bodily nourishment. To be united with God, his only love, was the object for which his soul strove by mastering every earthly hindrance and distraction, whether they arose from the requirements or the sufferings of his earthly nature. By the strength of his holy love he trod this earthly nature more and more under foot, and overcame all the attacks of the wicked enemy, who neglected no sort of temptation that might turn aside the warrior of Christ from his aim. But Simeon was already a master in the holy science of prayer; he suffered hell to rage, and held fast to heaven with his will.

On Easter Day the venerable Bassus again approached the mandra, not alone, but accompanied by all the ecclesiastics of his district, with many others, and by all the inhabitants of Telnesche and its environs. The mandra was opened in the presence of these witnesses, all of whom greeted Simeon with great rejoicing. A holy man of the name of Maris, convinced that the prayer of this great penitent must be agreeable to God, had brought a vessel of oil with him, and humbly begged Simeon to bless it. He did so, and as if God wished to typify His grace, the oil overflowed the vessel in such copious streams that all present eagerly and devoutly procured some of it, and Maris took the overflowing vessel home with him where it remained for many years miraculously filled. Bassus fed Simeon with the Bread of angels, leaving him in his mandra with increased love and veneration; and filled with the spirit of prophecy, he said to the assembled people, " The Lord will work miracles by this holy youth, such as He has never yet worked by His prophets or apostles. The kings and the great ones of the earth will come to greet him, to revere him, and to beg his prayers on their knees."

From this time began the miraculous cures of ailing bodies and souls which spread Simeon's fame far and wide. The first person he cured was a maiden of eighteen, belonging to the neighbourhood, who had been paralytic from her childhood. He enkindled in her at the same time so great a desire for perfection, that her father, who was a rich man, built a convent for her where she thenceforward led a holy life. When Theodoret speaks of the crowds that thronged to Simeon, after enumerating various Eastern nations, he says, " Even the nations from the setting of the sun came to him, from Spain and England, and from France, which lies between those two countries. Of Italy it will suffice to say, that in the renowned city of Rome the holy Simeon was so highly honoured that people placed his image in every room and workshop, to recommend themselves thereby to his protection. In consequence of his desire for undisturbed solitude with God, Simeon wished to withdraw himself from this throng of people, and had the door of his mandra walled up for three years, so that he became invisible and inaccessible to all. There only remained a very small opening in the wall, through which holy communion was given to him. Bassus pressed upon him a vessel of lintels and a pitcher full of water, and also persuaded him to reduce the period of his seclusion to eighteen months.

Simeon followed the advice of his experienced friend with great humility, putting so little trust in the weakness of his own nature that he had his right foot fettered by an iron chain, and the chain fastened to a heavy stone, thus making flight impossible. The Bishop Meletius of Anticch, however, remarked to him that a firm resolution springing from the will of God could fetter the body without any chains, and then Simeon had them taken off again, and gathered up his strength for his arduous spiritual combat. The trials which God sent him became more and more heavy in order to cleanse him in the crucible till he became an instrument of pure gold, worthy to be used by the Hand of God. The temptations of the devil alternated with heavenly revelations, painful terrors with overflowing consolations, deceitful apparitions with supernatural visions which enlightened his soul. By this interchange of pains and joys, Simeon became as practised in spiritual mortification as he already was in bodily austerity. Nothing seemed sweet or desirable or comforting to him, save only serving God in the way He wishes to be served; whether that were among roses or thorns, was perfectly indifferent to him. In the fire of incomprehensible torments he became like a garment of asbestos which is thrown into the flames to be purified, and is not consumed, but becomes purer and more pliable. In the stillness of night, or in the early morning, the shepherds and peasants sometimes saw angels bearing crosses on the wall of the mandra, or they heard beautiful music, like that of a choir, sung by supernatural voices. The mandra was usually looked upon with deep reverence; nevertheless three rough fellows once dared to make an assault upon Simeon and to climb over his walls at midnight. With sword and lance they advanced to attack the holy man of prayer, but they were suddenly arrested by an unseen power, and fixed immovably in one spot. There they stood, and continued standing, till the next evening, for not till then did Simeon come out of his extasy of prayer and, beholding them, ask who they were, and what they wanted. One of them mustered courage to tell him that they were robbers and had wanted to kill him, and Simeon said, "Go in peace, and do no more harm to any man lest something worse should happen to you."

Thus passed the eighteen months of Simeon's complete seclusion, and his holy friend Bassus came for the third time to open the wall, accompanied by innumerable crowds. The universal admiration and joy at finding Simeon alive and well was changed into devout astonishment at the grace of God, when Bassus opened the vessel of lintels and found them untouched. The people begged to have them, and priests and deacons were six hours in distributing the blessed provision. Although Simeon was now again accessible to men, and came to their assistance with his advice and his prayers, yet his soul remained in uninterrupted union with God. The vocation which God had given him became ever dearer to his soul, to be a preacher of penance by word and example, to announce the unfathomable depths of God's mercy, grace, and love by his teaching, his miracles, and his whole life; and at the same time to show in his own person the all-conquering and expiating power of penance when it springs from holy love of suffering, and pours itself like a little brook into the ocean of atonement on the Cross. It cannot be supposed that any self-torturing caprice could have driven a man so humble, so self-denying and so thoroughly poor in spirit, to shut himself up for forty-seven years in his mandra. He tortured neither himself nor others. He was, as all holy friends of God before and after him have been, of a friendly and sympathising disposition; but no saint has ever taken the world as the rule of his conduct. For the very reason that he was now in more frequent intercourse with men, his zeal for penance increased. His fasts grew more severe, his prayer more fervent, his mortification more austere. In order still more to subdue the flesh, he persevered in standing during whole days and nights on the one spot in his mandra where he was accustomed to pray.

At that time the press of people began to be immense. Many came out of curiosity, but they went away with devotion and reverence, and before long every one desired to hear the word of salvation, or to plead for favours from the miraculous servant of God. The sick, the crippled, and other sufferers had themselves brought to him from immense distances, despite every difficulty, to implore for health; the oppressed and illtreated came and begged his protection, the poor and afflicted sought relief from their necessities. Simeon listened to all their complaints with patience and love, comforting all, advising all, praying for all; by the power of God working innumerable cures of sickness and infirmities, countless conversions of poor sinners, and at times even bringing punishment on the obdurate, letting none depart without so dealing with them as to prove that the Spirit of God had chosen him as His instrument. Simeon had no preferences, and made no distinction between great and small, between high and low. A glorious vision had taught him to care for all, because each afflicted and oppressed soul is poor, and every mortified man a beggar, only the one begs for the Divine blessing on heavenly things, and the other seeks the things of earth. Simeon, therefore, implored wisdom and humility for kings: justice and respect of laws for judges; charity for the rich, contentment for the poor, selfdenial for priests, readiness of sacrifice for monks, steadfast faith in the Divine doctrines of Christianity for all. Therefore, also, Simeon was in no fear of the great ones of the world when they oppressed those beneath them, but stood forth as the protector of widows and orphans, of the poor and needy, and demanded their rights if they were violated or infringed.

In this life so insupportable to the natural man, Simeon found nothing burdensome save the marks of honour that were heaped upon him, and the tumult of men that surrounded him. He feared the besetting human weakness of vanity and dissipation of spirit which destroys union with God. But God, whom Simeon so ardently and sincerely longed for, protected him from these perils and gave him fresh grace, that is to say, new means of mortification. In the beginning of the year 423 Simeon began to get up upon columns, thereby increasing his unparalleled penance of continual standing. In the interior of the mandra there was a stone nearly seven feet high; on this stone Simeon saw in extasy a glorious man in warlike array, with shining countenance, who folded his hands, bowed himself down low, then raised himself again, and after continuing to make these inclinations for some time lifted up his eyes and hands to heaven. In the intervals he looked steadfastly and piercingly at Simeon. This glorious apparition lasted through three whole nights, from evening till morning, alternating between those two attitudes of prayer. It then disappeared, and Simeon felt so strongly impelled to imitate it upon the stone himself, that he stood and began to copy its gestures. His soul was immediately filled with untold sweetness, for it was now clear to him where God would have him be. He stood upon this stone for three months and then upon columns. During the first seven years he stood upon columns of twenty-five, thirty-eight, and fifty feet high, and at last he caused the renowned column of about ninety feet high to be erected, upon which he stood for thirty years, living those thirty years as though they had been one day, and finally closing his life upon the same. The diameter of the column was scarcely three feet, and the top on which the saint stood was surrounded by a balustrade, and had no roof. Whoever wished to speak to Simeon, the priest who gave him holy communion, his disciples who brought him a small quantity of coarse lentils once in the week, or at times an article of clothing, and who generally remained in the neighbourhood at his disposal, all had to use a ladder to approach him. His clothing was that of a monk, namely, a long tunic of coarse woollen texture, with a girdle round his waist and a hood to cover his head, and for the depth of winter a little mantle of sheepskin. His thin form was remarkably supple, and of great nervous energy, his countenance was beautiful and pleasing, always shining with interior holiness, at times glorified in the extasy of prayer, and later commanding reverence by his long grey beard. Thus he stood upon his column, hovering betwixt heaven and earth, and uninterruptedly occupied in that affair for which the world with its thousand occupations has never time—namely, prayer. The angels are immersed in everlasting worship; Simeon's love of God emulated the angels and made him resemble them by his unceasing prayer. Our earthly nature rebels not only against the practice of this continual prayer, but even against the belief in its possibility, considering it moreover an excess. But asceticism destroys the ascendancy of our earthly nature, and freeing the soul from its oppression, enables it to rise towards union with God and rest in Him. This desire and striving of the soul for union with God is the intrinsic part of prayer, and has in it nothing impossible or incredible. And as to excess, the excess in neglect of prayer by many many thousands is certainly far more incredible. There are millions who never think of giving God the honour that is His due, and no one is surprised at it. One person thinks of it day and night and thinks of nothing else, and the whole world is amazed. This amazement, which so clearly and sadly shows the aberration of man from his destined path, caused a continual concourse of people to that column on which Simeon stood and accomplished his mission. During the whole night, and till three o'clock in the afternoon, he laid before God his own necessities and those of his brethren, that is to say of all mankind, with humble and fervent prayer, praising the fulness of His glory and the excess of His love, and sorrowing over the coldness and faithlessness of the fickle hearts of men. Twice daily he preached, or gave instructions to the people, impressive, fiery, and loving, as the Holy Ghost inspired him. Exhortations to detach themselves from earthly things, to despise the world, to take by storm the kingdom of heaven, to fear nothing save the punishment of hell, to think nothing hard except to be banished from the sight of God in eternity; these formed the chief subjects of his discourses. But they were varied with glowing entreaties to be firm in the Catholic faith, in attachment to the pure traditional doctrine, in submission to the bishops and priests, and total abandonment of idolatry, heresy, and Judaism. Besides these two general discourses, he readily and affably spoke separately with each one who asked his advice, consolation, or intercession. At nightfall he laid aside worldly affairs, dismissed the crowds, and let them detain him no longer from sinking into the deep peace and solitude of prayer from whence he drew light and strength. He had adopted the habit of expressing his worship at times by deep reverences, bowing so low that his forehead nearly touched his feet. One of Theodoret's companions once counted twelve hundred and forty-four of these adorations, one after another, and then grew weary of counting. But on Sundays and holidays Simeon always stood upright for twenty-four hours with his hands raised up to heaven. In the first part of his standing on the column he had a stake fastened upon the top, and caused himself to be bound to it with cords lest he should be overpowered by fatigue and fall over the railing; there was no room within it to lie or sit down. He was obliged therefore to accustom himself to stand, and he succeeded so perfectly that he was able afterwards to procure as much refreshment from a light sleep taken standing or leaning against the railing as his nature, grown unearthly, required. What made his heroic patience and perseverance still more admirable was the terrific bodily suffering which this standing, fasting, watching, and want of shelter brought upon him. The soles of his feet peeled off, his spine suffered, ulcers broke out upon his feet, he grew blind three times. Those only of his disciples who served him knew the pains he underwent, and they but imperfectly, for he never complained. They remarked indeed his blindness, but no stranger ever heard of it, for Simeon strictly forbade them to speak of it. "God knows it," he said; "that is enough for me, for Him only do I suffer, and He alone can help me." Men were to him for God's sake beloved brothers, whom he had to serve according to his ability, but their pity, their praise, or their admiration he desired not. He therefore quietly averted all honours from himself. He generally said to the sick, whom he sent away whole, "If you are asked who has healed you, say, God. You must never mention my name. If you do, you run the risk of grievously offending God, and of being punished by Him. His is the power and grace, let the glory be His as well." Once a priest came to the column, and, seized with astonishment, called out to Simeon, "Who art thou, O wonderful being? Art thou a spirit? Art thou an angel? Canst thou be a man?" Those present were annoyed at these questions, but Simeon humbly begged the priest to ascend the ladder, and then he showed him his hands and feet, and the fearful ulcers; told him when and what he was accustomed to eat, and spoke of all these extraordinary things as indifferently as if they had been the commonest things in the world. The priest was convinced that Simeon was a man, and left him still more astonished at such great humility and mortification than he would have been had he seen an angel. But Simeon's mode of life excited at first disapproval and blame from such as knew not by what spirit he was moved. The spiritual children of an Ammon and a Macarius, the anchorites of Nitria, who thoroughly understood holy asceticism both of body and soul, sent, therefore, a message to Simeon in order to try him in that virtue, which is the touchstone of all others, and of Christianity itself, the virtue of obedience.

The deputy of these venerable fathers of the desert spoke to Simeon in their name of their blame of so strange a mode of life, and commanded him to come down from his column and to live henceforward, either as anchorite or monk, according to the rules handed down by tradition. The messenger had hardly announced his commission before Simeon prepared to abandon his beloved column, although he firmly believed the Hand of God had placed him there. The sublimest and noblest mind may be deceived and misled by private judgment, but never by obedience; in obedience there is always somewhat of the spirit of Him who "was obedient even to the death of Cross." As soon as the messenger perceived Simeon's willingness to descend, he called out to him according to his instructions, "Stop; remain upon your column, it is the will of God; persevere unto the end!" If Simeon had refused he would have been forcibly taken off his column. The monks of Tabenna also blamed his mode of life at first, as scandalous both for its novelty and exaggeration, and sent to tell him that they would hold no communion with him. But when their messengers arrived at the spot they learnt better to know his virtues and his sublime life, and on their return they gave a very favourable report. This being confirmed on all sides, another embassy appeared before long at the column to express the joyful reverence and admiration of the monks.

The most singular scenes were frequently enacted before this column, some of which are related by Theodoret as an eye-witness. "A tribe of a barbarous and unknown nation appeared before Simeon, and the chief begged the blessing of the saint upon himself and upon his people. At the same time another tribe that was at enmity with the former one went thither with the same intention. The chief of this one raised a great complaint against the new-comers, and implored Simeon not to bestow his blessing upon them, and above all not upon their leader, who was a very wicked and unworthy man. The accused began with equal vehemence to defend himself and to revile his accuser; both hordes took part with their chiefs, and the quarrel grew so violent that it very soon became a battle. I was present at the moment and sought to pacify the combatants, assuring them that Simeon would give his blessing to both tribes. But one tribe would not allow the other to receive it because they asserted that its chief was an unworthy man. At last Simeon was obliged seriously to threaten the combatants in order to quell the tumult. And I have related this as a remarkable example of the trust they put in Simeon's blessing, since they would on no account permit their enemies to receive its sacred power."

"Another time," says Theodoret, "I nearly incurred danger of death in this place. I have already said that the Persians and other nations from the heart of Asia repaired to Simeon and, captivated by his sermons and exhortations, were converted to the faith and baptized. The sons of Ismael (probably wandering Bedouius) also came at times, in bands of two or three hundred or even a thousand men, and laid aside their errors, destroyed the idols which they carried about with them, and being instructed by Simeon in the fundamental doctrines of Christianity, demanded holy baptism. Simeon, who had a great respect for the priesthocd, advised one of these newly-converted tribes to take advantage of my preseuee, and to ask for my priestly blessing. The good people did so at once with the double impetuosity of their new fervour in the faith, and of their natural wildness. They rushed upon me; **the nearest seized** hold of me, some by the cloak, others by the beard and hands, those farther off stretched out their arms towards me, while those at a distance pressed forward so boisterously from all sides into the tumult that I was dragged hither and thither by the crowd, and in danger of being crushed. Simeon had great difficulty in commanding peace and procuring order, to protect me from the pious throng." Theodoret further says: "I was myself an eye-witness of a very celebrated miracle of the holy man. A Saracen prince begged Simeon to pray for the restoration to health of one of his retainers who had lost the use of all his limbs. Simeon asked the sick man if he would renounce infidelity, and he professed himself to be ready to do so. 'Dost thou believe in the True God, the Father, the Only-begotten Son, and the Holy Ghost?' asked Simeon.

I believe,' was the answer. ' Then,' said Simeon, 'if thou dost believe, arise, take thy prince upon thy shoulders and bear him into his tent.' And the lame man arose in health and strength, and did as Simeon had bidden him. All present burst forth in praise of the omnipotence of God. In this miraculous cure Simeon did the same as our Blessed Lord had done when He commanded the man sick of the palsy to arise and take up his bed. And since He Himself has said, ' Whoso believeth in me shall do the works that I do, and shall do greater than these,' we cannot be surprised when He fulfils His prophecy, as He has done from the beginning. He never worked a miracle by His shadow; the shadow of Peter, on the other hand, conquered sickness, infirmities, and evil spirits,[1] because it so pleased our Lord and Saviour. And by the power of His Name and His commission, Simeon also worked countless miracles."

The people of Lebanon sent an embassy to

[1] Acts v. 15.

Simeon with the complaint that the wild beasts made it almost impossible for them to live in their mountains. They congregated in troops, and penetrated into the villages, carrying off all the cattle, and also little children, and even attacking full grown people. No one dared to go alone into the mountains or to cultivate the fields, and even when many went together the wild beasts were with difficulty scared away, and only for a short time. Simeon answered to their complaints, "God sends you what you have deserved. You have forsaken Him and His mercy to turn to idols, who can do you neither good nor harm, therefore God gives you in prey to the wild beasts. Call now upon your idols and see if they can help you" The delegates confessed that all their prayers and sacrifices had proved to be powerless, and with loud wailings they threw themselves on the ground before the column and implored Simeon's intercession. Many people were then assembled at prayer. They all supported the entreaties of the delegates, and Simeon said, "See now! if you will open your eyes to the mercies of God, Whose great compassion would see you converted to the true faith, if you will have a firm purpose of being instructed in holy Christian doctrine and receiving baptism, then I will beg God to remove His scourge from you, and to let His Countenance shine upon you." They answered with one voice, "If thou wilt pray for our deliverance from this tribulation, and the terrible scourge shall cease, we will promise thy holiness to renounce our idols and to become Christians." Simeon was deeply touched by the unspeakable mercy of God who made use of the wild beasts to convert these poor ignorant people from their errors, and said, "Place stones at all the boundaries of your domain in the Name of our Lord Jesus Christ, beg the Christian priests of your neighbourhood to mark each stone with the sign of the holy Cross, watch beside them for three days and three nights, and I hope in the Lord Jesus that the beasts will henceforward hurt no man." Full of joyful confidence the messengers returned to Lebanon, and followed his instructions, and it was immediately seen that his mouth had proclaimed the will of God, for the beasts of prey herded together with fearful roarings, and left the country. The inhabitants of the villages came one after another to Simeon, men, women, and children, joyfully announcing their deliverance from the public calamity, and begging for instruction and baptism; and after staying some time near Simeon they returned to their homes, singing songs of praise for the twofold grace that had given peace to their lives for time and for eternity. These converts became, in their turn, messengers of the faith to the neighbouring nations, and from Lebanon the fame of St. Simeon spread even to Yemen in Arabia Felix, from whence the infidels came to find health and the true faith through the servant of God.

His prayers were a powerful protection to the Christians, even in remote countries. Christianity had been early spread and firmly rooted in Persia, and had given a considerable company to the army of martyrs. The acts of the Persian martyrs are distinguished by an excess of barbarity; the Oriental imagination is inexhaustible in inventions of terrible tortures, and one shudders at the very thought that men can practise such cruelty on their fellow-men. Nevertheless, Christianity was not extirpated. But as the kings were still unconverted and persevered in the worship of fire, the Christians were never safe from oppression and tribulation. The magicians who were honoured by the Persians as priests of the fire-worship, and also as wise men and sorcerers, were ever seeking to extinguish the true faith, and their chief renewed the attempt just at the time when Simeon's name had become known in Persia as that of a miraculous protector of the oppressed. The king Jezdegerd gave the chief magician full powers to persecute his Christian subjects, and to leave no means untried to induce them to apostatise The scourge, the rack, and the sword tortured and sacrificed the lambs of Christ. Three hundred and fifty of the faithful, men and women, priests and laity, were kept in fetters in one horrible dungeon, in order that hunger might weaken their consciences, and bring them to apostasy; but they preferred all the tortures of this horrible death, and remained unshaken. When these heroic confessors had suffered hunger for ten days, the Holy Ghost inspired them to implore God's mercy in union with Simeon's prayers. They continued in childlike prayer, full of humility and confidence, till midnight, when they were rejoiced by a consoling vision. Simeon stood in their midst, shining with light, in white garments, with a glorious countenance, and encouraged them, promising a speedy end to their sufferings. Calvary was everywhere prominent in his life; wherefore should not Thabor be there also? After he had inspired them with such great joy that they completely forgot their prison and their tortures, he appeared to the chief of the magicians, angrily threatening him with punishment, and filled him with such supernatural terror that he did not dare to oppose this powerful protector of the Christians, but begged King Jezdegerd to discontinue the persecution. When the king learnt the cause of this surprising request, he immediately ordered the Christians to be set at liberty in an honourable manner, and their churches to be restored to them, for he feared some divine chastisement such as had befallen the magician. The apparition had said to him, "As thou dost worship fire, fire shall burn thee, and then thou shalt see if it can bring thee help." Attacked by fearful pains, which burnt out his entrails, he died in great agony.

The bishops scattered through Persia were not a little amazed at the sudden cessation of the persecution, and upon making inquiries, they learnt the supernatural occurrence; and writing an account of it, sent it to Simeon by an embassy of three priests. These messengers remained with him for three weeks, and frequently read the history to those present. It was not in vain that Simeon stood on his column under the open sky. His life and works were publicly attested, and the eye-witnesses might be counted by hundreds and thousands. A king of Persia, whether it was Jezdegerd or another is not known, sent an ambassador to Simeon with the request that the saint would pray for his son who had suffered from palsy of the whole body for fifteen years. Two costly carpets were sent to procure the hearing of his request. Simeon refused the honourable present, saying, "Go home in peace in the Name of our Lord Jesus Christ; take your carpets with you, cover the sick man with them, and say, ' The poor sinner, Simeon, orders thee in the Name of Jesus Christ to arise.'" The ambassador did as he was commanded. The king's son was restored to health on the spot, and was so moved by the grace and omnipotence of God, that he embraced Christianity, received baptism with his mother and sister, and then appeared before the column of his holy benefactor to seek his blessing.

Simeon was not only a missionary to the unbelieving, but also a preacher of penance to the faithful, and if his column served him for a pulpit at his daily instructions, it was also a judgment-seat, whilst the mandra represented a court of justice. An epistle which was sent to him by the clergy and people of Phanir in Cœle-Syria, shows that he well understood how to awaken the spirit of the Gospel in the minds of others, and to invite them to perseverance. It also shows in what veneration he stood, how fruitful were his works, and how holy his aims. It is not stated whether he ha impressed upon the hearts of these people the obligation of a truly Christian life by his oral discourses, or by his writings. The first part of the letter contains greetings from the parish of Phanir, whose priest, Cosmas, became Simeon's friend, and the writer of his life.

"To our father and master, the faithful, the chosen one, who is worthy of a greeting from heaven; to the glorifier of the Church of Christ, the preacher of life, who stands between God and His creatures; to him who practises the three most sublime virtues, love, hope, and faith, as his master the Apostle St. Paul taught him; who loves his Lord in truth, and serves his God in justice, who rejoices his Creator by his virtuous works, and fulfils the commandments of his Redeemer; to him who despises passing and perishable things, faithful as Abraham, gentle as Moses, holy as Josue, zealous as Elias, miraculous as Eliseus, victorious as Job; to our master Simeon, who in name and works resembles Simon Peter, the rock on which the Church is built,—Cosmas, priest of the place called Phanir, together with the deacons and lectors, and the whole ecclesiastical community, sends many greetings." Then it continues: "With regard to the commandment of the fear of God which thy greatness gave to our littleness, we write to thee, O father, in perfect love. Friday [1] and Sunday shall be kept holy; we will have no double measures, but one measure of honesty, and one weight of justice; no one shall alter the boundaries of land; no one shall with-

[1] In the early Church many pious Christians kept Friday as a holiday in honour of the Passion.

hold their wages from the labourers; the rents shall be reduced one-half; as to usury, what has been already received shall be returned; we will judge great and small aright, letting no distinction of persons weigh with us, and accepting no bribes. Moreover, we will not calumniate one another, nor have fellowship with robbers or magicians, but we will punish evil-doers and transgressors of the law, and diligent in prayers we will work out our salvation in the Church. No one shall dare to transgress these laws, to commit violence, to practise injustice, to bribe the judges, to oppress the widows, orphans, and poor, or to carry off a woman. We will, in truth, conscientiously observe what thou hast commanded us, and what we have undertaken, and we rejoice therein. We swear by God and His Christ, and by His living and Holy Spirit, and by the conquest of our lord the emperor, that we will, according to thy word, O master, and also of our own accord, punish any one who presumes to transgress these precepts, and drive him from amongst us. His offering shall be no more accepted in the Church, his dead shall not be accompanied to the grave. Pray for us, O righteous and excellent master, that through thy intercession we may persevere, firm and steadfast in our resolution, with the assistance of Christ. Pray for us that we may neither be disgraced before thee nor guilty before our God, but that we may work all good in justice with joyful confidence, and receive life therefrom. Pray for us, O master, that we may be helped on all occasions by thy intercession, and that mercy, hope, and salvation may be poured out upon the whole world for ever. Amen. May each one that observes all this be blessed. May he who presumes to transgress it be accursed. And may all the people say Amen!"

Love God above all, and thy neighbour as thyself. This simplest and first commandment of the Gospel requires to be constantly repeated, because it is constantly being forgotten. Simeon chiefly insisted on the fear of God and love of your neighbour, and he led back the parish of Phanir and many many souls besides, to these virtues which every one ought to practise, and which he himself exercised to so heroic a degree.

The inhabitants of Anadris in Lebanon had cast his words to the winds, and so neglected the observance of Sunday that they watered their fields on that day. Then the spring dried up which supplied the country far and near with water; and as in spite of all their labour they could not open it again by digging, their conscience reproached them, and going to Simeon they confessed their guilt. At first he was very angry at their breaking so holy a commandment, but at length he said to these afflicted people, "Why have you not followed my instructions? I give them to you only for your salvation. I seek nothing but to place your souls in safety before God full of joyful confidence. Obey Him and go in peace." After this the spring of Anadris flowed more copiously than before.

Simeon's great love of souls showed itself in him, as in all the saints, by true tenderness towards great sinners. A culprit of the name of Jonathas kept Antioch and the whole of its environs in terror by his wickedness and crimes. But the hour of retribution came, and with it came grace. Jonathas was so long and closely watched that, driven from one lurking place to another, he could no longer find a safe refuge. To this distress was added the still greater one of an evil conscience. In his despair he hurried to the mandra, and embracing the column burst into tears. Simeon asked him who he was, and with what purpose he came. Jonathas made himself known, and told him of his desire to do penance. Simeon encouraged him to confide in the infinite mercy of God, who sacrificed Himself for sinners, but warned him against hypocrisy, and against falling back into his evil ways when the danger should be over. Jonathas reiterated his earnest intention of being thoroughly converted. In the meanwhile some officers of justice arrived from Antioch, and demanded from Simeon the surrender of the sinner, for without the saint's permission they did not dare to tear the miserable man away from the column. "My children," said Simeon, "I have not led him here, it is God Who has done it; He is mightier than we are, and He has often before now come to the assistance of penitent sinners. Take this one away if you will, I cannot deliver him over to you, for I fear God Who has sent him to me in a penitent spirit." After this declaration from the venerable man, they had not the courage to lay hands on Jonathas. They went back to Antioch and he staid seven days by the column, listening devoutly to Simeon's exhortations, praying and shedding tears of repentance. After seven days he said to Simeon, "Now, my kind master, dismiss me." "Wherefore?" asked Simeon, anxiously. "Wilt thou return to thy wicked life, and add new sins to the old?" "No, gentle master," answered Jonathas, "but my time is fulfilled." And with these words the penitent sinner peacefully gave up his spirit. But in Antioch the execution of Jonathas was anxiously desired, that the town might be freed from all fear; and soldiers were sent to the column to demand the surrender of the criminal. Simeon answered them, "God Almighty led him hither, reconciled him with Himself by contrition and penance, and has taken him away. We poor men have no more power over him."

Simeon's mother, after the death of her husband and the entrance of her sons into the cloister, had lived like a Christian widow in strict retirement. Many a year had passed; the fame of her son filled the world, and she was inspired with an earnest desire to see him once more before she died. She left Sisan and went to the celebrated mountain of Telnesche. In the course of time the wall surrounding the column had disappeared, and its place had been taken by large buildings on all sides, which afforded shelter to strangers, and contained a dwelling for Simeon's disciples and a church for the faithful. In the midst of these buildings was an open square like a courtyard in which the column stood. Simeon could not be seen from without. Whoever wished to see him had to enter the courtyard, or mandra, and its entrance was strictly forbidden to women. Simeon prudently excluded the whole female sex from a place where there was such an influx of men of all sorts. A woman, infatuated by curiosity, had once put on men's clothes, hoping thus to be able to enter the mandra. But she fell down dead at the gate, and the fear of a similar fate had ever since repressed curiosity. Simeon's mother had also heard of this prohibition, but she imagined that her son would make an exception in her favour. She was mistaken. When she begged for admittance it was denied her, and Simeon sent to say to her, " Have a little patience. After a little while, by God's grace, we shall meet again." The poor mother was not prepared for this answer; she began to weep, to groan, to lament, to entreat, so that she not only moved those without the mandra to tears, but Simeon himself, when her voice reached him, covered his face with both hands and wept bitterly. " Beloved mother," he sent to say to her, " have patience for a little while longer, then shall we meet again with great joy in everlasting bliss." And he kept to this resolution. For her and for himself he trusted to the promises of God, which insure a hundredfold reward for the sacrifice of any earthly happiness.

Simeon had at heart the affairs of the Church no less than the conversion of sinners, the improvement of society, and the spread of Christianity amongst the infidels. He attacked, without respect of persons, all usurpation of her rights by the civil power, and all abuses or faults of the spiritual power in her government. He exhorted emperors and magistrates, bishops and priests, to fulfil their duties with the utmost punctuality, because it was as necessary for them to save their souls as for the meanest beggar.

Simeon stood in great consideration with the Roman emperors of Constantinople, Theodosius II., Marcian, and Leo I., as a man of prayer, whom God deigned to enlighten. They did not disdain to ask his opinion upon weighty matters. They thought that a man of so pure and sublime a mind must have a deeper insight into the concerns even of this world, and a sounder judgment of them in proportion as they were without any personal interest to himself; and that being undisturbed by political passions, courtly intrigues, or selfish ends, he must have a clearer knowledge of what was right and needful.

The Emperor Theodosius II., a gentle and noble sovereign, to whom nothing was wanting save the genius and character of his sister Pulcheria, was too complaisant towards those persons who pleased him, or on whom he bestowed his confidence, particularly towards his beautiful and intellectual consort Eudocia. Her life, a most romantic one for an empress, also came into contact with Simeon. She was born at Athens, of a Grecian family, being the daughter of the learned and celebrated heathen philosopher Leontius. She was called Athenais, and was richly endowed with all natural gifts. When she was in the full bloom of youth, Leontius died, leaving behind him a most curious will, he was very rich, and he devised his whole property to his two unworthy sons, Valerius and Genesius, with the condition that they should hand over a hundred gold pieces to their sister; for, as the will stated, she stood so far above her family, that her talents would be of more use to her than property. Athenais sought by prayers and tears to induce her brothers to set aside this unjust disposition, and to give her a fair share of their patrimony, to enable her to support herself. It was in vain, the brothers paid her the legacy and turned her out of their father's house. She found refuge with one of her female relations, who not only received her with kindness, but went with her to Constantinople to seek to have the will annulled.

Another young maiden, full of genius and talent, was then living in Constantinople, who was not a beggar but an empress, called Pulcheria. She was the grand-daughter of the Emperor Theodosius the Great, who left his kingdom to his two sons, dividing it into the western and eastern empires; Honorius received the western, and Arcadius the eastern portion, which existed for a thousand years as the Byzantine empire, whilst the western fell to ruin before the migration of barbarians, to rise again to new life through the vigorous action of Christianity. Arcadius, the first Byzantine emperor, died young, in the year 408. The eldest of his children was Pulcheria, then nine years old, her brother Theodosius II. being seven. Out of the whole family the spirit of Theodosius her grandfather had descended to this little maiden alone, and she possessed it in so eminent a degree that, at an age when others are still in need of education, she already superintended that of her brother and her two sisters. In her fourteenth year she made a vow of perpetual chastity, and on this solemn occasion she gave to the Church of Constantinople a magnificent altar inlaid with gold and precious stones; on its lower border was an inscription, stating that she offered it to obtain a blessing on her brother's reign, and as a pledge of her vow of virginity. Far removed from all the dissipations of youth, and the enjoyments of earthly greatness, Pulcheria led an earnest and holy life, fulfilling every duty. The anxious cares of government alternated with works of mercy, and serious studies with pious exercises of devotion. She recited the Divine Office at the appointed hours of the night and day, with her sisters Arcadia and Marina, who had likewise devoted themselves to a life of virginity. She took her meals with them and appeared in public only in their company. No strange man ever entered the interior of her palace. With this exception, she was very accessible, and ever ready to help others; charitable towards the poor, respectful to the bishops, intent upon erecting churches, hospitals, and monasteries, and careful above all of the education of her brother. She sent for the most renowned teachers for him, drew up herself the plan of his studies, and chose some boys of good character and happy disposition to be his fellow-students, that their example might urge him on. At the age of fifteen she became Augusta, or co-empress.

Athenais betook herself to Pulcheria, to make good her cause against her brothers. She was as agreeable as she was beautiful, and she stated her case in so touching a manner that Pulcheria was entirely won by her, and on making inquiries as to her character, found to her great joy that it was blameless. Theodosius was then twenty years old, and of an age to marry. Pulcheria found united in Athenais all the qualities Theodosius could desire in a wife, and after he had seen and spoken to the beautiful young pleader he was of the same opinion. Athenais was still living in infidelity, not from choice, but because her father had brought her up in it. Her noble mind was easily won to the truth of Christianity. Bishop Atticus instructed and baptized her, giving her the name of Eudocia. On the seventh of June 421 her espousals with Theodosius were celebrated. The strange prophecy of her father was fulfilled, and instead of the birthright denied to her she received the imperial throne. She always retained a predilection for science and poetry, and as empress she translated into verse the books of Moses, Josue, and Ruth, and the Prophets Daniel and Zacharias. She sent for her brothers to Constantinople and showered honours upon them, and her father's brother Asclepiades was made, at her request, governor of Syria. He was probably converted to Christianity only out of consideration for his imperial niece, remaining a heathen at heart, for he took every opportunity of expressing hatred of the Christians. In the year 429 he obtained an imperial edict, ordering all the synagogues in Syria, which in the course of time had become Christian churches, to be given back to the Jews. The Syrian Christians were filled with grief, the heathen rejoiced, the Jews triumphed, and did not regret the great gifts they had made to Asclepiades; but the Syrian bishops turned in their trouble and embarrassment to Simeon, made known to him the edict, and begged him to take the Christian cause under his protection. Thereupon Simeon wrote thus to the emperor,

"Because thy heart has been lifted up, and thou hast forgotten the Lord thy God, Who gave thee an imperial throne, and a time-honoured crown; and because thou hast become the friend and favourer of the misbelieving Jews, the chastisement of the justice of God shall suddenly overtake thee and all who in this matter have furthered thy will. Then shalt thou lift up thy hands to heaven, and exclaim in thy tribulation: 'With justice is this punishment come upon me, for I have acted faithlessly towards God the Lord.'" Theodosius entered into himself, and deploring his compliance with the governor's wishes, deposed him as a punishment for his corruption, at the same time revoking the edict against the Christians.

But far other storms were now to threaten the innermost being of the Church, and to inflict wounds upon her which are not perfectly healed at this day. The heresies of Nestorius and Eutyches aroused these storms. Nestorius, a priest of Antioch, of austere morals and great eloquence, but proud, violent, and destitute of deep theological science, was called in the year 428 to the Episcopal See of Constantinople. The doctrine of the Incarnation of God, of the Divine and human natures united in one and the same Person, had been from the beginning an abomination to the natural man. On account of it the Jews would have stoned Christ[1] long before they crucified Him: and when the Christian Church of the Incarnate God formed itself, making His Crib her foundation and His Cross her token of victory, then heresy also arose and rejected the saving Catholic faith in manifold ways, and with a thousand dissembling words. As the Church had waged a gigantic warfare against Arianism in the preceding century, so in this she had to carry it on against Nestorianism. Then, as now, the heresiarchs joined falsehood to rebellion, and asserted that the Church disputed obstinately and frivolously about a mere empty word, which they, however, made the great warcry of their party. Thus Arius asserted that he was thoroughly orthodox, only he denied the Consubstantiality of the Father and the Son, upon

[1] John x. 30, 31.

which precisely the Divinity of Christ rests, and which the Church therefore steadfastly upholds. Nestorius rejected the expression Mother of God, or "Deipara," (Theotokos,) by which the most Blessed Virgin Mary was designated, and which had never hitherto been rejected by any Father of the Church, but had been used by many, as for instance, by Dionysius and Gregory of Nazianzen. For Nestorius taught thus: Jesus Christ is a mere man, who had received the power of God in a very perfect way. Jesus of Nazareth, the son of Mary, is not true God, He is only a man who is filled with God more than any other saint or holy man, and He is called God, because by His relations with the Godhead He shares in its honours and privileges. The Eternal Word is not born of the Virgin; but has only made His dwelling in Christ Whom she bore, therefore she cannot be called Mother of God, or Deipara.

The East, that hotbed of heresies, had fallen through them into such feebleness of mind, that this new error found much acceptance, especially in Syria, where John, the Patriarch of Antioch, did not at once oppose it, perchance out of personal friendship for Nestorius. The bishopric of Cyrus belonged to this patriarchate, and it is with grief that we find Theodoret, the learned bishop, the disciple of holy anchorites, and the admirer of Simeon, amongst the followers of Nestorius: happily not for ever. But in the East also arose the great vindicator of the Catholic dogma and champion of this doctrine of the Incarnation so frequently attacked, Cyril, Patriarch of Alexandria, a successor of the great Athanasius. He says: "However intimate an union we may imagine between the son of Mary and the Eternal Word, if it is not an intrinsic and substantial one, it can never be a sufficient ground for adoring him as God who is not God; but who is, on the contrary, not substantially different from a creature. Worship is due to God alone; and if, nevertheless, according to Nestorius, Jesus should be adored because He has become the Lord of all things; this is directly contrary to the first commandment; a man cannot become equal to the Eternal because he has served as an organ to the Eternal Word. Neither can we say that the Son of God is our Redeemer, if it was not He Who suffered death for our sins; He would then have had no other share in our redemption but that of preparing, teaching, and encouraging Jesus, whilst St Paul says: "God has not spared His own Son." Cyril thus expresses the Catholic doctrine: "As the mother of a man is mother of his whole person, and not only of his body, although his soul has come to him from elsewhere, because she has borne not only the body but the whole individual as it consists in the true and substantial union of body and soul; so is Mary truly and indeed Mother of the Eternal Word, although she by no means brought forth the Godhead by which He is of the same being as the Father. For she brought into the world the very Person of the Eternal Word clothed with our flesh, and she formed His Flesh. This union of the Eternal Word with man is a true and intrinsic union of the Divine and human natures in one Person. Therefore the words of the authors who treat of Christ should not be separately referred either to Christ as man, or to the Eternal Word. He is one and the same Who said, "I am the resurrection and the life;" and Who exclaimed upon the Cross: "My God, wherefore hast thou forsaken me." And to this one and undivided Emmanuel an undivided worship and praise must be given." Yet Nestorius persevered in his heresy, and said, "Anathema to him who calls Emmanuel true God! Anathema to him who declares the man conceived in the Virgin to be the Only-begotten Son of the Father!"

Although this heresy was enkindled, embraced, and combated only in the Patriarchates of the East, yet Cyril and Nestorius deemed it impossible to settle their dispute without a decision from Rome, so unquestioned was the authority of the Pope as Head of the whole Christian Church. They referred the disputed question to Pope Celestine, who had it maturely weighed and examined; and in the year 430 he declared that Nestorius must recant his heresy, or be deposed from his bishopric and excluded from the communion of the Church. Cyril was commissioned, as Papal legate, to execute this sentence. In the meantime, the controversy was so widely spread and propagated by books, sermons, and the persecutions of which Nestorius and his followers were guilty, that bishops and priests, monks and anchorites, and laymen of all classes, both men and women, took an active share in it. It was to receive its final decision at the Council of Ephesus. According to a very ancient tradition, the most Blessed Virgin Mary had lived in Ephesus with St. John, from the death of her Divine Son until the end of her life. In Ephesus the question was to be determined, whether the Angel's greeting to the "blessed amongst women" had been a falsehood or not. The Council was opened on the twenty-second of June 431, in the great Basilica of St. Mary, under the presidency of Cyril as representative of Pope Celestine. By his side sat a hundred and ninety-eight bishops, and before them lay the Gospels, for they were to judge between the eternal truth of revelation, and the heresy of deluded man. Nestorius was in Ephesus, but far from recanting his error, he never even appeared in the assembly, although he was three times summoned to it. In the meantime, writings and acts relating to the subject were read aloud, and at last the sentence was solemnly pronounced: "By the holy Canons, and the letters of our holy Father and Brother Celestine, Bishop of the Church of Rome, we are constrained to declare with many tears, that our Lord Jesus Christ by His holy Council deprives Nestorius who has blasphemed Him, of his episcopal dignity, and excludes him from all ecclesiastical communion." Then the hundred and ninety-eight bishops all signed it. The sitting lasted from early morning till nightfall, although it was the longest day of the year. The whole population of Ephesus had surrounded the Basilica, and in hopeful expectation and prayer awaited the decision. When it became known, and they learnt the deposition of Nestorius, all the people broke forth in cries of joy, praising God that the enemy of the faith had fallen, and blessing the fathers of the Council. Instantly the town was festively illuminated, and when the bishops left the Basilica they were conducted to their dwellings by a thousand torch-bearers, whilst women preceded them carrying censers in which costly incense was burning. The next morning the sentence against Nestorius was proclaimed and written up in the public places of the city, and the bishops addressed the people in the two principal churches of St. Mary and St. John, upon the mystery of the Incarnation of God and the honour of the most Blessed Virgin Mary. Bishops of the party of Nestorius gave in their adhesion to the decision of the council by degrees, and on the day on which six of them added their signatures, Cyril made a discourse, which is a song of rejoicing for the triumph of God's Mother. "We greet thee, O holy and mysterious Trinity, Who hast assembled us in this church of Mary the Mother of God. O Mary, we greet thee also, thou precious treasure of the universe; thou lamp that never diest; thou crown of virginity; thou sceptre of orthodoxy; thou indestructible temple, Mother and Virgin, through whom, in the holy Gospel, He is blessed who cometh in the Name of the Lord. We greet thee whose virginal bosom embraced the Infinite, the Incomprehensible. We greet thee! Through thee is the most Holy Trinity glorified and adored, the Cross is honoured, Satan is precipitated from heaven, fallen man saved for heaven, the whole of creation freed from idolatry and led to the knowledge of the truth. Through thee holy baptism and the anointing of unspeakable joy flow over the faithful. Through thee is the Only-begotten Son of God arisen as the Light for all that sat in darkness, and in the shadow of death. But what mortal man could worthily praise thee, O thou incomparable Mary!" Thus did the ancient Church praise and honour the holy Mother of God. The third Œcumenical Council of Christendom was called into existence solely because Nestorius dared to attack her glory.

Several Oriental bishops, however, did not assent to the condemnation of the Nestorian heresy, although it encroached so dangerously upon the Christian faith. They found support in John, the Patriarch of Antioch, who, out of predilection for Nestorius, wavered irresolutely to and fro. Discord in doctrine ever brings in its train discord in political life. Therefore it was of no less paramount importance to the Emperor Theodosius II., than to the orthodox bishops to re-unite the Oriental bishops to the one fold of Christ. The emperor looked upon Simeon Stylites as influential in this affair, and summoned him by letter to contribute to the restoration of peace and unity in the Christian Church, saying, "We know very well that the whole of thy saintly life is devoted to God, and that thy conduct is such that thou canst unfailingly call down the mercy of God upon us. This encourages us to recommend to thee the affair whose right solution is so important to our times. Do thou procure that peace may strike root in the Church, and be no more disturbed by the intrigues of the wicked one. We trust with confidence to the prayers of thy holiness, and to thy pious and convincing exhortations. If the Patriarch John of Antioch, who fears God, would sign the deposition of that sower of discord, Nestorius; if he would declare that he does not in any way assent to his foolishly invented doctrine, but that he agrees entirely with the decision of the fathers and bishops of the Council of Ephesus, the reunion of the divided members of the Church would follow. All in the East and West who confess the Catholic faith hold themselves in communion with the pious Cyril, Patriarch of Alexandria, and nothing is more desirable or more worthy of thy prayers, than to see all united by God's grace in the harmony of the orthodox faith. Therefore do thou also fight for this holy work the good fight against the assaults of Satan, and it will be reckoned thy most glorious victory."

In the year 433, after incredible exertions, peace was so far restored that the heresy could make no further progress. Nearly all the Oriental bishops subscribed the sentence of the Council of Ephesus. The emperor would not bear with those who persevered in rebellion against the Divine authority, but banished them from their bishoprics as false shepherds of his people. A similar punishment overtook the originator of all this evil, Nestorius, who had withdrawn after the Council of Ephesus into his old monastery at Antioch, but who was now banished by the emperor to an oasis in Egypt, where he died without being converted from his heresy. Thus a bulwark was erected between Nestorianism and the West, but it opened a path for itself in the East, where it was fain to serve under the colours of political parties. The kings of Persia found it conformable to their policy against the Byzantine emperors that their Christian subjects should not be orthodox but Nestorian, and they therefore favoured and protected this heresy, and supported it against the Catholics with the power of the sword. And as the sectarian hatred of the Church of God has its origin in the opposition of falsehood to truth, the Persian kings might be sure that the heretical Christians of their dominions would be fundamentally estranged from the Catholic interests. To this day Nestorianism is one of the numerous sects that lacerate the mystical Body of Christ in the beautiful Levant.

In the midst of all these complications and divisions, Simeon stood upon his column, peacefully devoted to that One Whom he sought, loved, and glorified in stormy as in tranquil times. He grew old and he suffered, as man formed of dust must suffer according to the laws of nature, but his life continued to be what it had ever been, a life of prayer, benediction, grace, and love. He saw terrible days. Barbarian nations from unknown wildernesses, Vandals, Huns, and Goths, rolled like enormous waves over the Roman empire, and Attila, the scourge of God, threatened the nations and the Church. And the Church, so severely visited from without, had to carry on a still more severe warfare within against a new heresy, produced by Eutyches a monk of Constantinople, in his exaggerated zeal against Nestorianism. Nestorius had falsely taught that there were two *Persons* in Christ, one Divine and one human, who were united in Jesus of Nazareth. Eutyches now denied the two *natures* in Christ, and falsely taught that His Human nature was absorbed in the Divine nature, whilst the doctrine of the Catholic Church is that

Christ is a Divine Person and not a human, nor a Divine and human Person. For He is the Second Person of the Most Holy Trinity, the Word; and this Person took upon Himself human nature and united it to the Divine. The followers of Eutyches were called Monophysites, on account of his doctrine of one nature, and they rapidly spread far and wide, the more so as the Emperor Theodosius and the Empress Eudocia suffered themselves to be gained over to it. Theodosius died in the year 450, and Pulcheria, who ascended the imperial throne, and bestowed her hand upon the noble Marcian in a virginal marriage, remained firm with him in the Catholic faith. The Council of Chalcedon, the fourth Œcumenical Council of Christendom, in which five hundred and twenty bishops, under the presidency of four Papal legates, took part, condemned in the year 451 the Monophysite heresy. The sublime Pope, Leo the Great, came forth to do battle against it with all the weight of an enlightened Father of the Church, whose noble spirit was in unison with his holy soul; but nevertheless the evil spread grievously, and fell like a spiritual blight upon whole nations, who are to this day still infected with it. The Armenians became disciples of the new heresy, and as such separated themselves from the Catholic Church. They are at present very influential in the East, because they have a great spirit of commercial enterprise, and thereby acquire considerable riches. The Egyptians also became Monophysites in great numbers, and two centuries later, when Islamism arose in Arabia and went forth to the conquest of the whole world, their conduct showed how deep is the hatred always felt by heretics against the true Church, and against orthodox believers. Egypt was subdued by the Arabs in 640, and the

Monophysites afforded them willing aid, readily taking upon themselves the Mussulman yoke, because by so doing they widened the chasm between themselves and the Church. In the beginning the infidels left them their churches and their possessions, and did not extend to them the oppression with which they treated Catholic Christians. But when the Mussulman felt himself secure on Egyptian soil, the Monophysites also fell under his tyranny, which quickly diminished their numbers and suppressed their churches. In our day the Copts are the descendants of the ancient Egyptian Monophysites, still constant to the mournful doctrine which robs man of the holy example of the Incarnate God, and of the joyful consolation of adoring Him as his Redeemer, and at the same time loving Him as a Brother. Whoever has been in the melancholy house of prayer of the Copts in Old Cairo can see that no ray of the glorious joy which the Incarnation of God has poured into every creature has ever rested upon these children of darkness.

Eudocia, the widowed empress, was a powerful supporter of the heresy of Eutyches. After the death of her husband, she had repaired to Palestine, which had been so stirred up against the Catholic doctrine by the Monophysite monk Theodosius, that he had even ventured to drive away the Bishop of Jerusalem, and to usurp his throne. Neither this scandal nor the anathema pronounced by the Council of Chalcedon against the Eutychian doctrine induced Eudocia to abjure her error. She lived very piously and benevolently in Jerusalem, as many Christian widows of that time were accustomed to do, and this gave a false lustre to her erroneous faith. Pulcheria saw with deep grief the perversion of her sister-in-law, and implored the holy Pope Leo the Great to leave no means untried to save Eudocia's soul. He fulfilled this difficult commission with the most delicate prudence. He wrote to her on the fifteenth of June 453. He presupposes that living in the Holy Land, she cannot but believe in the mystery of the Incarnation, and he thereupon begs her to use all her influence in bringing back the monks of Palestine, who had imbibed the heresy from their fellow monk Theodosius, and in inducing them to acknowledge the decrees of the Council of Chalcedon, and to repent of their cruel persecutions of the Catholics. The holy Pope further writes: " As childlike faith and peaceful humility alone can lay hold of the mystery of our salvation, how desirable is it that these deluded souls should be persuaded to believe simply what they read in the Gospels and declare in the Creed, instead of embracing blasphemous inventions! For as the Catholic faith has condemned Nestorius because he taught that there are two Persons in one Jesus Christ our Lord, so does she condemn Eutyches because he denies that the Eternal Word took upon Himself our human nature in the bosom of the Virgin Mary. If thy exhortations assist in converting these poor souls, thou wilt acquire imperishable honour; and I beg of thee to make known to me this joyful news as soon as possible, that I may have a twofold gladness, for thee because of the blessed fruit of thy works, and for them because of the mercy of our gracious Lord." But Eudocia was not to be easily won, nor quickly released from the spiritual bondage which had grown dear to her. She withstood the gentle warnings of the Holy Ghost, and therefore the Hand of God laid heavy strokes upon her heart. The Emperor of the West, Valentinian III., her son-in-law, was murdered in the bloom of his youth in the year

455, and her daughter Eudocia was compelled by the murderer out of ambition to marry him. But revenge and hatred induced her to call Genseric, the Vandal king, out of Africa to assist her against the hated husband forced upon her. Genseric came, plundered and devastated Rome, and carried off Eudocia the younger and her two daughters prisoners to Carthage. Such visitations of God bring the dews of grace to noble souls. Eudocia entered into herself. Anastasius, Bishop of Jerusalem, appeared one day before Simeon's column, and delivered to the saint a letter in which Eudocia exposed the state of her soul to him, and asked his counsel. He answered her: " Satan saw the fulness of thy virtues, and determined to tempt thee. He used as an instrument the dangerous monk Theodosius, who filled thy soul with uneasiness and darkness. It was necessary for thee to be winnowed like corn and purified. But take courage, thy faith has not yet succumbed. I am, however, surprised that thou dost pursue a little stream in the distance when thou hast already near thee the source of wisdom in the holy Euthymius. Follow his advice, and thou shalt save thy soul."

Euthymius was a holy abbot who had retired to the desert of the Dead Sea to avoid all this confusion and controversy, as well as the violence of the schismatic usurper Theodosius. There, a quarter of a league from the Jordan, the anchorite Gerasimus had erected a laura and a monastery. The laura consisted of seventy cells apart from one another, in which the elder monks lived who were already mortified by obedience. The monastery was for the novices and the newly arrived monks, and was situated in the midst of these scattered cells; and every Saturday and Sunday all the solitaries assembled thereywith their younger brethren for the Offices of the

Church and holy communion. Eudocia determined to follow the advice of the saint, and to confer with Euthymius. But as she knew that the holy abbot did not come to Jerusalem, where the sight of so many heretical and fanatic monks grieved his heart, she had a building erected near the laura, where she wished to converse with Euthymius upon the faith; and she sent two distinguished ecclesiastics to invite him to come thither. But he had fled eastward into the desert from these imperial preparations, and he could with great difficulty be found, and with still greater difficulty be induced to agree to the desire of the empress. When at length he came, and Eudocia saw him, she fell on her knees and exclaimed, "Oh, my venerable father, I see by thy presence how good God is towards me." The holy old man blessed her, and simply said, "My daughter, thou hast fallen into pitiful errors from want of caution, and thou hast persevered in them with unreasonable obstinacy. Renounce them, submit to the decision of the general Council of Chalcedon, and return to the holy communion of the Catholic Church." Giving her his blessing once more, he left her. Eudocia performed what he had told her as faithfully as if God Himself had spoken to her. She returned to Jerusalem, where she abjured the Eutychian heresy, and joined herself to the Catholic Bishop Juvenal, who had in the meantime again taken possession of his see. Many laymen, priests, and monks followed the example of the empress; but, alas! not all. The Christian life gradually died out in this desolate sectarianism, which was constantly bringing forth new branches, but without blossoms and without fruit. The followers of this sect bear now in the East the name of Jacobites, after one of their teachers, of the name of Jacob Baradai.

After Simeon had beheld from his column the world tossed by so many and such various storms, he had yet to witness in the year of his death the terrible misfortunes that befel his Syrian home. On the eighth of June 459, a tremendous earthquake converted Antioch and many neighbouring cities into a heap of ruins. It was in the night between Whitsunday and Whitmonday. The luxurious inhabitants had kept the feast of the Holy Ghost in most unholy ways, and had been guilty of excesses worthy only of beasts. A few shocks, repeated from time to time at uncertain intervals, overturned the vast and magnificent city, with its innumerable palaces, as though it had been a house of cards. Many lost their lives, many their property, and all were struck with terror. Then they thought of God and eternal punishment, of which this temporal one reminded them, and they wished to be able to storm Heaven with prayer, a thing they had otherwise little desired, and even despised. They felt the need of holy intercession before the throne of God, and they flocked by thousands to Simeon in daily renewed crowds to put themselves under the shelter of his prayers. They went thither as pious pilgrims in solemn array with the clergy at their head, preceded by the Cross, with waving banners, with incense and lights, weeping and mourning. When Simeon saw his column surrounded by this sad and sinful crowd, and heard their lamentations over earthly distresses, he cried out with bitter grief: "Be silent! Hitherto ye would never listen to me, and never follow me. All have turned away and become worthless, vying with one another in covetousness and wickedness! Injustice has overbalanced the scale, therefore be ye silent now, for I cannot speak with the unfaithful. Let me speak to God alone!" He then betook himself fervently to prayer, whilst the shocks of earthquake continued, and made his column shake like a reed in the wind. The danger increased. Then Simeon commanded the crowds to repeat the Kyrie eleison, and when that prayer was finished, he humbly said: "My brethren, one soul among us all has been heard. To convince you of this I will point out to you the man." And from the midst of the crowd he called out a simple countryman, and said to him: "Thou art he, my brother! but tell me, wherefore art thou so pleasing to God?" The man timidly answered: "Forgive me, my father, I am not he, for I am quite an ordinary sinful man."—"Speak, as I enjoin thee," replied Simeon. Then the man said: "I am a day-labourer, and my mode of life is that I divide my wages into three parts; one I give to the poor, another I pay in tribute to the state, and the third I use for my daily expenses. And I have always acted thus." Then all thronged in veneration around the poor man who was so pleasing before God in his simplicity and lowliness. The earthquake ceased; but it left such terror in the minds of the people, and impressed them so deeply with the nothingness of all earthly existence that all business was at an end. Men were still a prey to the indescribable terror of feeling the ground tremble beneath their feet, and seeing the walls fall upon them. They hardly yet dared to enter their houses again, or to go to work in the fields. Only near Simeon's column did they feel themselves secure. The mandra was to them the only place of safety. The saints are the favourites of God; whatever happens, no evil comes nigh unto them, for they turn evil into good; and the unbounded confidence in Simeon of a people usually so dissipated was an involuntary expression of this opinion. He bade them bear the suffering in punishment for their sins, pray and do penance, and reconcile themselves to God. The season of penance lasted fifty-one days, and the concourse of the people to the column went on increasing. Cosmas, his Syrian biographer, writes: " It seemed as if God had stirred up half the world to hasten towards His well-beloved servant, to honour him, to take leave of him, and to make his end more glorious than that of any man of his day." On the twenty-ninth of July a great public solemnity took place; namely, the holy communion of this people, now reconciled to God. It was the last communion that Simeon received in this world. His mission had come to an end, the wonderful mission which he had held for thirty years on one and the same spot, and he knew that it was drawing to a close. Like a tender and judicious father speaking to dear children, he now dismissed all with consolation, exhorting them to keep the commandments and laws of God, and bidding each one go back to his home and begin his day's work in the Name of the Lord, he promised that God would then be merciful to him.

The saint continued his wonted manner of life for another month. He then became suddenly insensible in the presence of his disciples, and remained in a state of death-like unconsciousness for three whole days. The disciples went up to him by turns, and his favourite and biographer, Antony, staid by him faithfully all the time, never leaving him day or night. He was the first to remark the token of grace, the wondrous odour of sanctity that encircled this poor half lifeless body like a breath of Paradise. It was as though floods of fragrance out of invisible censers floated around this blessed column. At first the fragrance was only perceptible at the top. but by degrees it sank lower, and like invisible clouds of incense, filled the whole mandra with a sweet and grateful perfume. Every one below remarked it, but none knew what it signified. Antony spoke affectionately to his beloved and holy teacher, saying: " See,

O my master, how God loves thee! The air of Paradise already surrounds thee; now He will call thee hence, and lead thee where thou deservest to be. But first give the fulness of thy blessing to thy servant." With trembling hand the old man blessed the youth.

On the second of September Simeon recovered his strength, called for all his disciples, marked out two of them as superiors over the others, and recommended them all to God. Then he bowed himself down three times, and looked up joyfully to heaven. The mandra below was always full of people. It had created great surprise and grief that Simeon was silent for three days, and had neither preached nor spoken to any one. Therefore the joy was great when he raised himself up again and resumed his accustomed posture. All cried out to him, " Bless us, O master!" Simeon looked towards all the four quarters of the world, and lifting up his hands blessed them, and recommended them to Almighty God. He then spoke a few words of love to the two disciples whom he had named superiors, and striking his breast three times, he leant his head upon Antony's shoulder, and died in the Lord.

The reverence which those of his own age paid him was so great that the Emperor Leo I. wrote to the Patriarch of Antioch to beg for his corpse as a precious treasure, and a holy advocate for Constantinople and the empire, and also in order that due honour might be paid to the great servant of God. As soon as the intention of the emperor was known a loud wail arose in Antioch, and the whole population addressed a petition to Leo, humbly representing to him that the terrible earthquake had destroyed their walls, and that the holy body would serve them as a wall and a protection. The emperor unwillingly granted their request, and a special chapel was built in Antioch where

Simeon's relics were solemnly deposited, and honoured with great devotion. The mandra also continued to be a place of devout pilgrimage, and the monastery that surrounded it contained during many centuries a numerous community of monks. In the tenth century it was devastated by an Arab chief, and even in the last century its vast ruins were to be seen on the declivity of the hill, seven miles from Antioch.

Although such superhuman exertions and difficulties were involved in this mode of life, it yet found numerous imitators. In the seventh and eighth centuries there were very many who stood upon columns. They existed in Syria down to the twelfth century, and in Mesopotamia as late as the fifteenth. One of the most famous was Daniel, a disciple of Simeon, who ascended a column near Constantinople the year of his great master's death, and died upon it after thirty years, at the age of eighty. Like his holy predecessor, he was held in great esteem by princes and peo le, and was remarkable for the gifts of miracles and prophecy. Another renowned Stylites was Simeon the younger, who died in 596, after he had stood for sixty-eight years upon columns. His contemporaries describe him as a marvel of virtue and holiness. When he was a little boy, wandering among the mountain heights, he caught a panther in play. The wild creature let itself be led tamely by Simeon's girdle to the monastery where he was being educated. His teacher, also a Stylites, asked him with amazement what he was bringing. "A cat," answered the boy simply. This triumph of innocence over the evil in creation seemed to the superior to be full of meaning, and he agreed to the long-cherished desire of the boy, and permitted him to mount a column. The little Simeon was then six years old, and he stood at first six years upon a low column, under the eye of his spiritual director, and then eight years upon a higher one. When he reached the age of twenty he went to what was called "the marvellous mountain" near Antioch, where he remained until his death; and by his heroic virtue, adorned with all the gifts of grace, he became the spiritual brother of the elder Simeon whose name he bore.

This is called folly by the unbelieving world, and by the believer the holy folly of the Cross. Simeon is thus mentioned in one of the hymns of the Maronites, the pious and industrious Christian inhabitants of Lebanon: "The just man drank of the wine that was pressed out by the lance upon Calvary." It was so indeed with him: his life was an inebriation of heavenly love; it was a note of the song of joy of the holy Psalmist: "My chalice that inebriateth me, how goodly is it:"[1] a parallel to the exclamation of his great fellow-countryman the holy martyr Ignatius, Bishop of Antioch: "My love is crucified! let me be an imitator of the sufferings of my God." God does not require all men to do what this blessed soul did out of love for his crucified Saviour; but He may require that one saint should, out of his boundless and inspired love, do what none would else have done. He gave to all the highest commandment— "Love God above all." Millions fall far below this standard; if Simeon acted up to it, shall it be called folly?

[1] Ps. xxiii. 5.

ST. NILUS.

"You have not chosen me, but I have chosen you."—
JOHN xv. 16.

CHRISTIAN asceticism took up its abode in all quarters of the world, in every climate, and under every sky, because it is not of the earth, and cannot therefore be confined to any particular country or nation. It had, however, its favourite spots, and they were always those in which the earthly man was invited to renunciation by the surrounding scenery, and where the spiritual man found fulness of nourishment in holy contemplation. One of these places was Mount Sinai, in Arabia Petræa. It rises like a gigantic promontory on the northern coast of the Red Sea, with the family of neighbouring mountains and hills, of jagged peaks and steep precipices that surround it. It stands forth like a huge lighthouse. The commandments of God are the light that shines out from it, those plain and simple ten commandments that seem so easy, but yet fall so heavily upon sinful man that the Son of God had to come and deliver him from sin to enable him to keep them. Round about is the desert, the mighty desert, thinly interspersed with little oases formed by a few palm-trees, and scanty springs. The disciples of St. Antony the Great and St. Hilarion wandered on from Egypt and Palestine to Sinai. Some lived on the mountain heights, in the cells nature had provided for them in the rugged limestone, where they established themselves as far as possible from one another, so that each solitary had to travel for an hour before reaching his nearest neighbour. The others settled on the lower summit, which is called Horeb. There, Moses was guarding the sheep of Jethro his father-in-law, when the Lord appeared to him in the burning bush and commanded him to lead Israel out of Egypt into Chanaan. A church had been built there, and by its side a monastery, inhabited by priests and monks, who did not feel a vocation to absolute solitude. But they only formed one community with the solitaries, and Sunday brought them all together for the celebration of the most Holy Mysteries, for holy communion, and to receive encouragement in the love of God and their brethren. It was the same combination of separate and common life that we find amongst all the unions of monks and hermits of that time.

About the year 390, a young man, with a little boy who had hardly emerged from childhood, entered the rocky desert of Sinai, and retired into one of the most remote cells. The man was called Nilus, and the youth Theodulus; and they were father and son. They had forsaken worldly happiness and prosperity, impelled by an invincible desire to make that sacrifice by which man gives himself to God, and God in return gives Himself to man. Nilus belonged to a rich and noble family of Ancyra, in Galatia. He had received an excellent education, for he studied the sacred sciences under St. John Chrysostom; and going to Constantinople he became Prefect, and was clothed with dignities. He had married early, and a tender love bound him to his noble and pious wife. Two children gladdened and adorned this marriage. But it was not easy to live at the court of the Emperor Arcadius with a pure and undefiled soul. Luxury, ambition, lust of fame, avarice, and sensuality, were the idols that enslaved the hearts of all the courtiers. A spark might easily fall upon the mind in an unguarded moment, and might leave a hateful brand, even if it did not burst forth into a sinful flame. Nilus weighed this in his tender conscience, and a terrible struggle began within him. On the one hand, he wished to separate himself from the joys that lay waste the heart, and the honours that bring danger. He desired to sacrifice many goods, and to receive instead one all-embracing Good. On the other hand, he had to sacrifice not himself alone, but also his wife, to whom his heart was attached with all the warmth of his nature. And she on her part would not hear of separation. Who can say what tribulation they suffered whilst they were outwardly surrounded by every happiness, and all that man's heart can desire and enjoy! Our Divine Saviour rightly said that He did not bring peace, but the sword. All the saints have had to wield this spiritual sword, and to divide therewith the bonds that bound them to every selfish enjoyment, be it even the most refined. Christianity has its bitterness for those of whom our Blessed Lord says: " He that can take, let him take it." It has its balsam also which distils from the cross. It is, indeed, in direct opposition to that Christianity which, in order to gain followers, represents the Christian life as easy, smooth, and compatible with the world and its atmosphere. But our Divine Saviour did not bear His Cross to Calvary along a path of roses, nor crowned with flowers; therefore that man is not His follower who will not walk upon rough ways and among thorns. The struggle lasted long, but Nilus chose the thorny path, and a great victory rewarded his courage. He separated himself from his wife; she went with her daughter to an Egyptian convent, and he repaired with Theodulus to Palestine, and afterwards to Sinai. He took up his abode in a remote cavern, and occupied his time in prayer, the singing of psalms, and the study of the Holy Scriptures and other pious books. He was dead to the past with all its habits, occupations, and pleasures. He lived as austerely as the strictest anchorites of Sinai, very seldom eating bread, but generally wild fruits and raw herbs; and he found in Theodulus a docile disciple and a fervent companion. Sometimes in the evening, after having accomplished his day's work, he visited the monks that lived in community on the declivity of the mountain, and held pleasant discourses with them upon the joys of seclusion, and the graces that God pours upon the lonely and unselfish heart. He faithfully underwent the interior strife of the flesh against the spirit, without letting his sufferings trouble the peace of his pure and beautiful soul.

The world, though so apt to forget, did not forget him, but seemed to understand what is usually beyond its comprehension; that by asceticism he had entered, not into darkness but into spiritual light. He received letters asking his opinion and advice on various matters; and he answered them partly by letters, partly by longer treatises. The Emperor Arcadius recommended himself with his family and kingdom to the holy man at the time, when, after the banishment of St. John Chrysostom, earthquakes, fires, hailstorms, and all the terrors of the elements visited Constantinople, and the empress died in childbed. Nilus replied to the emperor: " How canst thou hope to see Constantinople freed from the visitations of God, so long as great crimes are committed there, and vice stalks abroad unrestrained? Since the holy Bishop John, the pillar of the Church, the light of truth, the trumpet of the Gospel was banished, injustice and wickedness reign supreme. But thou hast thyself banished that light of Christendom, thou hast foolishly let thyself be persuaded to this act by unworthy bishops. Consider well what thou hast done, and enter into thyself."

Monastic life had then, as now, very active opponents in such men as think all too much that is done directly for God, and who condemn a whole state of life for the frailty of some of its members. In his treatise upon the monastic life, Nilus spoke very strongly against irregularities in the ecclesiastical communities, but he proves at the same time even out of the Old Testament, that there have been men at all times who have striven after perfection by complete renunciation of the world. He says: "The spiritual combat in which we kill our passions, to put on the new man, is the most difficult of all the arts. We must never weary of this labour, but fight the holy fight fervently and perseveringly. Jesus Christ came down from heaven to earth to point out the way that leads to true happiness, and the first Christians imitated their Divine Master in all things. They left the world with its riches and pleasures, in order the more easily to subdue their passions, to tame their sensuality, and to exercise themselves in virtue. The ascetic life consists only in striving after holiness according to its model; it is destroyed by the vices of its members. Solitaries especially must expect the greatest difficulties, and must be tried by an experienced master before they follow their vocation."

Nilus himself had to undergo the most violent temptations, and he recommends to others the weapons that he had victoriously used; fervent prayer, pious readings, humiliation before God; patience, voluntary abasement, and the holy sign of the Cross. In another treatise on the deadly sins, he points out the especial danger of ambition and idleness. "Ambition," he says, "is like a reef hidden under water; when we strike upon it, we make shipwreck of our virtue. He who is addicted to this vice is glad to pray in public, he who has conquered it, prefers prayer in solitude. A fool displays his riches, and thereby attracts the cupidity of robbers. Hide thy interior riches carefully, for the enemies of thy salvation beset like robbers the narrow path that thou must tread. If a religious is prone to idleness it is easily detected by his frequently lifting his eyes from his book to contemplate exterior objects, by his being attracted to his door by the slightest noise, by his acquitting himself lazily or over-hastily of his duties, by his giving up his appointed devotional exercises, and attempting new ones, beginning many things and finishing none; by his looking out for novelty, and running restlessly hither and thither under every pretence, even under that of visiting the sick. A religious who does not stay in his closed cell, is like a withered branch planted in the desert, that can never bear fruit, because it has no root."

In the book on prayer, he says, "We must first ask of God the gifts of prayer and tears; and call upon the Holy Ghost to excite those fervent and pure desires in our hearts which are ever heard, and to make our souls blind and dumb with respect to creatures, and our hearts free from every inordinate attachment. If thou wilt rightly pray, mortify thyself at all times. If thou art patient in suffering, thou wilt be joyful in prayer. If thou dost love God, thou wilt understand the great art of prayer; and if thou dost pray aright, God will love thee more and more. Prayer is, therefore, the divinest virtue, because it is the expression of perfect love. If in prayer thou dost attain to a joy far surpassing all other joys, thou hast attained to true prayer."

There were at that time in Ancyra, the native city of St. Nilus, about ten thousand women and virgins consecrated to God, two thousand of whom practised virtue heroically in works of mercy and penance. Amongst so many sublime souls, Magna shone with the brightest glory. She herself would have chosen the state of virginity, but her mother's wish leant towards her marriage. Magna prized the virtue of obedience so highly, that she agreed to her mother's wish, and was betrothed. She succeeded in inducing her future husband to grant her willingly a few days' longer freedom, and behold! in this interval, he fell sick and died, leaving her great riches. Magna's heart was deeply touched by this event, and she blessed the Providence of God, and lived henceforward for her heavenly Bridegroom alone. She gave her possessions to the poor, and served them, and the sick in the hospitals. Her own house was a convent, in which she and her whole household lived according to an established rule, and punctually fulfilled every Christian duty. She only left it to perform works of mercy, and to visit the churches. Her greatest enjoyment consisted in watching whole nights before the altars, immersed in contemplation of the infinite perfections of God, and of the eternal truths. The spiritual recollection in which this holy virgin always kept herself, and her union with God, was expressed in the gentle seriousness of her countenance, which inspired not the people alone, but also holy priests and bishops, with a true reverence for her. The imperfect are always easily satisfied with themselves, the perfect never. Therefore, Magna asked Nilus for a few ascetical precepts, which he gave her in the treatise upon voluntary poverty; representing it as one of the fruits of the ascetic tree of life, whose remaining fruits should be obedience, peace, humility, purity, and concord.

The warlike and rapacious nation of Saracens, which for full a thousand years harassed the Eastern Roman empire, having won for itself by slow degrees province after province, and city after city in Asia, finally crossed the Bosphorus, and by the conquest of Constantinople overthrew that empire. These Saracens or Arabs at that time roved about on the borders, and made frequent predatory incursions into the unprotected parts of the country. Hardened by their nomadic life, and accustomed to privations, the deserts so little deterred them, that they even penetrated to Arabia Petræa. Nilus and Theodulus had one evening visited the monks on Horeb, and had rejoiced with them in pious conversation on the peacefulness of their existence. The night came and went without the holy men growing tired; one of those soft Eastern nights, that are neither cold nor dark, but seem to veil the world with peculiar sweetness. Towards morning, the priest who had charge of the church, said: "Who knows whether we shall ever meet again so happily here?" Arising, he called all to the church, and they offered up to God their matin psalms of praise. These were hardly ended, before fearful cries were uttered on every side. A horde of Saracens surprised the monastery, to plunder all that could be plundered; namely, the winter's provision, consisting of dried wild fruits; and they carried off the younger monks, to be used as slaves, or sold. The aged were robbed of their clothes, and then allowed to escape. The holy priest and two of the solitaries were murdered. Then the gang departed with their plunder and with the youths, amongst whom was Theodulus. Towards evening the dispersed monks ventured to return to their monastery, and found the holy priest still living. He had gently said, "God be praised," and made the sign of the Cross when he received the deathblow. He was now lying at his last gasp, and exhorting the brethren to worship the holy Will of God. He gave them all the kiss of peace and died. They buried him and their other dead with great sorrow, but they were still more concerned at the lot of those who were taken prisoners. Nilus grieved most of all for his son Theodulus; but he unexpectedly received some news of him. A refugee sought shelter upon the mountain, not one of themselves, but a young slave, who, with his master, had likewise fallen into the hands of the Saracens. His master was called Magadon, and was a senator of the city of Pharan, which was situated in Arabia, but belonged to the Roman empire. They had let him escape out of fear of the Romans, but had appropriated his slaves and his goods. The young slave then related to the afflicted monks that the Saracens had destined Theodulus and himself to be sacrificed to the goddess Venus, whom they worshipped as the morning star. He had ventured to fly in a propitious moment, but what had become of Theodulus he knew not. The grief of his father was unspeakable, that Theodulus should have to sacrifice his pure life to this goddess of impure love.

In the meantime, the authorities of the city of Pharan had heard from Magadon of the violence of the Saracens, and sent an embassy to their emir or chief, to demand satisfaction. The emir promised to restore the plunder, and said that all who had claims were to make them known to him. They formed an expedition under safe convoy, which Nilus joined, in hopes of finding, if not his son, at least some information or trace of him. The emir was friendly, and assured Nilus that Theodulus had not been sacrificed but sold, and that he was living with the Bishop of Elusa. Revived by this hope, Nilus determined to set out thither immediately, and the emir gave him guides, who brought him safely to Elusa, a border city between Arabia Petræa and Palestine. St. Hilarion had converted the inhabitants of Elusa. Whilst they were still idolaters, and were celebrating one of the festivals of their idols, they heard that the saint was near. They went out to meet him, begged his blessing humbly, and received it gladly and joyfully. This childlike reverence drew down great grace upon them, and opened their hearts to the Christian faith. Elusa was now the see of a bishop, and Theodulus was really dwelling with him. Nilus received his son as Abraham had received Isaac, and made him relate exactly all the circumstances of his wonderful deliverance. The two victims had been chosen, Theodulus and Magadon's slave; the altar was erected, the knife of sacrifice sharpened, the cup, the incense, and the flowery wreaths prepared; and the time appointed for the solemn ceremony was the hour before sunrise, when the morning star shines beautiful and clear in the rosy dawn. The Saracens spent the night in dissolute revels, and the young slave fled; but Theodulus waited, bent to the earth in devout prayer, knowing that God would save him by surer means than a hazardous flight. He prayed thus: "O Lord! suffer not my blood to be spilt for the evil spirits, nor my body to become a sacrifice to the demon of sensuality! O Lord! my father calls upon Thee, and hopes in Thee, let us not be put to shame!" When morning broke, there was indeed a purple streak in the East, but instead of its rising higher and higher, and spreading over the whole eastern sky, instead of that marvellous spectacle presented by each morning in the desert, thick clouds on the horizon covered the dawn and the morning star. The Saracens slept till the sun penetrated the clouds; and then the hour of sacrifice was past. They broke up their camp and journeyed farther. When they reached an inhabited country they offered Theodulus for sale. No one would give the high price that they set upon him; as being a strong and handsome young man. At length they grew weary of carrying him so long about with them, and they publicly exposed him at the entrance of a large village, with a sword hanging round his neck, which signified that they would rather kill him than sell him under the price they asked. Then a stranger, a traveller from Elusa, took pity on him, bought him, and took him home, and the holy Bishop of Elusa redeemed him, detecting something unusual in the youth. Thus Theodulus was installed as an inmate in the house of the bishop, who soon became attached to him and finding him fitted to fill the priest's office, bestowed minor orders upon him. Instead of being sacrificed on the altar of Venus, Theodulus was to offer sacrifices on the altar of God; and the happy Nilus found his son again. Thus do all things turn to the advantage of those who love God. The Bishop of Elusa kept them both some time with him, to edify himself with their virtues. But they longed for their solitude, and begged for dismissal. The bishop agreed to their departure only on the condition that they would both receive priest's orders, in order to serve their forsaken brethren in the desert, by dispensing the holy sacraments. Thus father and son returned once more to their quie solitude of Sinai, with the purpose of serving Godtstill more fervently than before. And thenceforth they disappear from human sight. Not even the time of their death is known.

ST. JOHN CLIMACUS.

"My flesh and my heart have fainted away: Thou art the God of my heart, and the God that is my portion for ever."—Ps. lxxii. 26.

GOD created man with an insuperable desire for happiness, for He created him after His own image. He gave the soul of man the capacity to know Him, to love Him, and to possess Him, and an immense magnitude which can be filled by nothing short of an immense good; that is to say, by God. Contentment in God is its truest, highest happiness. No other happiness can satisfy it, for every other good is less than itself. Sin blotted out from the human soul the knowledge of its sublime destiny, but not the desire for infinite happiness; and because it had lost God, and was separated from Him whose possession bestows that happiness, it turned to external things, and sought from them its satisfaction. The images of creation gave it agreeable impressions, and it mistook these fleeting sensations of pleasure for happiness, and strove to retain them or to call forth new ones. Thus has man lived since his fall, imagining that external objects can make him happy. This error springs from the inclinations of his fallen nature; it is nourished by the enjoyment of sensual pleasures and by ignorance of spiritual ones, and strengthened by intercourse with other men who are entangled in the same delusion. For man is determined to be happy, and it is his right. Therefore, St. Augustine says, in his Confessions, out of the treasure of his own experience, "Continue to seek what you now seek, but seek it not where it is not to be found, seek not a happy life in the regions of death." And St. Bonaventure gives an illustration of this advice in his Guide of the Soul to God, where he says, "As happiness consists only in the possession of the highest good, and as the highest good is above us, no man can be happy who does not rise in spirit above himself. Now we cannot rise above ourselves except by power from above, for we can do nothing without Divine assistance. However, Divine assistance is granted to those who ask for it humbly and piously from their hearts in fervent prayer. Prayer is, therefore, the beginning of the elevation of the soul to God."

This way of elevation, this ladder of Christian perfection, beginning where man breaks with the world and sin, and ending where he arrives at the possession of the highest good, rest in God, by the three theological virtues of faith, hope, and charity, has been described by a peaceful hermit in the desert of Sinai in a book so renowned for its beauty that it gave the author his name of Climacus, from the title it bore of "Climax," or ladder. He had himself climbed all the steps of this ladder before he described them. This book shows to what height the ascetic life had then reached. For it sets before us a type, not by any means as an abstract idea, but as a model which a man who loves God may imitate by grace and perseverance if he follows the counsels and exhortations here given him, which are drawn from divine inspiration and rest upon experience.

John came originally from Palestine. His Christian parents gave him an extremely careful education, which developed the rare endowments of his clear and penetrating mind, and his depth of thought. His progress in science was so great, and his learning so vast, that he gained in early youth the name then so honourable of "Scholasticus." Yet he did not set the smallest value upon his knowledge or his talents or the prospects that opened before him in the world. He soon saw clearly that all this world's privileges and pleasures may astonish but can never satisfy man, and he early turned aside from a career that offered him perishable goods in the place of the highest good. At the age of sixteen he entered the desert of Sinai, which had long been inhabited by anchorites and monks. The Emperor Justinian had built a large monastery in honour of our Blessed Lady on the top of Mount Sinai, which afforded shelter to a numerous community of monks. John did not betake himself thither. He was a man of clear intellect and lively imagination, and loved the interchange of thought in conversation, and he feared that this taste might lead him into vanity and dissipation, and that he might find dangerous temptations amid the intercourse with so many brethren. He preferred the remote hermitage of the aged and venerable Martyrius, and begged him to undertake the guidance of his soul. In holy silence John made the sacrifice of his learning to God, and by obedience he offered up his will. He practised submission to Martyrius to such a degree that he seemed to have no will at all of his own. This virtue impressed somewhat of the perfection of the obedient Son of God upon all his works. He never attempted to be his own pilot among the reefs and shoals of the interior life, but letting himself be conducted by an experienced mind and a firm hand, he happily avoided all those rocks upon which self-confidence is so easily shipwrecked. His pure and humble soul attained to a great height of perfection, and from that holy mountain raised itself to the contemplation of the Sovereign Good, and of all the beauties and joys that are hidden therein. Martyrius observed with silent joy the fulness of grace that fell to the lot of his holy disciple, and the zeal with which he faithfully corresponded to all its movements. He therefore exercised him in every kind of mortification of self-love and self-seeking.

St. Basil the Great by his monastic rule had given the clue to the regulation of the exterior and the formation of the interior monastic life in the East, as Pachomius had done for the monks of Egypt. The rules of St. Basil enjoined that the vows of religion should be taken after a long and mature trial and consideration; that is, those who believed they could, by God's grace, live according to the Evangelical counsels of poverty, chastity, and obedience, strengthened and sanctified this resolution by the solemn engagement to seek henceforth their riches, their joys, and their will in God alone. This resolution is above nature, for nature invariably loves its riches, its joys, and its own will, and knows nothing of the love of suffering which is the brightest blossom of the work of grace. The most perfect fruit of this blossom is the resolution which finds expression in the three religious vows. John considered for four years whether he could, without presumption, follow the attraction of grace which drew him to give himself completely to God; submitting willingly to all trials, and accepting thankfully all instruction that might enlighten him on the subject. The nearer the day of his sacrifice approached, the more did his desire for prayer, fasting, and watching increase, that he might prepare his soul as a pure hearth for the fire of the Holy Ghost.

When he gave himself to God by the holy vows Martyrius advised him to live henceforward as a solitary. Martyrius did not long survive the day of the solemn consecration of his holy disciple, and at his death the little cell was deserted, and John repaired to the desert of Thola, which lay at the foot of Mount Sinai. There he buried himself in a hermitage two hours distant from the Church of our Blessed Lady. On Saturdays and Sundays he assisted at the Church services of the community, and received holy communion with all the brethren, both monks and hermits; at other times he lived entirely apart from all human intercourse, solely intent upon hearing and understanding the inspirations of God. He kept himself always in the presence of God by prayer, in recollection of spirit by study of the Holy Scriptures and the works of the Fathers, in untroubled purity of heart by the contemplation of divine truths and heavenly mysteries, and by the sweet consideration of Eternal Love in an extraordinary readiness to fulfil His will in thought, word, and deed, and to be His submissive instrument. His soul was adorned with the choicest talents, but he concealed them more carefully than other men hide their deficiencies and faults, because in his prudent humility he dreaded vanity and ambition. For the same reason he avoided everything extraordinary with respect to bodily austerities. He followed the ordinary rule, and ate whatever was not forbidden, though always within the bounds of extreme mortification. He had begun so early to discipline his higher powers, and to subdue his will, that the lower powers were already mastered, and his struggle with them was less severe than that of the other ascetics.

The little imperfections and failings which are inseparable from the condition of man here below grieved him so sorely, and filled him with such great contrition, that his heart poured forth its sorrow in loud lamentations, and his eyes streamed with tears. He wept over the desolation and disorder which has entered into the whole of creation in consequence of the fall, and which seeks to assert itself in each individual. He wept over the lost image of God in man with that boundless sorrow which can be felt only by one who knows what a loss it is, and what a treasure of happiness is lost with it. This lamentation increased so much at times that the solitaries going to the monastery, or the younger brethren going to their teachers, often heard his heartrending moans. But as John was unwilling either to give scandal to the brethren or to cause them alarm, he made for himself, with great labour and patience, a cave that extended far into a hill, with only a very low and narrow entrance. His sighs in this cavern could reach no human ear, and thither he went at times to implore the mercy of God, and weep for the sinfulness of men.

In this ascetic seclusion he became ripe for the designs of God. A young monk, called Isaac, was so fearfully assailed by temptations that he hovered on the brink of despair. Fortunately for him he bethought himself of going to the peaceful and enlightened John to beg from him spiritual weapons for his terrible struggle. This childlike confidence met with its reward. Isaac expressed to John the needs and anguish of his soul more by his sighs and tears than by his words, and John said kindly to him, "Come, my brother, we will have recourse to God in prayer." They both fell on their knees imploring assistance from Heaven. Whilst they prayed, Isaac's temptations departed never to return, and the young monk gratefully blessed the salutary effect of the prayers of the great ascetic who so carefully concealed his extraordinary graces. From that time the life of John was another proof of what has been shown to men by thousands of holy ascetics both before and after him, namely, that souls supernaturally purified possess also supernatural gifts and light. A young solitary of the name of Moses pursued John so long with entreaties to undertake the charge of his soul that he gave way at length, and accepted him as the first of his disciples. After this, many came to him from the world with their various necessities, tribulations, and doubts, and each one went away consoled, instructed, or strengthened. However great may have been the temptation to distraction, arising from intercourse with so many men, John overcame it, and always kept himself spiritually recollected in the presence of God. It was because they misunderstood him, that some hermits, who had not yet attained to such intimate union with God, blamed him for wasting his time in useless conversations, and wishing to attract the favour and admiration of men. This misapprehension did not cause John the slightest pain, and instead of feeling it an offence, he thought that he owed them the greatest gratitude for their kind warning. He immediately imposed upon himself strict silence, and kept it unbroken during a whole year.

This humility disarmed the suspicious solitaries, and convinced them that John never, either in speaking or keeping silence, sought his own glory, but was always solely intent upon glorifying God. They now joined all the other hermits and monks in begging him to hold converse once more with men for the good of souls. He broke his silence as cheerfully and humbly as he had kept it, and the fame of his heavenly wisdom and of his experience in spiritual matters, penetrated from the deserts of Sinai into the whole world. John was held to be a man upon whom the Spirit of God rested, and people from far and near sought so enlightened a counsellor. Thus many years passed away.

The monastery of Raithu was situated in Arabia on the Red Sea; its abbot at that time was a very holy man, also called John, who venerated so highly the virtues of his great namesake, that he expressed a wish to see the spiritual fruits thereof preserved for the use of future times. He therefore begged John to collect together in writing the precepts he was in the habit of giving to the individual souls that ardently longed for Christian perfection. John answered that this was beyond his power, as he only gave to people the advice which God inspired him to give at the moment; that he did not know how to compose, and could not believe that a sinner such as he could be called to instruct others. The abbot of Raithu was not to be deterred by this denial, and only insisted the more strongly on the fulfilment of his wish; and John, humble as ever, gave way at length, and wrote his far-famed book, "The Ladder of Perfection," which is full of his spirit, and from which he received his name. But he did not imagine that he had written anything good, or likely to be successful; and he wrote to the abbot of Raithu: "I have done what I was able, from fear of throwing off the holy yoke of obedience, which I have always considered the root of all virtue. Yet, I very much doubt, whether I have brought to light anything useful; because, being a disciple, I could only make an imperfect sketch. A perfect master, such as thou art, will put the finishing touch to the work, and make it fit for use."

He divided this Ladder into thirty steps, by which man may climb from sinful imperfection to the heights of sanctity. Every imperfection which a man roots out, by gaining for himself the opposite virtue, brings him one step higher and nearer to God. As he raises himself more and more above earthly things, he feels a diminution of the labour and sadness which are very great at the beginning, because of the unwonted exertion. On the topmost step he finds God, and the blissful joy of rest in Him.

Of the first step, "The renunciation of worldly life," John writes: "To draw back from the world means voluntarily to hate what the world loves and praises, and to deny self, in the intention of attaining to those things that are above nature. If any one has fled from the world out of love of God and horror of sin, let him not cease to pray with burning tears and piercing sighs, until Jesus comes unto him and rolls away the stone of stubbornness from his heart, and frees Lazarus, that is, the spirit, from the bonds of sin; saying to the angels: Deliver him from all uneasiness of heart, and let him enter into the peace of the spirit, free from all infirmity of sin. Truly, those men who strive to journey heavenward, with the burden of the body, must use unceasing violence, and suffer much tribulation, and spend many bitter hours, until, purified by persevering contrition and penance, they enkindle divine love in their hearts. But they would deceive themselves if they tried to tread this thorny path without an experienced guide. In the exodus out of Egypt, Moses was the guide, as an angel had been in the flight from Sodom. Life in the cloister is not for every one, and all are not fit for solitude; but the endeavours of every true

Christian must be directed towards examining, with the help of a spiritual adviser, what condition and state he is to choose. If he lives in the world, I say to him, do all the good that lies in thy power; deceive no one, hate no one, exalt thyself above no one; keep from lying; live in peace with thy lawful wife; never give scandal; have pity on the poor; be not absent from church, and from the Divine Office; if thou dost these things, thou art not far from the kingdom of heaven. But a monk is constantly doing violence to his nature; he uninterruptedly guards his senses, and seeks to lead the life of the angels in an earthly body; he has divine things alone before his eyes; and while his soul lives in contrition, his spirit is flooded with divine light. He who gives himself up to this painful, but glorious and divinely-assisted struggle should know that he has, as it were, to precipitate himself into a purifying sea of flame, if he desires that the fire of divine love shall be enkindled within him."

John writes of the fourth step, " Blessed and praiseworthy obedience:" " He who by the spiritual vow has put off worldly garments, and taken upon himself the yoke of Christ, enters into the service of obedience, to be recompeused for it by eternal liberty, and lets himself be borne over the stormy sea of life without any cares, supported by the hands of others. As he entrusts his guidance to another, with the object of gaining humility, and working out his salvation, he has already, as it were, arrived at what is good, spiritual, and pleasing to God, for obedience is the perfect abnegation of the earthly man, the burial of self-will, the source of humility, the blessed life of one dead to the world."

John afterwards speaks of a monastery in which he had lived for some time, whose abbot was a very holy man, who, by his instructions and example, enkindled in his spiritual children an ardent love for obedience, and thereby led them to the highest perfection. Many of these monks arrived, under the guidance of obedience, at a wonderful degree of abnegation and self-conquest. One of them was called Abbacyrus, and of him John relates that he had been, as it were, the butt of all manner of persecution, and that even the lay brothers had treated him so badly, that they often refused him his necessary nourishment. John once said to him, "How comes it, my brother, that thou art so often sent away from table, and forced to retire hungry to rest?" "Oh, my brother," answered the blessed Abbacyrus, "my fathers are trying whether I am fit to be a monk or not. They are not in earnest; and because I know their kind intention very well, I bear all easily and gladly. Fifteen years ago, when I entered the monastery, they told me that they were in the habit of trying for thirty years those who devoted themselves to obedience and renunciation of the world. And they are quite right, for gold is not cleansed without fire." Two years later, Abbacyrus went to God. With his dying lips he said to the abbot: "I thank God and thee that thou hast constantly tried me for my salvation. Behold, on this account I have been free for seventeen years from all temptations of the wicked one."

Another monk, called Lawrence, was a noble and amiable old man of eighty, who held the first rank in the monastery after the abbot, because of his priestly dignity. Once the numerous community had just sat down to their dinner, when the abbot with a loud voice called the holy priest, Brother Lawrence, to come to him. He hastily rose, left his place, and approached the abbot's table, where, after kneeling down and receiving the customary blessing, he stood up again and waited for the abbot to give him further orders. But without saying a word to him, without vouchsafing even to look at him, the abbot left him standing before the table. The noble old man stood there for a whole hour before the entire assembly. When they rose, the abbot gave him no further command than to recite the thirty-ninth psalm, which he did with great fervour. John afterwards said to him: "What didst thou think of, reverend father, whilst thou wert standing before the table?" Lawrence answered: "I saw Jesus Christ in our abbot, and believed that I was executing the command of God imparted to me through our superiors. Therefore, I did not stand before the table of men, but before the altar of God; and whilst I addressed my prayers to Him, my confidence in our holy abbot increased."

The purveyor of this monastery was called Menas, and was a highly gifted man, prudent, gentle, humble, as few are, and, at the same time, so able, that even the temporalities of this poor monastery throve under his management, and all the brethren had the necessary support of life. The abbot once accused this excellent brother of some fault, without any grounds, and caused him to be expelled from the church. John, who did not yet know this great abbot's mode of dealing with his spiritual sons, and who also knew for certain that Menas had not committed this fault, went afterwards to the abbot to enlighten him about the innocence of Menas. The abbot gently interrupted him, and said, with a smile, "I know his innocence, but a guide of souls must endeavour to prepare as many crowns for his pupils as he knows that they can bear, whether it be by injurious words, humiliation, or contempt. I knew that I could do Brother Menas no greater injury than that of robbing him of the heavenly reward which he will one day gain by his meek acceptance of an undeserved injury" John replied that the race of men at that time was no longer strong enough to bear such severity, and that many would on that account leave the community. "No," answered the abbot, "a soul which is united to its shepherd by Christ in faith and love will not leave him, especially if he has healed the wounds of its sins. But a soul that is not sufficiently rooted in Christ to follow its guide with unconditional obedience, would derive no benefit from staying amongst us." And he continued to make Menas a victim of perfect mortification. One evening Menas returned to the monastery, from a journey on business, half dead with fatigue, and prostrated himself at the abbot's feet, according to custom, to ask the favour of his blessing. The abbot left the holy old man, who had already lived fifty-nine years in the convent, lying on the ground till the next morning. Then he blessed him and bade him arise, but reproached him with being a hypocrite, and inwardly impatient. To the great edification of the whole monastery, Menas bore this penance magnanimously, and when John asked him afterwards, whether he had neither been vexed nor sleepy all that time, he answered meekly that he had been thankful to use it in reciting the whole Psalter.

A respectable citizen of Antioch, named Isidore, once begged admittance of the abbot. The abbot wishing to prove whether any worldly curiosity had brought him, sought to humiliate him, and said: "If thou hast truly undertaken to carry the yoke of Christ, I desire that thou shouldst exercise thyself in obedience." Isidore replied: "I give myself into thy hands to be moulded as the blacksmith moulds iron."—"Well then, my brother," said the abbot, "go and stand at the gate of the monastery, bend the knee before each one that goes out or enters in, and say to him: 'Father, I am a sinner, pray for me!'" Isidore obeyed the abbot, as an angel obeys God the Lord. He stood and prayed outside the monastery gate for seven years. Then the abbot joyfully admitted him amongst the brethren, and wished to have him ordained priest, because he held him to be a very perfect man. But the humble Isidore begged to be spared so high a dignity, and to be left in the place that was fittest for his unworthiness, outside the monastery gate. The abbot, much moved, acceded to this request; but after ten days Isidore left his place, not to enter the monastery but to go to heaven. John once asked Isidore, in what dispositions he had been during those seven painful years. Isidore answered: " In the first year I felt like a slave that was punished for his sins, and bitter grief filled my heart, so that I threw myself disconsolately at the people's feet. In the second year my sorrow vanished before the hope of reaping one day the reward of my patience. But in the third year I considered myself entirely unworthy of being received into the monastery, and of all the graces of the spiritual life, and my heart was more humble than my gesture as I implored the prayers of the passers-by for me a poor sinner. And in this mood I have ever since remained in my place, peaceful and contented." How pure must have been the soul that had attained to such a knowledge of self and of God!

John leads us ever upwards on his ladder to Paradise, and describes, step by step, how the Church, by the power of the Holy Ghost dwelling in her, delivers man from sin, by gradually teaching, exercising, purifying, and strengthening his soul, and divinely healing its mortal wounds. But man must prepare himself for this absolution by perfect penance. To this John dedicates the fifth step, and calls it " a second baptism, a baptism of tears, a judgment that a man passes on himself, a lasting refusal of all consolation, a voluntary endurance of all tribulation, and a wounding of the soul, for the purpose of self-conquest. Penance is a turning away from sin, that is, from all the old sinful man." The thought of death incites us to penance; salutary sorrow for former sins accompanies it, bringing forth three virtues: purity of thought, patience in suffering, and perseverance in prayer. Whilst penance attacks, one by one, anger, hypocrisy, sloth, covetousness, lust, pride, and all the vices, it gradually roots out the evil passions by implanting their opposite virtues.

On the twenty-fourth step, John thus speaks of the sweet virtue of meekness: "The morning light shines before the sun, so does meekness precede humility. Meekness is that unalterable condition of the soul in which it remains always the same in praise as in blame, without confusion, without disturbance, and without vexation. Meekness aids obedience, and is a quality of the angels. A meek soul is enlightened by the spirit of discernment, and is the seat of simplicity. The simple soul is far removed from all vain, curious, and perverse thoughts; it goes directly and sincerely to God, as a scholar to his master. As God is simple by nature, and without any combinations or admixtures, He wills that pure and guileless souls should come nigh Him. Blessed is the simplicity we gain by many labours, and by struggles with our own wickedness; an exceeding reward is prepared for it, for it opens the road to the deepest humility. It has never been seen more perfect or more beautiful than in Paul, surnamed the Simple. Its sister is innocence; that serene peace of the soul which excludes every evil thought."

Of humility, John says, on the twenty-fifth step, that the fathers of the monastery of Sinai being once gathered together to discourse upon it, some of them had said: "Humility is a constant forgetting of our good works; humility is the knowledge of our own infirmity; humility is the feeling of a contrite heart, and the denial of our own will. It is humility to take ourselves for the last of men and the greatest of sinners." Then he adds: " Humility is an unspeakable grace for the soul, a priceless treasure, an especial gift of God. Christ says: ' Learn of Me, (not of men, or of angels, or of books, but of Me,) for I am meek and humble of heart, and you will find rest for your souls.' When this queen of virtues reigns in our souls, we consider all the good we do as nothing; then we fear daily to increase our load of sins; and the fulness of the grace that has been bestowed upon us, and of which we are unworthy, raises in us the fear of eternal punishment; then we receive with joy every injury and contempt, because they are medicines for our spiritual disorders of pride and ambition; then we not only call ourselves sinners, not only think ourselves so in our hearts, but we rejoice that the whole world should think us so as well. Humility is a divine shield and veil which conceals our good works and virtues from our own too curious eyes. Penance awakens us; holy sorrow knocks at heaven's gates; humility opens them. This virtue is the only one that no devil can imitate. If pride made demons out of angels there is no doubt that humility could make angels out of demons. He who endeavours to escape from the dangerous and tempestuous sea of pride will do his utmost, employing prayers and tears, till with divine help he guides the little ship of his soul by a lowly mode of life into that calm haven of repose, humility; and when he has arrived there, like the publican, he can easily overcome the other sins. Humility is the door of the kingdom of heaven that lets all enter who approach it. Through it, as I believe, the Lord Himself entered. Many have attained to salvation without prophecies, extasies, or miracles, but without humility none can be admitted to the marriage-feast of the Bridegroom. He who has reached this step should have courage and confidence, for he has imitated Christ."

The purified soul rises from brightness to brightness. This divine illumination is the "gift of discernment" which lies upon the twenty-sixth step, and is thus explained by John. "Discernment is a sure and true comprehension of the Divine Will, at all times, in all places, and in all matters. Those only who are pure in heart, words, and body, have this discernment, for nothing so disturbs and confuses the spirit as impure desires, thoughts, and works. He who wishes to learn the Will of God must first mortify his own will and deny himself, he must pray with faith and simplicity, and ask the fathers and brothers in a childlike manner for their advice. A spirit freed from all sensual desires sees heavenly things. Solitude, silence, and continual vigilance give to the soul a peace favourable to contemplation and prayer. Many have obtained remission of their sins in one moment by perfect contrition; but none have suddenly arrived at the highest repose of the soul, for that requires time and labour, and special assistance from God. A lover of the peaceful solitude of the soul can penetrate the depths of Divine mysteries where no dissipated worldling can enter, only after he has heard, seen, and conquered the tumultuous storms of the passions and the devils. In peaceful solitude our ears hear great things from the Lord. He who lives in solitude requires the protection and the virtue of an angel; because to live in solitude means to stand in perpetual adoration before God. Therefore the true solitary is the earthly likeness of an angel. He falls only when he interrupts his prayer. Prayer is in its nature confidential intercourse with God and the union of man with Him.[1] It is the illumination and nourishment of the soul, the source of all virtues, the fountain of Divine graces, the foretaste of future glory. Prayer is a holy violence which man uses with God. The fruit of prayer is mastery over the passions and over the enemies of our salvation. Weary not, neither be slothful, but be ever strong in thy combats, call constantly upon the heavenly King for help, and thou shalt have God Himself for a Teacher in thy prayer. We cannot procure for ourselves the gift of sight by our own exertions, for it is a gift of nature. So also in the science of prayer God is Himself our Teacher, and gives the gift of prayer to him who is faithful in prayer."

As a consequence of being freed from all passions, the soul rises above herself " to the blissful peace of the soul, the earthly heaven," of which St. John Climacus says, in the twenty-ninth step, " See, how even we, although we are lying in the deepest sea of ignorance, in the darkness of confusion and unrest, and in the shadow of this body of death, have ventured to speak of the earthly paradise. For I hold the peace of the soul to be nothing else but the heaven of the soul in the heart. And as the stars are the ornaments of the firmament, so are the virtues the ornaments of this heaven. He who has purified his body from every spot of corruption, and subjected all the senses to the spirit, raising his spirit above all created things, and placing his very soul before the eye of God, has arrived at the celestial haven before the resurrection of his body, and enjoys the rapturous delight of heaven, contemplation of God. St. Antony possessed this peace of the soul, when he said: ' I do not fear God; I love Him.' Likewise St. Ephrem the Syrian, when he said: ' Withhold from me, O Lord, Thy streams of grace.' He who has no fears

[1] St. Nilus says, " Prayer is a raising of the soul to God."

and no desire for spiritual sweetness is either completely plunged in the peace of Divine love, or his soul is dead. He who reposes in this peace of the soul lives no more himself, but Christ lives in him. But as the crown of victory is not composed of only one precious stone, so the peace of the spirit is not perfect if even one single virtue is neglected."

"In a soul thus purified, the virtues of faith, hope, and charity, act without hindrance, and man is thereby raised to the highest state of sanctity in body as well as in soul, and the Divine image is restored in him. He is pure, he rests in God, he is lord of nature. For by faith he can do and undertake all things; by hope he can strengthen and conquer all things; but love, which is in its nature and quality a resemblance to God, in so far as mortals can attain to it, love is mightier than faith, and stronger than hope, for it shall be called God. God is charity."[1]

To what peace of soul must this holy and experienced man have attained to be able to write such a work! How far he must have entered into the rest of the soul so to receive the inspirations of the Divine Spirit! How holy he must have been so to illuminate the way of holiness! How full of love so to unfold the work of Divine love, the redemption and deliverance of mankind from sin, from its very source to its completion! How perfect a child of God he must have become to labour with so humble and glowing a desire for the extension of God's kingdom! Two of his own beautiful sentences may be applied to himself. "Peace of the soul, love, and acceptance as a child of God differ from each other only in name, in reality they are one and the same, just as light, fire, and flame, have one nature and effect, but separate names." And, "The origin and cause of the peace of the soul is obedience springing from humility."

[1] 1 John iv. 16.

Whole pages might be filled with his beautiful sayings, but only one must be inserted here. "The Providence of God appears in all His creatures, the help of God in all faithful Christians; the mercy of God in His especial servants, and the consolation of God in those who love Him."

One small work by St. John Climacus is in existence besides this "Ladder;" it is an epistle to the holy abbot of Raithu, which he calls a pastoral letter, because therein he describes and inculcates the duties of a spiritual pastor towards his flock. He thus addresses the holy abbot: "Thou art saved by God; do thou then save others. Thou art thyself snatched by Christ from death, do thou, therefore, snatch others from the dangers that lead to death. This is the great office confided by God to thee and to those who have the strength for it; an office that excels all the works of the most virtuous of mortal men; to be the companion and fellow-labourer of Jesus Christ, and by thy zeal, thy cares, thy ardour, thy love, and thy prayers to seek the lost sheep, to lead it to penance, and to present it before God as a pure sacrifice. No gift is more agreeable to Him than to lead a saved soul before His throne. The whole world is not worth as much as one single soul; for the world passes away, but the soul is immortal and eternal."

In the year of grace 600, St. John Climacus reached the seventy-fifth year of his age, sixty of which had been spent in the desert. The fame of his holiness had then risen so high, and had been so widely spread by his life and writings, which were alike distinguished by Divine wisdom, that he was unanimously chosen abbot of the monastery on Mount Sinai, and superior of all the monks and solitaries in the whole of Arabia. He submitted himself with holy fear to this dignity, which came upon him at an evil time. Arabia, and the neighbouring parts of Palestine were suffering from a direful famine. The sky seemed as it were parched, no cloud ever dissolved in rain, the terrific drought robbed the earth of its fruitfulness, and the people were dying of want, misery, and disease. In times of tribulation the afflicted always betake themselves for assistance to the chief personage of their day; and this was St. John Climacus. He had long been looked upon as a Moses to whom God spoke; he was now to become an Elias, and never to desist from prayer until God had bidden the plague of drought to cease. It pleased God soon to hear the prayers of His faithful servant, and streams of rain fertilised the arid country far and near. At the same time Gregory the Great, the saintly Pope of the race of the Anicii, wrote to the holy abbot to recommend himself to his prayers, and sent him a considerable sum of money for the house for pilgrims at the foot of Mount Sinai. For four years John bore in trembling the heavy responsibilities of his office, and fulfilled its duties with great perfection. But then, with the foreknowledge of his approaching death, his desire to spend his last days far removed from every temporal solicitude increased, and his spiritual children allowed him to prepare in peace for his journey home. He laid down his office and withdrew to his dear solitude of Thola. He gave himself up to prayer with unspeakable joy and fresh fervour. The holy joy of being, as it were, lost in the love of God, and plunged in the delights of union with the Object of his long lasting desire, shone forth from his countenance. In like manner, Moses was surrounded by a heavenly glory when he had been favoured with the sight of God the Lord. On the thirtieth of March 605, St. John Climacus passed into eternity. This holy patriarch of Christian asceticism, this sublime guardian of the monastic life, this apostle of the state of perfection was a contemporary of the man who, six years after his death, came forth and desolated the world by the doctrine, "There is one God, and Mohammed is his prophet."

THE DAUGHTERS OF THE GRACCHI.

THE fourth century began with the bloody martyrdom caused by the persecution of the Emperor Diocletian, and ended in the unbloody martyrdom of holy asceticism, to which the flower of Christendom devoted itself from love of the imitation of Jesus. God on the Cross, and God in the Blessed Eucharist formed the centre and lifespring of these two martyrdoms. Our Blessed Lord willed that His holy Passion, as well as His humiliation, should be perpetuated in the most favoured members of His mystical Body. The East,—with the advantages of a warm climate, a serene sky, and the peculiarity of large tracts of land of such a quality of soil as attracts only those settlers who do not look upon the amassing of gold and possessions as the chief object of their life,—the East offered, above all other lands, the outward conditions necessary for the development on a large scale of the ascetic life, whether in solitude or in a monastic community. The East possessed also a supernatural attraction; it was the earthly home of the Incarnate God. In the "Holy Land," as the strong faith of the middle ages so rightly named it, the Sun of justice had arisen, and its rays allured men to those spots where the marvellous mysteries of the Christian faith had come to pass, and where those circumstances had occurred which prepared the way for them, or had been connected with them. Egypt was one of the most attractive places in this respect. Thither the children of Israel had once joyfully journeyed under the guidance of their patriarch, and had remained contentedly in that land until its rulers laid the yoke of slavery upon their shoulders. And there they would have succumbed beneath their burdens and sufferings, had not a messenger from God saved them by innumerable signs and miraculous power, and led them back, purified by new afflictions and struggles, to their own country. But the bondage in Egypt, and the passage of the desert, and the return to the promised land were not only historically interesting facts; the Christian soul recognised therein a type of the paths and destinies of its own life, and found in this knowledge an inexhaustible subject for holy contemplation, and a sharp spur to fervour. And in the fulness of time, the Incarnate God, the heavenly Fugitive, the poor persecuted Child Jesus went to Egypt. He went from the throne of the Most Holy Trinity to the Crib at Bethlehem, from the Crib to the strange deserts of Egypt; for the foxes have holes, and the birds of the air have nests, but He had no safe place where to lay His holy Head. There is a legend which says that as soon as His foot trod Egyptian soil, all the idols, which were more plentiful in that land than in any other, were shivered in pieces, and fell to the ground as though they had been struck by lightning. The Christian soul longed to share exile and the desert with the God of his heart, Whose blessed coming had also crumbled into dust the idols of that very heart. At the close of the century Egypt resembled a mystical garden where Christian asceticism brought forth blossoms in profusion, like countless lilies amongst thorns. Writers such as Palladius, Rufinus, and Cassian, who travelled through Egypt at that time, and remained there many years in order that the intercourse with holy men might have a beneficial effect upon themselves, give numbers which are almost appalling to us, because the spirit of the present day is so opposed to perfection. But at that time asceticism was dominant in the Christian world. It was aided by the outward pressure of the times, which led many souls to seek in the peaceful cell a haven of protection from the menacing storms. The advance of the barbarian tribes from the north-east against the ancient Roman Empire, which the Emperor Theodosius the Great with difficulty held together in his powerful grasp, filled all minds with a dark foreboding of the overthrow of the established ordinances of the world. It is often remarked that at the close of epochs, and on the threshold of world-stirring events, a sultriness is felt in the spiritual atmosphere similar to that which occurs in the physical one before the coming of an earthquake. Every one perceives a sort of insecurity in existing relations, and seeks on all sides some safe spot in which to cast anchor. Those minds alone that are entirely superficial and immersed in exterior things perceive it not, or only perceive it sufficiently to become more eager for the enjoyment of the apparent goods which they are, perchance, soon to lose. But there are moments in which even the frivolous become thoughtful, and the thoughtful turn to higher and more serious things, whilst the deepest minds fasten with their whole strength upon eternal and heavenly things, and thus become richer rather than poorer by the loss of temporal goods, and the overthrow of earthly prosperity. If, on the one hand, the storms that raged in the world drove souls into the peace of the cloister, on the other hand the discord that heresies sowed in the Church was the cause of many of the faithful seeking to withdraw to as great a distance as possible from all parties, that they might avoid the unspeakable anguish of seeing fraternal dissensions in the bosom of their Mother the Church, and the danger of being themselves drawn into them. And, finally, it happened here, as elsewhere, that some souls entered into the holiest places not with a pure intention, but rather from mixed motives. As in the time of the Emperor Constantine, the heathen in great numbers, following outward impulses, professed the Christian faith without any Christian dispositions; so now many Christians determined to embrace the monastic life who were not called to it by the Holy Ghost. This is sufficiently proved by the rude interference of many monks and abbots in religious disputes. These considerations make the numbers given by Palladius and Cassian seem less fabulous.

Palladius says: There were at that time monasteries in every part of Egypt, the oldest and most ancient being those founded by St. Antony, in the Lower Thebaid, near the Red Sea, on the mountains of Colzim and Pispir. Most of his disciples lived there, and their numbers amounted to five thousand. St. Isidore governed another community of a thousand monks by a very severe rule; the enclosure was so strictly observed, that no one was suffered to enter who did not come with the resolution of ending his life within it. A community of two thousand monks existed at Antinopolis, who lived partly dispersed in caves and cells. But the greatest wonder of the Lower Thebaid was the city of Osirinchis; this was, so to speak, peopled with monks, for their numbers were greater than those of the other inhabitants. Most of the buildings were monasteries, and monks dwelt also on the gates and towers of the city. The praises of God resounded day and night in psalms and hymns; for ten thousand monks, and even a greater number of consecrated virgins, devoted themselves with holy zeal to prayer. The remaining population consisted of good Catholics, unmixed with pagans or heretics; and withal so devoted to works of mercy that the public officials set watchmen at the gates of the town to give notice of the arrival of poor travellers and pilgrims, that they might be immediately received with hospitality. Tabenna, with its community of nuns, the creation of St. Pachomius, was in Upper Thebais. St. Jerome relates, that the monks of Tabenna formed an immense congregation, which yearly assembled together for the celebration of Easter, to the number of fifty thousand. In Egypt proper, was situated Nitria, with its five thousand monks, and the desert that was called the Cells, which was inhabited by five hundred solitaries. We have no details of the numbers that lived in the desert of Scete, on the borders of Lybia, although Cassian staid some time amongst them. There were two thousand monks in or near Alexandria; many thousands near Arsinoe, Canopus, and Pelusium. Five hundred monks lived under the guidance of St. Apollonius, near Heliopolis, the present village of Matariah. They were always clothed in white, that their very exterior might remind them of the necessary purity of the soul; and in order to raise this purity to the highest possible degree, St. Apollonius recommended daily communion to his disciples. Palladius gives the united numbers of the Egyptian monks in the year 395, at seventy-six thousand, and those of the nuns at twenty thousand seven hundred. St. Pachomius gave his sister the first rules for communities of women, which quickly increased, vying with the men in mortification, industry, humility, and devotion. They observed strict enclosure, and left it only on Sundays to go to church to receive holy communion. The Abbess Talida was superioress of one of these communities, in which she lived for eighty years. Her daughters were so firmly and holily attached to her, that although the gate of the monastery was never locked, not one of them ever opened it. Taor was one of these virgins. She was of such marvellous beauty, that the most holy men could not look at her without admiration. To avoid being seen she never left the monastery; and when the community went to the celebration of the most Holy Mysteries, Taor renounced this happiness, and remained in solitary prayer, seen by the Eye of God alone. These nuns considered illness as the greatest of blessings, because it gave them occasion to practise the virtue of patience, and therefore they never used remedies. Their monasteries were not a burden, either to the country or to individuals, any more than those of the monks. They cultivated in their own gardens the vegetables that formed their principal food; they span and wove the cotton for their garments, and they earned so much by their various manual labours, that it not only covered their own necessary expenses, but enabled them also to give alms, and especially to redeem prisoners in times of war. This was the case more or less in the whole of the East.

The ascetic life was differently constituted in the West, because it was developed under other circumstances. It has its source in the innermost core of Christianity, and can never be absent where the Christian life is fully and profoundly understood. In Rome, the centre of the universal Church and of the whole western world, the ascetic life had been practised from the first beginning of Christianity, by single individuals in the midst of their families, without altering their exterior circumstances. The persecutions, the sufferings, the discord amongst families and friends, offered so many opportunities of self-denial, that it required a man's whole strength to bear them. But in the beginning of the fourth century Christianity gained the ascendancy by the conversion of the emperors, and this ascendancy brought with it its accompanying evils of effeminacy, vanity, and pride of life; and then it was that the ascetic tendency took a more decided form, for it had to supplant the disorders of the heathen and of superficial Christians, and to uphold in contradistinction the sublime heights of the Christian faith and morals. The noblest mind of the century, Athanasius the Great, who, like the sun, spread light and heat wherever he went, raised the sparks to brilliant flames in Rome itself. His banishments were apostolates, his journeys missions of the highest Christian perfection. When he fled before his enemies, from Alexandria to Pope Julius, he was accompanied by two Egyptian monks, who might have passed for types of the ascetic life. One of these was called Ammon. His heart was so devoted to divine things, and his desire of them so ardent, that nothing earthly could engage nis attention. He went about amongst the glories of Rome, without ever observing them; like a blind man that refreshes himself with the better images of a blessed world, and remembers not that his eyes are shut to the beauties of earth. The other monk was called Isidore; and the purity of his soul, showing itself by his fascinating kindness, and his holy wisdom, so attracted the Romans, that even the pagans loved him. Holiness, that is, union of the soul with Eternal Love, shone forth so sweetly and sublimely in these holy men, that it inspired admiration for the state of life that had developed such souls. Athanasius strengthened the impression these two men had personally made by the History of Monasticism in Egypt, which he gives in his life of St. Antony. In this work he held up a model of the ascetic life, showed the way thither, and the rules by which to walk along that way; and he thus enkindled the fire of holy love in innumerable hearts, which had hitherto had nothing wherewith to nourish this holy flame. In voluptuous Rome, monks had heretofore been either unknown or despised; for in Rome paganism was then in full vigour; and one of Constantine's reasons for transferring his residence to Byzantium was that so few of the ancient Roman nobles were converted to Christianity. Their riches, power, and influence, had descended to them with the greatness of heathen Rome, and their hearts were bound up with these treasures. Our Blessed Lord said of them, and of all who resemble them, that it is difficult for the rich to enter into the kingdom of God. The world was conquered and ruled by these haughty Romans, and they themselves by their haughtier wives. But the day was to come when these haughty women were to be themselves conquered and ruled by Christianity.

It is difficult to form a correct idea of the luxury in which the Roman ladies of the consular and senatorial families lived, because of the overrefinement of their love of pomp and the fine arts on the one hand, and the boundless barbarity that sprung from their entire want of moral restraint on the other. They considered themselves not only the mistresses, but the goddesses of the earth. They were very rarely interfered with by their husbands, who had generally no objection to the magnificence and splendour in which their wives lived attracting admiration and envy; for it displayed the riches and glory of the family. The possession of slaves fortified the Roman lady in her delusion. A slave was considered less than a beast —much less than the favourite ape, parrot, or dog. These beasts were nourished and cared for, fed and housed, pitied and deplored; there was compassion, sympathy, and care for them; but slaves were only *things*, and no interest was felt in them, save in so far as they could be of use. The rich Romans had many thousand slaves divided amongst their houses and lands. Slaves performed every service the master required, from the cultivation of his fields to the attendance on his own person. The overseers brought the slaves by hundreds into the fields every morning, from the small prison-like rooms that gave them nightly shelter, in order to get the utmost possible labour at the smallest possible cost. They wore an iron ring round one foot, not as any especial punishment, but as the token of slavery. But however hard these poor field labourers had to toil, their lot was far happier than if they lived in immediate contact with their masters. It has happened that slaves have taken their own lives because they could not resolve to perform the shameful offices required of them. Those most to be pitied were, without doubt, the female slaves of the ladies. Five hundred of these for the personal service of the mistress, poor creatures who vied with each other in flattery and intrigue to alleviate by her favour their bitter fate, were not too many for her endless requirements. The dressing-box of an Asteria of the consular family of the Turci, of the beautiful silver workmanship of the fourth century, with fittings of massive silver, chiefly gilt, and weighing altogether one thousand and twenty-nine ounces, was disinterred at the foot of the Esquiline about sixty years since. The houses of the great were very beautiful and magnificent, with their inner courts surrounded by pillared halls, into which the chambers opened, and which were adorned with fountains, statues, and vases. Marble, bronze, ivory, alabaster, and precious stones were all employed in household utensils, so that every piece of furniture, every little table, every seat, every lamp might, as far as was possible, be a work of art. But the buildings behind these splendid palaces had a far other aspect, for they were crowded with slaves, as beehives are with bees. One wing was set apart for the female slaves, who had to sleep in small and miserable rooms, and to work in the larger ones. For their various labours h were divided into gangs, under the superintendence of an overseer; and they often had to suffer as much from her as from the mistress herself. The lowest and most despised gang was that of the spinners, because they were the furthest removed from personal attendance on the mistress. To be degraded from another gang to that of the spinners passed for a great disgrace. They span cotton and wool, and sought to enliven their heavy labour by singing. The second gang consisted of weavers. They wove the material spun by the others into the finest muslin and most delicate cashmere, and also into commoner stuffs. In former times the noblest Roman ladies thus employed themselves in the midst of their servants; even the Empress Livia worked with her own hands the garments of the Emperor Augustus. But an Asteria never troubled herself beyond giving new patterns to the overseer, and urging upon her greater zeal and diligence. The dressmakers were more highly esteemed, because their work brought them into immediate contact with the person of the mistress. Theirs was the very difficult task of fashioning the costly stuffs of the Syrian and Alexandrian merchants, so as to satisfy the vanity of their lady. The embroiderers formed a still higher class on account of the skill of their handiwork, and they worked together in a fourth large chamber which adjoined the actual wardrobe apartment, where the clothes-folders were occupied. The noble Roman ladies could not appear publicly except in the distinguishing dress of a matron, which might not be worn by any woman of lower rank or birth, or by any freedwoman, slave, actress, or even stranger. This apparel consisted of a white garment (tunica,) and a white mantle (palla.) Its material was the finest wool, or silk and wool interwoven. Everything depended upon giving these garments the utmost degree of brilliancy and smoothness, and folding them in a particular way. For this purpose special machines and presses were employed, and much practice and skill was required to use these machines properly. A flounce in many small folds was set into the lowest border of the tunic, and was always edged with a line of gold and purple; but it might also be embroidered, and studded with gold and jewels. In the country, and at parties of pleasure to which they went incognito, the Roman nobles were very fond of wearing coloured dresses. Besides this their garments were provided with some variety, either in the material or the ornaments, for every festival and all the seasons. Therefore, besides the pressing machines, the wardrobe held a considerable store of garments of all kinds. They were kept in large chests of valuable foreign wood, standing in rows along the walls, and their contents were written upon them, so that no mistake or search need be made. When a chest was opened a sweet fragrance issued forth. The superintendent of the wardrobe was always a very important person, as everything the workwomen had to do and to prepare was under her charge.

There was also a whole array of waiting-maids, who were likewise divided into separate companies. First came the painters with soaps and essences to preserve the freshness and delicacy of the skin, and to paint the cheeks red and white, the eyebrows and eyelashes raven black, and to cleanse and polish the teeth, or to insert false ones. This is so ancient a custom that seven teeth fastened to a gold plate have been found on opening an ancient Roman grave, showing that they were even left in the corpse. After the painters came the hairdressers. They had to make the hair soft and glossy, to dye it, plait it, wave it, and put it up.

The most precious ointments and the finest oil of spikenard perfumed the head-dress, and these were so costly that the revenue of a whole estate was often spent upon them. The poor hairdressers had a task that gave more occasion of impatience and ill-humour to the mistress than any other. It was the custom for the female slaves to leave their breast and arms entirely bare so long as they were in their mistress's dressing-room, so as to be able to receive immediate punishment at her pleasure. It was very common for the impatient ladies to use their long and thick gold hair-pins, which were always at hand, as daggers,[1] and to punish every fault by wounds in their breast, shoulders, or arms. It was fortunate when they did not put out an eye of the unfortunate maid, but contented themselves with a blow of the fist on the face, drawing blood from the mouth and nose. But even these were very gentle chastisements. Many were scourged to blood; and one of the most painful punishments was to fasten a block of wood, made for the purpose, above the knee of the unhappy delinquent, who had to drag it about with her day and night. A special corrector administered to the male and female slaves all the punishments which the master and mistress did not inflict with their own hands. One of the important duties of the toilet was that of the nail-cutter. Those northern inventions, stockings and shoes, were completely unknown in Rome, where the hands were always uncovered, and the feet were shod only on solemn festivals. Therefore great esteem was set upon them, the more so as no surreptitious beauty could be given them, as was the case with the hair, the teeth, and the complexion. Small feet, slender fingers, and finely formed nails could not be artificially procured, and they had therefore to be tended with

---

[1] The Roman masters had similar instruments of torture in the styles they wrote with.

the greatest care. When this slave had finished her operations with the small silver knife and tongs, and washed the nails with a little sponge dipped in spirits of wine, the fingers were adorned with rings, each hand bearing eight rings. Each season had its own set of rings, for the massive winter ones were too heavy for the heat of summer, and the bright colours adapted to spring were not in accordance with the sobriety of autumn. It was not enough to wear rings of precious stones, but each stone must be engraved by a masterhand. If one of these rings had a pedigree, that is, if it could be proved to have been worn by Cleopatra or Berenice, by Antony or King Agrippa, it would be bought for immense sums; for men and women outbid each other in this prodigal taste. The jewellers naturally bestowed most brilliant certificates upon their gems. This lavish expenditure rose to the most frantic height for pearls. At first the ladies wore in each ear a single pearl of such fabulous beauty that Julius Cæsar gave 60,000 sexterces, or about £480,000 for one pearl, which he presented to the mother of Brutus. Such pearls were called " uniones." But when the fashion descended from the consular matrons to the ladies of lower rank, the former gave them up and wore earrings of three pearls, hanging one from another, which were called marks of distinction, because they could be worn only by the very richest ladies, such an earring being worth a large estate, or two, and even three, inheritances. The jewels and trinkets were confided to a particular company of female slaves. The necklaces, rings, and bracelets, the earrings and head-ornaments, had their several keepers, whose duty it was to bring the sealed jewel-cases to the mistress, and display their contents before her.

The mirror consisted of a plate of silver, set in precious stones, overlaid at the back with a plate of gold. A pagan writer thus speaks of these mirrors:—" The dowry once bestowed by the Roman Senate upon the daughter of Scipio, is not now sufficient for the mirror of the daughter of a freedman." The mirror-bearer had to devote her whole attention to this mirror, in the first place to hold it in a convenient manner before her mistress, and then to keep it so carefully that its brightness might not be tarnished by the smallest speck; this was the object of her life. These unhappy creatures were brought to the perfection of a machine, or reduced, as it were, to become a piece of furniture, by the constant practice of the same thing; one for instance being, as it were, a candlestick, holding the torch immovably; another being like a table, holding the wash-hand basin motionless under the hands of her mistress. Others had to devote their lives to their lady's tenderly beloved menagerie—one to the lap-dog, another to the ape, and a third to the snake. For the great ladies even made favourites of snakes, of a small harmless kind, called Epidaurian dragons. They took great delight in these repulsive creatures, and let them coil around their arms and necks, taking them with them to table, and to pay visits. The waiting-maids, whose duty it was to dress the mistress, completed the number of her female slaves; but she also possessed male slaves, young pages, who waited upon her at table; strong men who, by six or eight at a time, bore her litter upon their shoulders, by means of gilt poles; swift-footed runners, black Africans of the race of the Mazices, chosen for this office because they were held to be the swiftest people in the world; and porters at the entrance of her rooms, which were not closed by doors, but by curtains of brilliantly coloured and costly carpet. Every word therefore was audible outside, and slaves kept watch to send away all undesirable listeners.

This was a high office at the imperial court. Finally, dwarfs were the especial delight of the Roman ladies, particularly when they were deformed, with large unshapely heads. They had to play the castanets, and dance, a spectacle that afforded great pleasure to their mistresses. Since nature did not create as many dwarfs as the Roman ladies desired, recourse was had to the inhuman device of procuring them artificially, and stunting their growth by pressure in chests made for that special purpose. The haughty Roman ladies saw nothing amiss in this mortal offence against God in His creature and image.

If the visit to the baths be added, which was with the Romans as it is now with the Orientals, a very ceremonious and tedious affair, it is evident that the toilet of a Roman lady oconpied a considerable portion of the day. And how did she spend the remainder? She read Milesian Tales (as romances were then called) and poems of the lightest description; or, perchance, a philosophical treatise, or she made her favourite slave read aloud to her. She also amused herself with the class of parasites that called themselves philosophers, whose whole wisdom consisted in pressing themselves into great houses, and procuring places at the tables of the rich at the cost of unspeakable humiliations. She would have her favourite philosopher, as surely as her favourite lap-dog or monkey, and she found great amusement in maliciously provoking him and wantonly teasing him. Then she visited the circus, in which were held the public chariot races, like the horse races of the present day. The drivers in the circus were divided into four parties, and dressed in colours corresponding with the four seasons. It was considered good taste frantically to espouse one of these parties, and make the livery of the slaves, and especially of the litter-bearers, of its colour, so that when the lady appeared in public every one could see at a glance which party had the honour of being under her protection. Their principal entertainment was that of the gladiatorial combats in the amphitheatre, of which we have already spoken, and in which the noble ladies took as vehement an interest as the common people. All their joys were of a morbid and spasmodic kind, such as belong only to corrupted souls and demoralised characters, who, in the depths of vice, have grown incapable of every higher feeling. It is impossible to delineate even distantly the domestic morals of a life passed in these circles.

Thus it was with the noble ladies of Rome's greatest families, with the descendants of a Cornelia, who even now enjoys, as mother of the Gracchi, a renown of two thousand years' duration, because she prized her children more highly than a few diamonds. Well was it for her that she did so. But virtue springing from a sort of proud self-consciousness is little calculated to produce seeds that will develope into fresh flowers of virtue, for it glorifies the individual rather than God. The mother of the Gracchi glorified herself through her sons with the ancient Roman pride. This pride rapidly increased from generation to generation, suffocating virtue, and nourishing self-love, and after a few centuries the daughters of the Gracchi and the Scipios became a degenerate race of women; that most terrible thing of all others upon earth. What power of renewing the soul must the Christian faith and holy asceticism possess to form saints out of such a race! What strength of will was required to rise from such a sea of indulgence to the cold shore of poverty and abnegation, and to keep pace with the leadings of grace! For even if all the noble Roman ladies were not sunk in excesses of selfishness, yet all grew up, even those in Christian families, not only with these images and examples before their eyes, but also surrounded by all the ease, luxury, and splendour inseparable from immense riches and great dignities. It certainly gave great glory to God's work, that where nothing could be expected from the natural man save weakness, effeminacy, and luxury, there heavenly strength and the sublime spirit of sacrifice shone forth, and, by love for the Incarnate God, impressed a totally different character upon the age.

ST. MARCELLA.

" He hath set me in a place of pasture; He hath brought me up on the water of refreshment."—Ps. xxii. 2.

THE Aventine, one of the seven hills on which Rome is built, was, in the old Republican times, the exercising ground where the Roman citizens assembled to make their preparations for war. In the middle of the fourth century it became an exercising ground of a different kind for such as went forth with heavenly weapons to the conquest of the kingdom of God. For Marcella's palace stood upon the Aventine. St. Jerome, the great Doctor of the Church, wrote her life and those of the other holy Roman ladies who sought his spiritual guidance and teaching when he came to Rome in 382. He was summoned thither by Pope Damasus to translate the Holy Scriptures from the Greek and Hebrew into Latin, a translation which has been adopted by the whole Catholic Church under the name of the Vulgate. The great St. Jerome had to suffer mockery, disapprobation, blame, and calumny, because he undertook the charge of the souls of these women. In what frame of mind he did so, and how much they deserved it, is shown by their whole lives. When he was blamed for it he answered that it was not his fault if the Roman men were not so much concerned for the salvation of their souls as the Roman women. There was nothing new in this, for three Maries stood under the Cross of Christ, and only one John.

Marcella was very rich and noble, being of consular lineage, of the house of the Furii. Her father having died early, her mother Albina remained a widow, and gave a very good education to her two daughters, Asella and Marcella. Both sisters were still young when St. Athanasius came to Rome. What they heard from him about St. Antony and the lives of the Egyptian solitaries, and about St. Pachomius and the rules he had given to his monks and nuns excited in them a lively desire to tread the same paths of salvation. In the little Asella, then ten years old, this desire was so strong that she dedicated herself to a state of virginity, and at the age of twelve made a cell for herself in her mother's house, in which she had not one of the comforts of life except a roof. Four naked walls surrounded her, she slept upon the bare ground, she ate bread and water all the year round, and deprived herself even of that in the seasons of fasting, spending many days of the week entirely without food. She only left her beloved cell to visit the churches of the martyrs, and always at such times as they were likely to be empty. There she prayed with great devotion, undisturbed and unnoticed. She also gave herself up with her whole soul to prayer and contemplation in her cell, so that she was always recollected in spirit, while she was continually occupied in needlework for the poor. Silence was her delight, and perhaps for this reason every word she spoke was edifying. She was always strong, always kind, always full of grace and charity, though she lived in the midst of luxurious and populous Rome as mortified and solitary as in a desert. Only under very great necessity, and with the utmost reluctance, did she allow men, even the holiest, to enter her solitude. Even her sister Marcella, whom she tenderly loved, could seldom see her, so completely had she devoted herself to God.

Marcella married, but lost her husband in six months, and she then resolved to lead the life of a Christian widow as perfectly as her sister did that of a Christian virgin. She was most beautiful, and she was wooed by Cerealis, the richest and most noble man in Rome, who was related to the Imperial family, and had been Prefect and Consul. Being no longer young, he intended in the event of his death, to leave her his whole property. Albina, the mother of these holy daughters, would have rejoiced at Marcella's brilliant marriage. But although Marcella was so submissive to her mother as to do many things out of obedience to her that were contrary to her inclinations, yet she could not resolve to marry a second time to please her. When Albina pressed her to accept the suit of Cerealis, Marcella answered that even if she did incline to a second marriage she would rather choose a husband after her own liking than for the sake of his riches. And so it ended. She refused Cerealis so decidedly that no suitor dared approach her again, and not the smallest breath of evil report ever tarnished the brightness of her fame during a very long widowhood in the midst of the corrupt Roman world, so much given to slander. She made her house a cloister, and became herself its active and pious superioress. Albina lived with her, and was always in her company. She never spoke to any man without witnesses. She never suffered any levity either in dress or words in her maid-servants, but insisted on their all being modest, chaste, and peaceable, and she held sisterly intercourse with them in return. Marcella's clothing was of the coarsest and simplest possible description. She sold all her jewels, and gave the price to the poor. She kept nothing of gold but her signet ring. The numerous locks and keys of our days were not then in use, and most things that could be stolen were sealed up. As the lady of the house had charge of everything, the opinion of antiquity decided that the seal of the house belonged to her, and the Father of the Church, Clement of Alexandria, who died about the year 217, allowed Christian mistresses to have a golden signet ring, in order to seal up the various articles of household furniture. Marcella therefore kept one, not as an ornament, but because it belonged to her position and vocation. Her table was as simple as her dress; she denied herself meat and wine, which latter was a great privation; wine mixed with hot water being the only customary warm drink, taking the place of the tea and coffee of later times, and being therefore considered indispensable. But Marcella found nothing too difficult that might help her to subdue sinful nature and its inclinations. Prayer, contemplation, diligent visiting of the churches, spiritual reading, the administration of her household, the care of the sick and the poor, and constant manual labour filled the life of the holy widow, and made her a pattern to the Christian women of Rome. They frequently sought her advice in the affairs of their soul, and some placed themselves temporarily or entirely under her guidance, and made with her their noviatiate in the ascetic life which they afterwards practised in their own houses.

Thus the palaces and villas of many great Roman families were dedicated to monastic purposes, although not under the same form afterwards given to community life by fixed rules. Sophronia, Paula, Eustochium, and Principia, were all the friends and spiritual daughters of Marcella.

She was already past middle age when she became acquainted with St. Jerome. This gave a new impulse to her noble spirit. St. Jerome had practised the life of an anchorite in the Syrian desert, and had profoundly studied the Holy Scriptures before he came to Rome, and these were the two points which irresistibly attracted Marcella, as the magnet draws iron to itself. Jerome was by no means an accessible person to any one; and he was, moreover, averse to having any intercourse with the Roman ladies; but Marcella's persistence overcame his holy reserve. She desired to gain by his means a deeper insight into the Holy Scriptures; for he says of himself in his humility, "I passed then for one versed in Scripture." He found in her so much virtue and intelligence, so much purity of mind and holiness of heart, that he says he dare not describe them, because he would not be believed; and he gave her all the explanations and instructions, and all the counsels for the interior life that she piously desired. She proposed questions upon the Holy Writings with great sagacity, and was not contented with short answers; but she was not impelled in the smallest degree by foolish curiosity, or an idle desire for superficial knowledge. She wished to know more that she might become better; she cared, not for sophistry, but for virtue. This pure motive so enlightened her penetrating and elevated mind, that St. Jerome thus writes of her: "All that I learnt with great study and long contemplation the blessed Marcella learnt also, but with great facility, and without giving up any of her other occupations or neglecting any of her duties. She had so profoundly studied the Holy Scriptures, as well as the treatises written upon them by the Fathers and Doctors of the Church, that when we" (he is speaking of himself and other holy and learned men) "were not unanimous on any question, we consulted Marcella either verbally or by letter, and every time we had occasion to admire the correctness of her decision. Intelligent and humble as she was, she always so shaped her answers as to ascribe her opinion to me, or to some other, that she might never pass for a teacher, but always continue to be thought a disciple." He speaks thus of her great zeal for reading holy books: " As often as I set before myself her diligence in holy reading, I cannot refrain from condemning my own slothfulness, that I, in a monastery, and even on this holy spot (namely Bethlehem) where I have my Redeemer's Crib ever before my eyes, do not accomplish what a noble lady does in the hours she saves from the complicated cares and occupations of her family and numerous household.".

After St. Jerome had spent three years in Rome, he returned to the East in the year 385; but he kept up an uninterrupted correspondence with Marcella and her sister; and he said, " We are always together in spirit." Before he embarked at Ostia, the port of Rome, he wrote thus to Asella: " Although some may call me radically wicked, and stained with all the abominations of sin; and although this retribution is very little in comparison with my sins, yet thou doest well in measuring others by thyself; that is, in holding the wicked to be good, for it is a dangerous thing to judge another." At the end he says: " Good Asella, thou perfect image of a virginal and pure mind, think right often of me before God, and calm by thy prayers the waves of the sea." This letter alludes to the many enemies he had made amongst the pampered Romans by his great frankness, which at times bordered on harshness, and especially by his having relentlessly denounced the faults of the spiritual life, if anything more severely than those of the world.

Marcella's influence was not confined to the

pious and fervent persons of her own sex; it was felt also in wider circles. The controversy of Origen filled the Church at that time. Rufinus, the learned priest of Aquileia, had translated a work by Origen called Periarchon, containing erroneous propositions, which were believed by the blind partisans of Origen to be doctrines of the Catholic Church. The most important were these: " The pains of hell are not eternal; our souls have existed before our bodies; the fallen angels will regain their lost dignity; Paradise is only a figurative representation of heaven; man will not rise again in the same body." Even in his lifetime Origen had asserted that the copyists of his numerous writings had not done their work conscientiously, but had occasioned grave misunderstandings, by which restless and subtle minds had profited to place him in a false light, to lay snares for many, and to give scandal to others. In like manner it was now attempted, through the lustre of his renowned name, to make these propositions dogmas of the Church. Although Jerome was a great admirer of Origen, and a friend of Rufinus of Aquileia of many years' standing, yet he came resolutely forward against errors disapproved by the Church, because these false doctrines had gained the assent and approval of many of the laity, clergy, and monks, and had even spread from the East to Rome. The more famous was the name of Origen, the more secure was the cloak for the heresy, which the holy man himself would certainly have been the first to combat; for, at the time at which he wrote, the Church had not yet given the decision of the Holy Ghost upon those propositions. And it is not error that makes the heretic, but a certain determined resistance to the Church which the Son of God founded upon earth when He said: He that heareth you heareth Me.

Marcella lost her beloved mother soon after the

departure of St. Jerome. Although Albina was a most virtuous matron, yet she was attached to her family with all the strength of natural affection, and as Marcella had not continued it, she left all her property to the children of her brother. Marcella would have rejoiced to possess it, that she might bestow it upon the needy; but she acquiesced in the withdrawal of it to avoid vexing her mother; and God, in His boundless love, fulfilled the wish of this holy soul: for this property, and much more, passed into the hands of the poor through Pammachius, one of Marcella's nephews. Asella was now made superioress of a community of newly converted women, and by her instructions she worked great things for the spread of the faith in R . Palladius saw and admired her there in the beginning of the fifth century, and says that men also had been converted to the faith by her exhortations. Marcella withdrew more and more from the world, and left her palace on the Aventine for a simple country house in one of the suburbs of Rome. But when the monstrous heresy of Origen broke out in Rome, she took the greatest possible pains to remove the tainted sheep from the flock of Christ, and to raise a barrier against the evil. It was difficult to trace the heretics, for the book Periarchon had been anonymously translated, and those who believed its teaching still asserted that they were Catholic and orthodox, and that its doctrines were not essentially opposed to the fundamental teaching of Christianity; in short, they followed the tactics observed by most heretics. Pope Siricius suffered himself to be pacified by these declarations. But Marcella in her retirement rested not. The Catholic faith was in danger; and on that very spot where the holy Apostles, Peter and Paul, had announced it, and had died for it, guileless souls were being estranged from that faith from which nothing can be taken away, and to which nothing can be added, if it is to remain the pure, true, and revealed faith; how then could she do otherwise than adopt every means in her power to prevent the tarnishing of the brightest jewel possessed by Christ here below? She went to work with the greatest prudence and reserve, and she succeeded in finding credible persons who deposed that such and such a one had instructed them in the heresy of Origen, by which means these teachers were called to account and their doctrines condemned.

Amongst the many devout souls that had relations with Marcella, she had chosen out one to whom she stood in the place of a mother. This was Principia, who came to Marcella in her early youth. She was an orphan, and descended from a noble patrician family; for St. Jerome thus writes to her: "All Rome rejoiced that thou didst find a mother, and Marcella a daughter." United with this beloved adopted daughter, Marcella devoted herself unceasingly to the spiritual and corporal works of mercy, and reached a great age, of which the last days were stormy and painful. King Alaric with his Goths rolled like a devastating flood over Italy, and even to the very walls of Rome. The Emperor Honorius was at Ravenna, busy with his favourite occupation of feeding hens, and the courtly flatterers who surrounded him so little dared to disturb him in this imperial pleasure, that they never even uttered the name of Alaric in his presence; still less would they tell him that this king with his barbarians was besieging Rome. This terrible siege took place in the year 410. Famine and sickness raged in the city, and on the twenty-fourth of August it fell by treachery into the hands of Alaric. He gave it over to his barbarians to be plundered, and they made havoc therein with fire and sword. Alaric and his Goths were Arians. Nevertheless, they had so great a veneration for the holy Apostles, Peter and Paul, that by Alaric's orders the two basilicas on the Vatican and on the road to Ostia, dedicated to them, became safe asylums for all fugitives. The following anecdote will show that this command was observed with the greatest fidelity by his rapacious Goths, although they were drunk with victory. An aged consecrated virgin had taken the holy altar vessels of the basilica of St. Peter under her charge, in her own house, and was waiting in prayer for whatever fate God might send her. A Gothic warrior with his followers forced an entrance into her house. He did not insult her, but merely demanded the surrender of her gold, silver, and jewels. She answered him that she had indeed great treasures, which she would show him, and she led him at once to the chamber where were the magnificent vessels, which rejoiced and astonished the Goths by their number, beauty, and weight. The holy virgin said to the Goth: "These vessels belong to the Apostle St. Peter; as I cannot defend them, I dare not keep them back. Take them if thou hast the courage to do so." But he had not. He apprised Alaric, through a soldier, of his discovery, and he commanded that the holy vessels, the consecrated virgin, and all the Christians that chose to join her, should be conveyed unharmed to the basilica of the Prince of the Apostles. The Vatican lay at the other end of the city, and thereupon commenced a solemn procession through the warlike tumult. The Christians bore, with great respect and devotion, the holy vessels which thus saved their lives, and soldiers marched on each side with drawn swords, while both Romans and Goths sang hymns in praise of God; and the more fugitives joined the train, the more willingly did the soldiers open their protecting ranks. Whence came this respect paid by heretics to the golden chalices and vases, if not from an instinct of truth in their souls which told them that they had held the Body and Blood of God?

Marcella had remained peacefully in her own house during this perilous time. For herself she feared nothing; but only for Principia. When a troop of soldiers attacked her, and judging by the size and grandeur of the dwelling, demanded her hidden treasures, she displayed her poor clothing, and assured them that she possessed nothing more. This seemed incredible, and they beat her with sticks; but she disregarded this, and only begged that they would not separate her from her daughter. God moved the hearts of her tormentors to listen to her prayer, and they led them both to the basilica of St. Paul. Then Marcella broke forth in praise of God, because imprisonment had not made her, but had found her poor, and because her Principia was saved. And after a few days she died in the arms of the beloved daughter of her adoption, and without illness or agony she gave back her beautiful soul into the Hands of her Creator.

THE BLESSED FABIOLA.

"I will please the Lord in the land of the living."—Ps. cxiv. 9.

ALTHOUGH this noble Roman lady was less perfect in her early life than St. Marcella, yet she was so heartily converted to God that her penitential spirit made her an equally edifying model to all who sincerely desire to save their souls. St. Jerome, in writing her life, brings her forward as a living monument of the mercy of God, Who sends enlightenment and proffers grace to every one who is of good will to return to the right path after having strayed along false ways. Pagan morals, customs, and opinions ruled supreme in heathen Rome, and even penetrated into Christian Rome, bound together as they were, by a thousand ties of family and friendship. A believing family was sometimes surrounded by a whole array of heathen relations. If the pure breath of the Christian life wafted to the heathen the perfume of the virtues of the saints, the sultriness of the heathen atmosphere on the other hand oppressed many a Christian. No corruption that had entered in consequence of the fall was so great as that which had destroyed the relationship between the two sexes, and what should be the highest and most beautiful expression of this relationship, namely, marriage. The history of the four centuries before Christianity is full of the abominations which, in consequence of this corruption, once drew down the deluge upon the earth; but which, alas! rose again out of the great waters with the new world. No wrathful judgment of God, no rain of brimstone, no deluge, no destruction of Sodom, described in Holy Scriptures, no submersion of the island of Atlantis, related by the ancient Greeks; nothing, in short, could put a stop to the unspeakable corruption that flowed in all men's veins, and made the relation between the two sexes one of nameless degradation. But what the anger of God could not accomplish, was done by the Blood of God, and by His love. Christ said to the Jews: " Moses, by reason of the hardness of your heart, permitted you to put away your wives; but from the beginning it was not so " He who gave the consummation to every law, who taught mercy towards strangers, love of enemies, voluntary poverty, and purity of heart, raised the divine law of marriage out of the mire in which it was buried and trampled under foot. He endowed it with the grace of a Sacrament, and St. Paul the Apostle shows how highly God would have it esteemed, when he compares the matrimonial union between a man and his wife to the union between Christ and His Church. A Christian is a supernatural man, and Christ has placed marriage on a supernatural footing. Whenever it is degraded from this position it incurs the danger of becoming boundlessly impure, and drawing humanity down into the seething crater of demoralisation. But if it keeps its true position as a type of the union of Christ with the Church, it produces a race of benediction, and is the salvation of the generations in time and for eternity. As a matter of course, it is indissoluble save by death; for in its inmost substance it is a union made by grace, and cemented by the Blood of Jesus. And it is also a matter of course, that this idea of marriage was unknown to paganism, and is disavowed by the sects outside the Church, because it is burdensome to the sensual man.

In the holy season of Lent of the year 390, a rare and soul-stirring spectacle was seen in Rome. Amongst the public penitents in front of the basilica of St. John Lateran, who begged to be received once more into the communion of the Church, stood Fabiola; the noble, honoured, and wealthy Fabiola of the ancient race of the Fabii. She was kneeling on the ground in a penitential garment, without sandals, with dishevelled hair and tearful face, with ashes on her head and neck, and dust in her hands, imploring with many tears the grace of being reconciled to God throngh salutary penance. Pope Siricius, the clergy, Fabiola's equals, and all the people of Rome, beheld her penance with edification and emotion. Fabiola had early espoused a husband who led such a wicked life that it seemed to her impossible to remain at his side. She was very young, and she thought she had the right to refuse to endure the great offences he committed against her. Her womanly delicacy forbade her to complain of him, and preferring to take upon herself the blame of the separation, she left her husband's house to return to her family. Moreover, all Rome was aware of this man's licentious life. After Fabiola had lived a certain time with her relations she thought herself justified in contracting a second marriage, because she had been separated from her husband by his own bad conduct, and not by inconstancy and fickleness on her part, nor by the impulse of blind passion. A second marriage during the lifetime of the first husband was allowed by the civil laws, and she was either ignorant or regardless of the ecclesiastical law forbidding it. She lived happily many years with her second husband until he died. The loss of her husband placed before her eyes the transitoriness of earthly happiness, and the folly of purchasing it at the price of eternal goods.

When the bandage fell off from the eyes of Fabiola's soul, she perceived what an offence she had been guilty of against God's law, and entered with great firmness upon the way of reconciliation with God. She willingly submitted to do public penance, which was a hard thing for a woman of her rank. Her sorrow for having offended God and given public scandal was so great that no humiliation could wound her more than this consciousness. After the outward acts of penance had been accomplished, and Fabiola had been raised out of the dust and ashes of sin, and restored to the purity of the children of God, it became evident how sincere had been the contrition which had laid the foundation of her conversion. " Many sins are forgiven her, because she hath loved much."[1] Fabiola comprehended this saying of our Blessed Lord, and therefore He who had forgiven her so much became the Well-beloved of her renovated soul. On the day on which she received Holy Communion, she descended for ever from the throne of ease and rank whereon she had been placed from her cradle, and betook herself to the obscure abode of voluntary poverty. Her desires of fasting, almsgiving, prayer, and humiliation, kept pace with each other, so that her exterior mortification was only the reflection of the interior. She laid aside for ever gay clothing, costly stuffs, fine linen, pearls and jewels, and assumed coarse garments; and yet she set no value on this mortification, although it is a very great one for a lady brought up in indulgence as she had been. St. Jerome says: " It is easier to cast off diamonds than pride. He who does not take complacency in the thought that he has given away gold and silver, becomes, perchance, proud of his mean clothing, and the praise of men indemnifies him for his poverty. But Fabiola has directed her intention purely to God's honour and good pleasure, and has never been ensnared by any motion of self-complacency." Her generosity knew no other limit than that of having no more to give; and to be niggardly in giving seemed to her unworthy of a disciple of an Incarnate God Who has given Himself entirely to us. The great city of Rome was too small for Fabiola's bounty. She, as it were, invited the whole world to herself, with the words of her Well-beloved: " Come to me all ye that labour." She travelled through all Italy; she sought out the monastic communities which were at that time just springing into existence; she visited the solitaries who were leading, amongst

[1] Luke vii. 47.

the Apennines, on the sea-shores, and in the neighbouring islands, the life of the anchorites of the East, and the only object of her journey was to bestow help where it was needed. But if she gave much, she did more. It was she who founded the first hospital in Rome, and received therein the sick, the poor, and the needy. She herself was the principal nurse in this hospital, and the daughter of the ancient Roman consuls and senators made herself the servant of the poor of Christ. With her own hands she dressed sores, bound up wounds, and tended the dying in their agony. She held in her own arms those of the sick who were torn by convulsions or attacked by spasms. She prepared couches for all, brought them soothing remedies, and gave them nourishing food; and all this she did with such heartfelt love, that the poor in the hospital who were in health wished to be sick in order to be tended by Fabiola. "I know well," says St. Jerome, "that many of the rich show mercy to the poor, but they do it by the hands of others. They give their gold, but not their personal services, because the sight of misery inspires disgust, and makes them ill. I will not find fault with this weakness, nor will I call it unmerciful. But I must be allowed to say that true love and perfect faith raise the mind above such infirmities, and make it strong for holy services of love."

Yet all this did not satisfy Fabiola. The desire of this great soul was turned towards the Holy Land, towards making herself a true burnt-offering of holy love, and living after the manner of the anchorites for God alone, supported by alms given for His love. She had already sent considerable gifts to Palestine, when she determined to journey to Jerusalem. Her friends and relations opposed it, and sought to retain her in Rome, but in Rome she was surrounded by pomp, dissipation, and

2 E

worldly pride, whilst she had espoused poverty; and she longed for the desert, as the prisoner longs for freedom. She embarked in the year 395, and arrived safely at Jerusalem, where her name and holy life were well known, and where she was welcomed with joyful respect. There, and in Bethlehem, St. Jerome learnt to know and esteem her. Fabiola's mind, like those of all her holy and renowned contemporaries, was so highly cultivated that deep study of the Holy Scriptures became her favourite occupation. St. Jerome writes: "She eagerly perused the Prophets, the Psalms, and the Gospels, asking searching questions, and imprinting the answers on her heart, looking at knowledge only as a means of increasing in understanding. Once when we had the Book of Numbers before us, she asked me many things concerniug the Israelite tribes and races, and was satisfied with my answers. But when she wished to know the secret and higher meaning of the places of encampment where the children of Israel pitched their tents during the journey through the desert from Egypt to the Jordan, and I was forced to confess my ignorance, she urged me so strongly to meditate upon the signification of these mysteries that I was unable to withstand her. And as I have dedicated the little book of explanation of a priest's vestments in her name, I will also dedicate to her, to this blessed Fabiola, who has journeyed through the desert of the world, and reached the heavenly tabernacles before I have, the Exposition of the forty-two camping places of the people of Israel." However, in spite of the joy she experienced in these studies under the guidance of such a master, Fabiola had by no means given up her intention of leading a solitary life. She knew by heart the Epistle of St. Jerome to Heliodorus, the former companion of his solitude, in which he summons him to return to the forsaken desert, an epistle that aroused so much disapprobation and so much sympathy; and she kept constantly in her mind the question addressed therein to Heliodorus, "Why art thou in the world, thou who art greater than the world?"

Jerome took great pains to seek out a spot that was fitting for a soul led by such extraordinary paths. Before he had succeeded in finding one, the East was thrown into fear and trembling by the marauding incursions of the savage Isaurians, who pressed with great rapidity through the mountain passes of the Taurus in Asia Minor, ravaging and plundering the country, and who, having assembled large armies in Syria, threatened Phœnicia. The inhabitants fled to the coast and on board ship to be ready to escape should the tribulation come upon them. The women were specially endangered, for the barbarians violated and carried them off. Under these circumstances, Jerome judged it best for Fabiola to return to Rome, and to seek for shelter in the very place where she had given shelter to so many, to be poor where she had formerly been rich, to live mortified, and as it were in a desert, amidst all the recollections of her brilliant past. It grieved him very much "to lose so costly a jewel from the Holy Land;" but Fabiola, who was a stranger everywhere, at all times ready for a journey, and who was detached from all permanent dwelling-places, renounced every wish that was not in unison with the dispositions of God, and willingly returned to Rome.

"This valiant woman," as St. Jerome calls her, edified and gladdened the Roman people for a few years longer by the holy and penitential life which she continued to lead in her hospital as servant of the sick and poor. Then, in the foresight of her approaching death, she summoned some holy monks to free her from the burden of her last remaining earthly goods, and to spend them in founding new communities, that she might thus multiply the intercessors who would help her speedily to reach the everlasting tabernacles. She was more desirous of death than others are of life, and she was at all moments ready to die, in order, like the Apostle St. Paul, to be dissolved, and to be with Christ. It was soon shown in what estimation Fabiola was held by the city of Rome, for she had hardly given up her spirit in the peace of the Lord before the population gathered together, making all the churches resound with prayer and praise. Her burial was grander and more solemn than the triumphal processions of any of her ancestors had been; for then men were rejoicing over earthly victories only; but now the angels in heaven went forth in exultation to welcome the poor converted sinner, on whom grace had been so prodigally bestowed, that she had victoriously triumphed over sin.

ST. PAULA.

"Hearken, O daughter, and see, and incline thy ear, and forget thy people, and thy father's house.—Ps. xliv. 10.

UNDER the church at Bethlehem is the Cave in which was accomplished the marvellous and humble mystery of God's exceeding love. It took place in the greatest concealment. A bare cavern in the rock which, according to the custom of the East, served as a stable; a poor little Child lying in the manger that was used to hold the fodder for the beasts; an unknown and delicate mother; a humble artisan; a few shepherds from the neighbouring fields; it was thus that He began His earthly life. Whom the Prophet Isaias had foretold a thousand years before as the "Wonderful, the Prince of Peace." The eye of faith alone can penetrate the veil that shrouds this mystery. The shepherds hear and see the exulting angels, and the kings in the far East follow the mysterious Star. In this mystical peace the work of the redemption of the world began. And in later days, the eye of faith rested with unspeakable love upon this holy scene, and pious souls panted after the grotto of Bethlehem as after a haven of repose.

Bethlehem presents a decided contrast to Jerusalem which is, as it were, petrified in dust and ashes. It seems as though the Birth of our Lord had cast an unfading hue of spring over Bethlehem, whilst His Death spread a lasting gloom over Jerusalem. Bethlehem is situated on a declivity between two hills richly covered with olive, fig, and almond trees. The fertile soil bears luxuriant crops, and here and there are diminutive green meadows as bright and smooth as velvet. Birds sing at Bethlehem, and that is rare in Palestine. The whole landscape is pleasant and spring-like, exactly fitted for the Idyll of Ruth, for the childish sports of the shepherd boy David, and for the cradling of the Divine Infant. The church is the very same that was built by the Empress Helena in the form of a basilica over the Stable and the Crib; the beautiful old marble columns with their rude capitals, which divide the interior into three naves, are still standing. The flat roof of cedar remains, but the mosaics on the walls are partly torn down, and partly plastered over by the Mohammedans. The whole of the limestone hill upon which the church stands is undermined by caverns and grottos, partly natural and partly artificial. The Christians of the first centuries took up their abode in them for life and for death. They range like little catacombs beside the grotto of the Birth of Christ, which is lined with marble walls, hung with silken tapestries, and adorned with paintings. It is lighted night and day by more than fifty golden lamps, always burning, to denote the Light of the world which has appeared to us in Christ. The altar erected over the grave of St. Jerome is in one of these caverns. Here he sought and found a resting-place after his laborious life. He said, " I will repose and dwell in the birth-place of my Saviour, because He chose and consecrated this spot." This was the mystical attraction which allured souls that "follow the Lamb whithersoever He goeth." This cave was Jerome's favourite sojourn. There he, the oracle of his age, lived immersed in mortification and study. There he passed whole nights in his work of translating the Old Testament from Hebrew into Latin. There he had ever before his eyes the last end of man; ever in his ear the trumpet of the Judgment; and by his violent penance, which impelled him to beat his breast with stones till he drew blood, he sought to subdue whatever impeded his taking heaven by storm. The grave of his disciple, the holy abbot Eusebius of Cremona, is in another of these caves. A third is dedicated to the remembrance of the innocent children whom Herod made the first-fruits of the flowers of martyrdom, who could not bear witness, but who could die for their Saviour. Outside of Bethlehem lies the little sanctuary known as the asylum of the Blessed Virgin Mary during her days of woe, which is held in especial veneration by the people, and even by the Mohammedans, who take their oaths upon it. In a fourth cave there is an altar over the relics of the two noble Roman women, Paula and Eustochium, the mother and daughter, who were led by their faith and devotion to a monastery in Bethlehem. These two last offshoots of the noble Scipios and the impetuous Gracchi were inseparable in life, and they now rest undivided in the dark and humble grave hard by the dark and humble Crib.

The race of ancient Romans succumbed according to the flesh, together with ancient pagan Rome, to rise again according to the spirit. With enlightened minds they surveyed the past which had made them rich and powerful, and given them the mastery of the earth now lost to them for ever. Noble souls cling not to temporal greatness, they turn away from it to seek true greatness as soon as they recognise it to be their rightful aim. We are taught by the Gospel and the Life of the Incarnate God in what this greatness consists.

The first senatorial family that was converted with all its members to Christianity was that of the Anicii, from which, two centuries later, St. Gregory the Great descended. Proba Falconia, to whom St. Augustine addressed a celebrated treatise on prayer, was of this house, which gave more saints to Christian Rome than it had supplied consuls to the heathen city. This family was rivalled by those of the Julii and Æmilii, which were united in the persons of Toxotius and Paula.

Paula was born at Rome on the fifth of May 347. Her father, Rogatus, was of Grecian descent, and claimed to trace his ancestry as far back as Agamemnon. Her mother's forefathers included the two noblest names of the Republic, Scipio and Æmilius Paulus. The riches of this family were proportionate to their nobility, and all this fell to the lot of Paula and her only brother. Nature had adorned her with the highest gifts of mind and heart, and when, at the age of eighteen she espoused Toxotius, who was her equal in nobility of birth and disposition and in the gifts of mind and fortune, all Rome rejoiced to see the union of two scions of these noble families. They led a Christian and very edifying life, giving a brilliant example in their high position. Paula's conduct was blameless, and admirable in the judgment of the world; but she was still far from Evangelical perfection. Her heart clung with passionate affection to her husband and her children, and she basked in the world's approval and in self-complacency. Her children were called Blesilla, Paulina, Eustochium, Rufina, and Toxotius. They had all inherited the excellent qualities of their parents, and the happy mother rejoiced inordinately in this living garland of sweetness and virtue. She enjoyed this untroubled and almost superhuman happiness for fourteen years.

At the end of this time, Toxotius, her husband, died. She had loved him so ardently that life without him seemed to her insupportable, and she longed to die of grief. She became entirely indifferent to the approval of mankind and the glory of this world, and could find no consolation or alleviation save in the hope of soon following him. She was utterly miserable, as every one must sooner or later be, who has forgotten that the creature should be loved only for the sake of the Creator. The mercy of God watched over her through this dark night of suffering. God would not permit that the love of this beautiful heart should be thrown away. He bade stars to shine upon her darkness, suggesting to her other thoughts and hopes than those which had followed Toxotius to his grave; and as she raised her mournful eyes to these new constellations, a supernatural light was enkindled within her. She had never sought earthly consolation for a single instant, she was therefore capable of receiving it from Heaven. The fairest blossom of earth had faded in her grasp, and she determined to detach herself entirely from all temporal things, and to attach herself with heart and soul to those of eternity.

In order to see clearly how she could best accomplish this, she left her home for some time, and retired to that house upon the Aventine, which had already served as a field of battle to many souls wrestling in unseen struggles, the house of Marcella, her beloved and revered friend. She hoped by Marcella's enlightened counsel to be able more clearly to learn, and more courageously to tread the path that leads to heaven. God so disposed that she should only take her daughter Eustochium with her to Marcella. Hence a steady and inextinguishable flame of Divine love was enkindled in the heart of this young maiden, perhaps the most talented of all Paula's highly-gifted children, which illuminated her whole life, and caused her early to form the resolution of choosing no other bridegroom but our Divine Lord Himself. Paula also determined to follow the standard of the Cross, which Marcella so bravely and perseveringly carried before her. In order completely to sever her past and her present, and to make herself more acquainted with the full austerity and severity of the ascetic life, she left Marcella's house for a little time, and repaired to a still greater solitude in a convent of women outside Rome. She left Eustochium with Marcella, who took the pious child under her own especial charge, in order to bestow constant care upon the cultivation of grace in this young mind. Paula examined in the cloister the purpose she had formed with Marcella, and when she was sufficiently acquainted with the holy yoke it laid upon her, and had implored with fervent prayers and tears the grace of perseverance, she returned to Rome, and lived in her splendid palace as though in a cloister. She did what our Blessed Lord's first disciples had done in such great perfection, she "arose and followed Him." This arising and with one step leaving all things is what our Divine Lord calls putting the hand to the plough and not looking back. Paula entered upon this heroic career of the saints, and devoted herself to the service of God with such unspeakable joyfulness that it seemed as though the death of her husband, which had led her to this service, must have been welcome to her. If her former sorrow is compared with this victory over self, it is clear that she had learnt to say with the Apostle St. Paul: "I can do all things in Him who strengtheneth me."

Although Paula had refrained from the excesses of an Asteria, she had, nevertheless, led the indulgent life that was usual amongst noble Roman matrons; she had been clothed in costly stuffs, adorned with precious stones, and nourished with dainty food. She had reclined on soft couches, and been borne by her servants in a golden litter; she had decked her hair with flowers, and perfumed it with valuable essences. But she now wore coarse garments, and beneath them a hair shirt; she slept on the hard floor, covered only with a rough carpet; she took neither meat nor wine, neither fish, eggs, nor honey, not allowing her vegetables to be prepared with oil, except on feast-days. She never again sat down to table with any man, not even with the holy bishops who came to Rome from distant countries and dwelt in her house. She never used baths except in illness. She so blinded her eyes with her tears and nightly prayers, and so tortured her body that Jerome himself, that austere saint, recommended moderation to her. But she answered, "May my face be evermore disfigured, which, against the commands of God, I have adorned with paint and foolish ornaments to please my husband and the world. I now seek nothing but to please my Lord and Saviour, even if my too tender body should be consumed thereby, for it deserves nothing better." She had a clear and refined intellect, which had fomerly caused her to find much pleasure in society. But she soon became convinced how quickly the loss of recollection follows upon intercourse with the world, and how little food the soul receives from any conversation, and she therefore renounced making visits. She, however, still spoke sometimes with pious persons upon spiritual things. All earthly joys were in her eyes despicable, and unworthy of a Christian, who ought to be a stranger here below. She still clung to her children, perhaps unawares, with a love so great that it counterbalanced her burning desire to make a pilgrimage to the East. But loving and kind as she was to these children, she was as much so to the poor, on whom she bestowed alms almost to extravagance. She strove to alleviate every want; she sought out the sick and tended them; she visited the dying and consoled them, and provided for their decent burial. If a hungry or a naked person had been fed or clothed by another instead of by her, she reproached herself for her negligence. She spent in alms not only all that she had re trenched of the former expenses of her house and person, which were very great, but also all that portion of her property which was at her own disposal. It never occurred to her to gather together gold and silver for her dearly beloved children. who had indeed inherited great riches from their father. Her relations reproached her for what they termed prodigality and robbery of her children; but Paula smilingly answered, "I do not rob my dear children; on the contrary, I hope to procure for them in exchange for a temporal inheritance, the eternal mercy of God." This and all other blame was highly welcome to Paula, and nothing was more painful to her than the praise and applause of men.

In the year 382 the holy Pope Damasus summoned several of the Eastern and Western bishops to Rome to investigate and decide some disputed questions in the Church. Paula had a great desire to hold pious intercourse with these holy men, and as she was held in high esteem, St. Epiphanius, Bishop of Salamis in the island of Cyprus, accepted her respectful invitation and came to lodge in her house. Through him she became acquainted with St. Jerome, who arrived in Rome at the same time, in company with Paulinus, Bishop of Antioch. Jerome was considered by many a rough zealot, but souls eager for salvation did not find him so; rather, they found in him such enlightened and sublime thoughts as to inspire them with the trust that he would lead them along the narrow way and through the strait gate to heaven. Paula was too noble and high-minded to wish for an easy and effeminate spirituality; she even required to have the love and fervour of her heart kept within bounds; and Jerome was the person sent her by God to teach her how to regulate her conduct in every circumstance by the love of God alone. She not only made him her guide in the spiritual life, but like her friend Marcella, she sought to draw profit for herself and her daughter from his extraordinary learning, by hearing his explanations of the Scriptures.

In order to be in a position more fully to understand the holy writings, and to imbibe the spirit of the royal Psalmist who has sung better than any other the praises of the love and mercy of God, Paula pursued the study of Hebrew, and with great success. Eustochium shared with her all her studies as well as all her works of mercy. The mother and daughter had never been separated except for the short time that Eustochium spent with Marcella, whilst Paula was in the monastery, perhaps the same that was governed by Lea, another holy widow of a noble Roman family.

They shared the same room, they had the same occupations, they lay down to rest on the same poor bed, they lived as it were with one and the same heart in two bodies. Eustochium looked up with reverence to her mother as a pattern of Christian virtue; Paula admired and respected the virginal soul of her consecrated daughter. There has never been a deeper or sweeter tie between mother and child. Paula had renounced the world, and the world had never come into contact with the mind of Eustochium. Her pure spirit unfettered by any earthly thoughts, readily turned to supernatural things, keeping pace with that of her mother, and being quickly developed under the sublime guidance of St. Jerome.

Paula's eldest daughter Blesilla had, in the meantime, espoused a husband whose name has not been mentioned, and who died in six months. Blesilla fell dangerously ill, and after her recovery she took the magnanimous resolution of dedicating the remainder of her life without reserve to God. She resigned herself so perfectly to God that she did not so much deplore the death of her husband as the fact of having bestowed her love upon a creature. She now emulated Paula and Eustochium in all the virtues of a soul that loves God, and led a life of mortification, prayer, good works, and contemplation of the Holy Scriptures, under the spiritual direction of St. Jerome. He says of her, that she had an unusually intelligent mind, and great grace in speaking. She was as fluent in Greek as in Latin, and she learnt Hebrew even quicker than her mother. In order to strengthen her in holy contempt for the world, which was so necessary for her at the age of nineteen and with her brilliant and amiable qualities, St. Jerome read with her the Book of the Preacher Solomon, and she obtained from him the promise to write an exposition of it, that she might be able in future to read it and understand it without him.

Paulina, Paula's second daughter, married Pammachius, so noble and great a man that he is numbered by the Church among the saints, the favourites of God. He deserved to be the son-in-law of Paula and the nephew of Marcella. Like Marcella, he was descended from the ancient family of the Furii; he was also a Roman Senator, and exceedingly rich. He was a great friend of St. Jerome, who submitted many of his writings to him for his opinion and judgment. Paula lived in constant intercourse with these intellectual and holy men; but God in His grace and mercy prevented her from priding herself upon having such a circle of holy children and friends. Envy, the offspring of wickedness, which hates what is beautiful and good because it is in itself hideous and evil, sought to scatter its poison over Paula. It was hardly possible to do so, for even in the world her reputation had been as spotless as her conduct. But envy often attempts impossibilities, and the assertion was spread abroad that her good conduct was mere hypocrisy. Paula feared not, neither did she bestir herself, but remained in perfect peace and silence, complaining neither of the calumny nor of the calumniators. She quietly said: "'Blessed are they that suffer persecution for justice' sake.'[1] If man suffers not on account of his sins, persecution in this world merits a heavenly recompense." Her virtue was so great and so firm that she peacefully rejoiced, like the Apostle, to be " accounted worthy to suffer reproach for the Name of Jesus."[2] It was once said of her before her face, that her ardent zeal for the faith and virtue made many think her mad, and that it was surprising her family did not put her in confinement, and under medical treatment, like one insane. She lovingly replied:

[1] Matt. v. 10. [2] Acts v. 41.

"'We are fools for Christ's sake, but you are wise.'[1] But this folly is better and wiser before God than human wisdom." No blast from the world could disturb the beautiful peace of her heart in which she had deeply engraven that saying of our Blessed Lord : " Because you are not of the world the world hateth you."[2] With these and similar passages of the Holy Scriptures Paula prepared for herself weapons of invincible patience and forbearance, which finally conquered and silenced even envy itself. The deeper she looked into the vanity and temptations of life in the world, the more clearly she perceived the dangers that surround every step, and the extreme difficulty of escaping from amongst them with unstained soul. Perfect souls fly more earnestly from the smallest speck upon their interior than the imperfect do from great stains, because their conscience is more tender and their love of God more fervent.

Her intercourse with St. Jerome, and with the holy bishops Epiphanius and Paulinus, strengthened her inclination for solitude, and heightened her desire to retire into complete seclusion, and to leave for ever the city of Rome, where she was obliged by her position to be in continual contact with the world, and where the eyes of men were ever upon her. To seek concealment with "the hidden God," as Isaias named Him, was the attraction of grace in Paula. But she still withstood it. The children, the beloved children, held fast the most tender of mothers. At length God came to her assistance, and the amiable and talented Blesilla died in her twentieth year. God rewarded the offering she had made to Him by an early death, and thus secured her sacrifice. But Paula fell once more into unmeasured grief. She was carried away from Blesilla's burial like a

[1] 1 Cor. iv. 10.   [2] John xv. 19.

corpse: she came to herself only to break forth into lamentations and mourning, and remained in a condition that occasioned the greatest fears for her life. Her heart had loved this her eldest child, if not the best, at least the longest. In Blesilla she saw her own likeness—the same mind, the same destiny, the same conversion. She had enjoyed a second existence in her daughter; and now her own life descended, as it were, with her into the tomb. She wept and mourned like the voice in Rama, that would not be comforted.

Jerome was much grieved to see this. He also deplored Blesilla's death, but he thought it incompatible with Paula's resignation to God, that she should grieve so immoderately for a person whose death was only the passing from time into eternity—the return home from exile. He sought to inspire her with courage and self-command, but in vain. He left her in this grief, and returned to the East in the year 385, because he found that one who undertook to expound the Holy Scriptures ought to be intimately and minutely acquainted with every part of Palestine. He wrote from thence a letter to Paula about her condition of mind, full of that holy severity which springs from the supernatural love of souls. "Thy daughter," he says, "departed from this life in the fervent resolution, fortified by cleansing penance, of dedicating herself entire y to God. Seest thou not that the Redeemer calls to thee and says, 'Paula, wherefore dost thou grieve because thy daughter has become mine? Thy tears are a rebellion against my Providence, an offence against my love.' I know that a mother must needs grieve somewhat, but she should not be under the dominion of such overwhelming sorrow. It does little honour to thy faith, and it brings discredit on the ascetic life. In so much as is possible in Blesilla's happy state, she grieves because thou dost grieve thy Saviour. She calls to thee from the heights of heaven: 'Oh, grudge me not my bliss! I am here near the Mother of God, and in the company of the angels and saints. Thou weepest because I have forsaken the earth; but I pity the banishment which places thee in so great danger.'" Jerome would not tolerate any feminine weakness in Paula, because he well knew of what perfection she was capable. He expresses this in another place, where he says: "She despised all earthly joys, but she sometimes let herself be mastered by earthly sorrow for the loss of her beloved ones, although it was according to the flesh rather than the spirit. This was her greatest fault—a fault that in others would be called a virtue."

His epistle produced a salutary effect upon Paula; she took courage, and made her grief become what grief should be to every Christian—a means of raising herself higher in the love of God. Blesilla was gone, and her other children might follow her at any moment; and this served to remind her that God had only lent her children to her, only entrusted them to her for a short time, without prejudice to the higher rights that He possessed over them. Wherefore should she not voluntarily resign to Him her best beloved? Wherefore should she not make the complete sacrifice of her sweetest happiness? The tie which bound her to them was so strong that it seemed easier to her to renounce this happiness entirely than to be perfect while enjoying it. She had to undergo a terrific struggle. On the one side was the attraction of grace and her vocation, the unceasing call that she heard above every other sound: "Follow Me; take up thy cross: he that loveth son or daughter more than Me is not worthy of Me;" on the other side, the drawing of her nature to that which, holy in itself, was commanded her as a duty, and supported by all around her—by the prayers of her children, the representations of her only brother, and the wishes of all her family. And her heart threatened to break at the bare thought of separation, voluntary, self-chosen separation, and yet longed for this separation. This was a battle indeed. Not the ordinary and daily battle between good and evil, between light and darkness, which every one must fight, but the battle of the saints, where perfection strives with higher perfection, and where virtue must be conquered by a stronger virtue. Such a battle never rages in ordinary souls; such a victory enters not into the thoughts of worldly people.

When Paula's resolution was irrevocably taken, she made every arrangement to execute it as soon as possible. Her youngest daughter, Rufina, was already betrothed to Aletius, a Roman noble, and she was to live with her sister Paulina until her marriage. Paula knew that the education of her son Toxotius could not be in better hands than those of her brother, and her son-in-law Pammachius. She arranged her property so as to leave to her children all that she had inherited from her departed husband, and as much of her own property as was theirs by right. She kept the rest rather for alms deeds and works of mercy than for her own use. In the year 385, when all was completed, and the ship was ready to sail from Ostia, at the mouth of the Tiber, which was to bear her for ever to strange and distant lands, Paula left the home of her fathers, with its thousand hopes and recollections, the place where she had been blessed by God with much happiness and much sorrow. All her family and kindred accompanied her, anxious to see her to the last moment. When the time of leave-taking arrived, their grief burst forth in tears and lamentations. Rufina wept inconsolably, and Toxotius, who was still a child, clung to his mother. But Paula repressed her tears and the sorrow of her heart, and recommending herself and hers to God, she hurried on board ship. Eustochium followed her, for both mother and daughter were animated with the same resolution of dedicating themselves to a monastic life in the Holy Land. The ship pushed off from the shore, and sailed into the open sea. Whilst all the other travellers looked back towards the shore where those left behind were waving greetings to them, and where the little Toxotius was stretching forth his arms towards his beloved mother, Paula alone was looking towards heaven, and saw the earth no more.

As she passed by the island of Pontia, where Flavia Domitilla had lived in exile for the Name of Jesus, and had attained the palm of martyrdom under Domitian, Paula felt herself inspired with joyful courage to go into voluntary banishment for Jesus' sake. She passed safely through the Straits of Messina, between Scylla and Charybdis, and then turning towards the East she landed in the island of Cyprus, where St. Epiphanius returned with joy the hospitality she had shown him in Rome. Paula did not spend her stay of ten days in Cyprus in repose, nor in enjoying the society of the holy old man, for whom she cherished childlike and affectionate respect, and whom she looked upon as the father of her soul. She visited the monasteries and the poor, she prayed and gave alms, edifying others still more than she was edified herself. Receiving the holy bishop's blessing, she sailed to Seleucia in Syria, where her sea voyage ended, and whence she travelled by land to Antioch. The archbishop of that place, Paulinus, was also glad to welcome her to the East, and kept her with him for a little while. She then continued her pilgrimage to Jerusalem, riding like a poor person upon an ass, which she found very fatiguing, accustomed as she had been to be carried in a smooth litter. But she would not travel luxuriously where the Son of God had lived in poverty and tribulation, and even in His triumphal entry into Jerusalem had only made use of an ass. She took the road along the coast, which was the same as the one that is now used on the sandy seashore, from Beyrout through Sidon to Tyre, and beyond to Ptolemais, now Acca, or St. Jean d'Acre, Cesarea, and Jaffa, the Joppe of the Bible. All these towns were well known to her from the Holy Scriptures, both of the Old and New Testaments. The burden of the fulfilled prophecies of Isaias lay even then upon the voluptuous cities of the Phœnicians, but Cesarea was populous and flourishing. Paula there saw the house in which the centurion Cornelius, the first of the heathen, was converted to Christianity, and which had been changed into a church. At Jaffa, where she thought of Tabitha awakened from the dead, and of Peter, whose faith had wrought this miracle, she left the seashore and turned inland towards Jerusalem, passing Emmaus on the way.

The devotion, self-denial, charity, and humility which she had practised during her pilgrimage were amply recompensed by the unspeakable joy she experienced in beholding and exploring Jerusalem. She had reached at length the goal of her laborious pilgrimage, and stood upon the very spot which the Son of God had glorified by His Life and teaching, by His Passion and Death. The governor of Palestine, who had known Paula and her family very well at Rome, and who also knew the splendour that there surrounded her, placed a large and magnificently furnished house at her disposal. But she had not come to Jerusalem to inhabit a palace; therefore she gratefully declined the offer, and went with Eustochium and her maid-servants into the poor cells of a monastery of nuns, perhaps the one that had been founded there by her great contemporary and compatriot, St. Melania. She lived in her cell as detached from all that gives joy to the earthly man, as poor in spirit and in heart as though she had never known or practised anything in her life but the severest asceticism. And yet it was only five years, but five years of a conversion as sincere as it was impetuous, that had advanced her so far.

She visited daily some one of the Holy Places, and remained long in prayer, and in contemplation of the mystery of divine grace that had been accomplished there. She sought out the Cœnaculum, the hall in which our Blessed Lord ate the Paschal Lamb with His disciples, and instituted the feast of the New Testament in His Flesh and Blood; and Mount Olivet, where the terrible and incomprehensible Agony began, that mystical Passion which heaped four thousand years of sins upon the Lamb of God, whose Blood was to make superfluous satisfaction for them all; and the long and painful Way of the captivity, from one unrighteous judge to another, from one torture to another, from the Scourging to the Crowning with Thorns, and from that to the carrying of the Cross to Calvary. She sank on her knees before the Holy Cross, and falling on her face she worshipped as if she had before her eyes our Blessed Lord bleeding from all His wounds, and dying thereon. And she covered with tears and kisses of loving devotion and blissful gratitude the Sepulchre which had received but had not retained the Holy Body of the Lord. She tarried on each of these blessed spots with such fervour, that it seemed as though she desired to die of love at each one of them. "Who will give me wings like a dove, and I will fly, and be at rest?" This heavenly desire of the royal Psalmist was Paula's only wish, and she felt herself more and more a stranger here below, whose only true citizenship is in everlasting life. Therefore she did not choose Jerusalem for the place of her repose, but she took up her pilgrim's staff once more and visited all the places that were connected with the history of the Israelites and the mysteries of the work of Redemption. Her intimate knowledge of the Holy Scriptures, which were never out of her hands, and her deep interior devotion so animated external things that she seemed to see with her own eyes whatever she read of or remembered. Her former struggles were rewarded with the sweetest joys that a pure heart can experience.

When Paula left Rome, or perhaps even earlier, she had given her slaves their freedom, and at the same time the means of procuring subsistence. But very many of her female slaves voluntarily remained with her as servants, and desired nothing better than to share the mortification and toils of their beloved mistress. She had taken all these with her across the sea to the East. In Jerusalem she was joined by other women desirous of salvation, who hoped to derive much enlightenment concerning the spiritual life from her instructions, and from intercourse with her. Thus she was always surrounded by a whole company of pious women who honoured her as their guide. Many of them accompanied her upon her journeys. After she had made devout pilgrimages through all Samaria and Galilee, as well as Judea, she journeyed with Eustochium and her numerous companions to Egypt, the country where the ascetic life had arisen and reached its highest perfection. They travelled to Alexandria across the Great Syrian Desert, composed of loose sand, in which the footsteps of travellers are immediately lost. From thence they visited several monastic communities in Nitria, where they were received with great marks of honour. But Paula was so humble that she threw herself at the feet of those holy men and honoured in them Him who lived in them, Christ the Lord. The poorer were their cells the better they pleased her, and the more she longed for the like seclusion.

Everywhere she gave alms to the sick and infirm with that humble love which never prides itself upon its gifts, but lays them in the loving wounded Hands of our Blessed Lord Himself. Then she took ship for Pelusium, and landing at Majuma, the port of Gaza, she made a pilgrimage through the country of the ancient Philistines, and returned to the Holy Land.

For there was one place that seemed to her sweeter and more attractive than all the world beside; one spot from whence a supernatural light diffused itself over all creation; and this was the mysterious Cave of Bethlehem. When Paula entered this Cave for the first time, she fell upon her knees in extasy, and the marvellous mystery of the Incarnation of God so penetrated and enlightened her soul that the dark Cave became for her a Thabor, upon which she beheld the glory of the Lord, and resolved to build tabernacles. Therefore, after her return from Egypt, she repaired to Bethlehem to put her purpose in execution. She took up her abode with Eustochium and her servants in a small and poor house where they had but scanty room. And this was her greatest joy. Could she indulge in comforts and conveniences by the side of the Crib where her Lord and God had lain upon rough straw, and where His most Blessed and Virginal Mother had undergone such privations? No; it was her desire to return suffering for suffering, and love for love, and she did not content herself with suffering and loving, neither did she shut herself up in her cell; but her love, like that of the suffering Divine Infant which gladdened the poor shepherds and the rich Magi, overflowed upon her neighbour in corporal and spiritual works of mercy. With tender devotion Paula built a home for pilgrims on the spot where the Son of God appearing in the flesh had found no shelter. And in order to cause the eternal "Gloria" of the angels to resound here below, she also built a monastery wherein souls espoused to God might sing His praises and exult in His honour.

Pilgrims from the East and the West, and from distant lands, such as Persia, India, Æthiopia, France, and England, were then often led by their devotion in great numbers to Palestine, in order to reverence the Holy Places of our salvation. Many were unable to tear themselves away again from the Holy Land, and desired there to serve God and their neighbour. Most of these remained in Jerusalem, where the caves and grottoes of Mount Olivet attracted those inclined to become solitaries, and where the great concourse of pilgrims, necessarily embracing many sick and needy, afforded occasion for the charitable exercise of brotherly love. In Jerusalem, the seat of an archbishopric, these wants were amply supplied, and moreover, the holy widow Melania lived there during twenty-five years, distributing her immense riches with open hand. Bethlehem being a small country village, had hitherto been without such support, and this was bestowed on it by Paula. Whilst she herself lived in a small and crowded dwelling, she built on the Jerusalem road a large hospice for pilgrims, joined to a monastery for monks. The monks undertook the charge of serving the strangers, a duty which not only monks, but even anchorites were bound to practise. In order that the means of hospitality might never be wanting to them, Paula herself took charge of their temporal affairs. In other things the monks were under the guidance of St. Jerome.

She built at the same time a monastery for nuns, of which she took possession with Eustochium and many pious widows and virgins, in the year 389, four years after her departure from Rome. As these women were of various ranks and capacities, of very different ages and degrees of health, and came, moreover, from divers countries, having been drawn together by the disposition of God, she erected three buildings under one roof. She appointed a special place in one of these three divisions to each one of her little flock, and each division lived and worked together under a superioress chosen by Paula, and addressed by the title of Mother. Paula herself was the principal superioress, and Eustochium assisted her. The whole establishment united in the oratory of the community early in the morning, as soon as the awakening call, "Alleluia," resounded, then again at Tierce, Sext, and None, (9, 12, and 3 o'clock,) in the evening for Vespers, and at midnight for Matins. Each sister had to know the psalter by heart, and daily to read and contemplate the Holy Scriptures. On Sundays, each company, under the guidance of their superioress, repaired to the church which formed the centre of the three buildings, and attended the solemn offices of the Church. All were clothed alike in coarse cotton stuffs. They used linen only for their towels. They performed all the household labour, and span, wove, and made their own habits as well as clothes for needy pilgrims, and above all for the poor. Paula carefully separated the noble ladies from their former servants, lest they might be reminded of their former position and tempted to continue the distinction in the cloister. No man of whatever age or condition he might be was permitted to enter the monastery. "In this way," St. Jerome observes, "every possibility of evil-speaking was cut off from those malicious tongues which so eagerly pursue it to palliate their own vices." Paula was the heart and soul of this community, brightly burning with faith and love, God's most humble child, and the tender mother of her spiritual children. She was the first and last everywhere, the first to serve and pray, the last to rest. She and Eustochium undertook the lowest menial offices, lighting the lamps, raking the fire in the kitchen, cleaning the vegetables, laying and serving the tables, and sweeping the house. Nothing was too mean or too laborious for them, since they were only doing what our Blessed Lord had done for thirty years in the little House of Nazareth. "He was subject to His parents." The subjection of their God, even to the death of the Cross, was the source whence these two holy souls drew their untiring readiness to serve others. Paula nursed the sick with the greatest care, and amply provided for all their wants. She arranged her alms and gifts according to the necessities of the recipient, with wise moderation and forethought, so as to be able always to give to all; but with the sick she overstepped this measure, giving them abundance of meat and wine, and whatever else could comfort them.

Inside the monastery a strict fast was observed, but not even the youngest or strongest of the sisters kept it as austerely as Paula herself. St. Jerome says that towards others she was all compassion and mercifulness, towards herself all severity and harshness. He adds, "The blessed Paula was once ill and very much reduced by a violent fever, which was increased by the insupportable heat of the sun so as to endanger her life. The omnipotence of God preserved her, and the physicians ordered her to strengthen her wasted body by taking wine. But she would not do so. The holy Bishop Epiphanius was then at Jerusalem, and he sometimes visited the blessed Paula at Bethlehem. I secretly begged him to persuade her, to command her, to drink wine, as I knew what childlike reverence she bore him. When he began to speak of it she said, smiling, that she knew at whose instigation he mentioned it. But Bishop

Epiphanius would not desist from his persuasions, and remained a considerable time with the sufferer. When he came out from her, I asked him how the affair had ended, and he said, 'It ended by Paula's nearly persuading an old man like me to drink no more wine myself.' I do not relate this," adds St. Jerome, "to praise such unsparing dealing with a weakened constitution, but to show her love for mortification."

Paula treated her spiritual daughters with gentle forbearance, which never degenerated into weakness, because she had always before her eyes the high destiny of souls consecrated to God; and by her example of self-sacrificing love, she knew how to inspire them with such affectionate respect that a sad look from her was a painful punishment to them. Violent and angry natures she wisely governed with the gentlest words, whilst she subdued them by manifold exercises of patience. She spurred on the slothful, and was inexorable towards offences against silence or sisterly union. If reproofs were fruitless, the sisters who committed these faults were made to eat and pray standing at the door, in order that the public humiliation might render them careful of giving such scandal to the community. Paula said, "The faults of which the world thinks little or even nothing, are great vices in the cloister." She possessed the spirit of penance in so great a degree that she bewailed her smallest imperfections with as much contrition as though she were guilty of grave sins.

Her love of poverty went hand in hand with that of mortification, and was expressed in her buildings. Not only the monasteries, but even the churches were low and unadorned, and provided with only the most absolute necessaries, for fear the poor might suffer. Jerome sometimes remonstrated with her upon her excessive generosity to the poor. Then, with great humility and in few words, she took God to witness that she gave away everything for Christ's sake, and that she desired nothing but to die a beggar, to be buried in a borrowed winding-sheet, and to leave not a single penny to Eustochium. To give back all to Him from Whom she had received everything on earth, and hoped for all in heaven, and to follow Jesus in the greatest possible poverty of heart and soul; this was the motive of her actions, for she never suffered herself to be influenced by natural compassion for the sorrows of others.

Eustochium was no less magnanimous in her love of God. With joyful heart and countenance she saw her whole inheritance pass through Paula's hands to the poor, whilst she herself never touched any of it. She considered her mother's generosity her own greatest treasure, and she was so obedient and submissive to her that she never left her side day or night, and never ate, drank, or went out without her. Jerome wrote thus of her to Furia, a young widow in Rome who was related to her: "Oh, if thou couldst see Eustochium and hear her pious conversation, thou wouldst be amazed at the strength of the spirit that inhabits so frail a body, and surprised to find that all the treasures of the Old and New Testaments flow out of her heart. Fasting is play to her, and prayer a joy. With a tambourine in her hand she leads in song, like Mary, the ranks of virgins, and trains singers and musicians in honour of the Saviour. Thus day after day passes, and with oil in her lamp she awaits the coming of the Divine Bridegroom." Like Paula and Blesilla, Eustochium was so skilled in Hebrew that she recited the psalms in that language. It was here in Bethlehem that both mother and daughter unceasingly assailed St. Jerome with entreaties until he consented to read the whole of the sacred Scriptures with them, and to initiate them in their deepest mysteries by his explanations and expositions. That great doctor of the Church dedicated to Eustochium his commentary on the Prophets Isaias and Ezechiel, and wrote for her a treatise on virginity, known as the Letter to Eustochium. He also translated into Latin, for the monastery of Bethlehem, the Rule of St. Pachomius.

The saintly and joyful life led by these two holy souls, exemplifying as it did the charms of the highest asceticism, is best described by themselves. Their friend Marcella had lost her mother in the year 389, and after her death had retired into the country, in the neighbourhood of Rome. But Paula and Eustochium wished that Marcella should come to the East, and if possible to Bethlehem; and they expressed this wish in an earnest and affectionate letter to her, in which they say, amongst other things, "Thou didst enkindle the first spark in our hearts; by word and deed thou didst encourage us to embrace this manner of life; thou hast gathered us together as a hen gathers her chickens under her wings. Wilt thou now leave us to fly alone without our mother? Shall the gentle, the loving, the most kind Marcella, who urged us forward to our new life by the magic of her eloquence, shall she become to us a harsh Marcella? Shall that most serene brow become clouded on hearing our request? We only urge thee to take that step to which thou didst first thyself allure us. How many martyrs, bishops, and doctors of the Church have visited Jerusalem since the Ascension of the Lord until this day! They felt as if something was wanting to their religion, their wisdom, and their virtues, if they had not worshipped Christ in the places where the light of the Gospel sent forth its first rays from the Cross. If we should rightly blame any one who studied Greek sciences in Rome instead of Athens, and Latin in Lybia instead of in Rome how can we believe that it is possible to attain to the summit of Christian wisdom without visiting Jerusalem? We do not, indeed, deny that the kingdom of God is interior, and must be within ourselves, or that there are great and holy men in other countries also. But we only say that the greatest and most excellent men in the world are gathered together here. We certainly are not of that number, but precisely because we are among the lowest, we have come hither in order to see the noblest and most distinguished men of all lands. Pilgrims, both monks and seculars, throng hither from all parts, and sing the praises of God in the most varied languages, but animated by the same faith. The purest concord reigns amongst all these strangers. If any seek to excel the others, it is in humility. The least is as much respected as the noblest. No value is set upon appearance, for no one observes the dress of his neighbour. Severe fasting excites no remark, while modest eating is not blamed. No evil speaking, no luxury, no criticism is to be found, and all practise the first of Christian virtues, purity and chastity of life. They visit with fervour and devotion the numerous Holy Places in Jerusalem. But as each one loves to glory in what he himself possesses, so will we speak to thee of Christ's little city, of the refuge of Mary. Here there is nothing but peace, quietness, and simple country life, for here is the Crib in which the Divine Infant wept, and it is best honoured in silence. Thou wilt find here none of Rome's glories, no pillared halls, no sumptuous chambers pannelled with gold, no palaces filled with slaves, and surrounded with the misery of the poor. We do love Rome, however, for a holy Church is there; and there shine the victorious trophies of the Apostles and martyrs; there Christ is truly confessed, and the faith was preached by the Apostle; there Christianity is now rising on high, whilst paganism sinks into the dust. But Rome's greatness and glory, Rome's innumerable population, that seeing and being seen, greeting and being greeted, speaking and listening, that praising and blaming, allow no time for the recollection of the contemplative life. If you receive visitors your peace is gone. If you shut your doors you are accused of pride. Also a visit must sometimes be returned. You must then enter magnificent palaces, and pass by troops of talkative servants, and tread on gorgeous carpets, but what gain do you bring home with you? How different is it here, in Christ's own land! Here nothing is to be seen save rustic simplicity; nothing to be heard save the praises of God. The singing of psalms alone breaks the stillness. The ploughman in the field, the mower in the meadow, the vinedresser in the vineyard, all encourage themselves in their tedious labour by singing psalms. The Psalms of David are the only love-songs of this land; all life here is animated by the spiritual life. And shall the hour never come, when a breathless messenger shall bring us the joyful tidings that Marcella has landed in Palestine? Oh, surely it will come. Surely the day will break on which we shall enter hand in hand the Cave of the Birth of Christ, shall weep together upon His Tomb, shall kiss His Cross and shall climb Mount Olivet, to follow after Him in spirit and longing desire. Then we will journey on and see Lazarus come forth from his tomb at Bethany, we will see the Jordan that flowed purer and clearer after the Baptism of Christ, the tents of the shepherds, the burial-place of David, the tabernacles of Abraham, Isaac, and Jacob, and the mountain caves where the prophets took refuge in the days of persecution. And we will go yet farther—to Nazareth, and the other flowers of Galilee; to Cana, where our Blessed Lord worked His first miracle; to Thabor, where we will contemplate Him not with Moses and Elias, but with the Father and the Holy Ghost in glory; to the Sea of Genesareth, upon whose waves He walked; to the desert, where He fed thousands by the power of His word, and to Capharnaum, the most familiar scene of His miracles. Then we will return and pass by other spots, finding everywhere Christian churches, like so many triumphal standards of Christ. And when we shall have accomplished this beautiful journey together, and reached our peaceful home once more, oh! then we will weep much before God in lively joy, and sing His praises, and pray unceasingly; and, wounded by the love of Jesus, we will call out to one another the watchword of love; "I have found Him whom my soul loveth; I held Him, and I will not let Him go."

But Marcella's path through life was a different one from that of these two "doves in the clifts of the rock." She withstood the loving invitation; and taking Principia into her house, she brought her up to be a second Eustochium.

The Hand of God continued to touch the most vulnerable part of Paula's heart. All her children at Rome died before her. She was, indeed, detached from all inordinate love in her spirit and will. She made the sign of the Cross, in which she fully trusted, upon her mouth and heart; and thinking that God says to each of His creatures by the Prophet Isaias, "I have called thee by thy name; thou art mine," she united herself to the adorable will of God. Rufina, who had grown up into a holy maiden, and espoused Aletius, never grieved her husband except by her early death. He was very intimate with St. Paulinus, Bishop of Nola, one of the greatest converts of that epoch so rich in conversions. In the letter of condolence which St. Paulinus wrote to Aletius after Rufina's death, he calls her "the daughter of perfection, the sister of virginity, and the bride of faith, for she was Paula's daughter, Eustochium's sister, and thy wife." She left no children. Paulina, Paula's second daughter, died in the year 398, also childless. She had lived with Pammachius in a very happy marriage, and like him had practised all Christian virtues in the midst of the world, avoiding the precipices to which high rank and great riches are so apt to lead. Active service of the poor was Paulina's chief occupation; and Pammachius did not consider it beneath his talents, and the dignity of his position as a Roman senator and a man of learning and science, to assist his wife therein. He did not think it incompatible with deep study and high offices, to practise works of mercy. He rivalled his wife in this humble virtue, which meets with its reward in heaven, but finds on earth a rich measure of ingratitude, misconception, and even blame. Paulina had hardly reached middle life, when God called her into eternity.

Pammachius had loved her tenderly. Her death detached him still more from the world, and drew him towards supernatural things. He wished to raise a monument that should be worthy of the holy love of her heart, and he therefore carried out alone with great zeal the plan that they had conceived together. He built a large hospice at Ostia, where the Tiber pours itself into the sea, and where the ships disembark travellers from distant countries; and he spent upon this building and its arrangements and endowment, not only Paulina's whole fortune which she had left to him, but also his own, keeping only a very small yearly income for himself. A hospice on this spot was a great benefaction. Rome was still the centre of the world. Crowds of men flocked to Rome from all the lands that were ruled by the sceptre of the Roman emperor, or that followed the shepherd's crook of the Prince of the Apostles. The

African and Asiatic coasts of the Mediterranean Sea were not then as lifeless as they have become under the rule of Islam. Mauritania, Numidia, Lybia, Egypt, Syria, and Asia Minor were blooming and cultivated lands, thickly peopled, and with many large towns full of refinement and commerce on a large scale. Innumerable bishops and the three patriarchs of Antioch, Jerusalem, and Alexandria, diffused the Christian life which they learned in Rome through all these countries and peoples. Rome stood in the same living and vivifying relation with Gaul, Spain, and Eugland. Hence arose many connexions that brought to Rome strangers of all tongues and from every climate. The hospice of Pammachius, at Ostia, the harbour of Rome, received with hospitality all who landed there fatigued, exhausted, or ill with the discomforts of a long sea voyage, and in need of rest and care before they began their land journey. This hospice was a lodging and hospital in one, and all without distinction who sought hospitality therein, were received lovingly and with generosity, but especially the poor and needy Even the travellers who came from Rome, and who often had to wait very long for a suitable ship or a fair wind, might live in the hospice, which was a great advantage to those without means. The throng was, therefore, very considerable; and St Jerome says, that even in the first year after the hospice was opened, the fame of the Refuge on the Roman shore had reached England, Persia, and Egypt, and had been blessed by the whole world. Rejoicing in his work, Pammachius sometimes left Rome, his studies, his scientific occupations, his labours for the Church and the faith, his correspondence with St. Jerome, his intercourse with the holiest and most learned men of his time, and hurried to Ostia, where, assuming the dress of a servant in the hospital, he went to meet the poor strangers, washed their feet, changed their clothes, served them at table, and prepared their beds. And he rejoiced more and more that he had sown in time these earthly goods, which after his death would perhaps have been dissipated in dissensions and discord, in order to reap in eternity a heavenly harvest, when he should bring in his sheaves. This just man lived in this manner twelve years from Paulina's death, and after surviving the tribulation of Rome, when it was conquered by Alaric, he departed in the peace of the Lord at the same time as Marcella, in the year 410.

Paula's only son Toxotius was no exception in this family of saints. He had married Læta, the pious daughter of the aged idolatrous priest Albinus. The branch of Christianity had been engrafted on this ancient stem, and had so transformed the wild stock that it brought forth fruits of sanctity. But the old man himself remained a heathen in the midst of his Christian children. The marriage of Toxotius was at first childless. The prayers of the two spouses, and their vow to dedicate their child to God, if He should give them one, gained for them a daughter, who was verily a child of grace, Paula, called the younger to distinguish her from her grandmother. These tidings filled St. Paula with unspeakable joy, which increased with everything that she heard of her granddaughter. In her cradle, the babe with lisping voice sang Alleluia! and the first names she uttered were those of Paula and Eustochium. Albinus had been a decided foe of the Christian religion, but this child — on whom his heart doted, and whom he bore in his arms, and unwillingly suffered to leave his side—this child of prayer changed his soul. Læta's marriage and virtuous life, her holy conversation with Toxotius, the pious and joyful manner in which they both accomplished their duties; the good teaching and example they gave to their household; all this had laid a secure foundation for the conversion of Albinus, which was completed by the prayer of innocence. He could withstand no longer; the holy and believing house sanctified the unbelieving old man, and Læta praised God for the great miracle. Her father, the Pagan high priest, in his old age, received new birth by baptism, and humbly suffered himself to be instructed in the Catholic faith and doctrine with the children and the simple. But in order that her cup of life might not be too sweet, God mixed with it wholesome bitterness. Toxotius died, and Læta made the resolution of practising every Christian virtue as faithfully in her widowhood as she had done as a wife, and of living solely for God, for the salvation of her soul and for her daughter.

In order to bring this daughter up meet to be spiritually espoused to Christ, she begged St. Jerome to give her some written instructions. The words of Jesus, "Suffer the little children to come unto me," find an echo in the souls of all the saints. The education of children is a high and holy office in their eyes. With admirable love, like that of a mother who watches little trifles that might escape a father's eye, the great doctor of the Church fulfilled Læta's wish, and did not disdain, in the midst of all his important labours, to occupy himself with the education of a little maiden. He writes to Læta: "If thy daughter is to remain ignorant of vanity and vice, bring her up in the temple like Samuel, and in the desert like John the Baptist. What she hears and sees must be fitted to lead her to God. Let no word reach her ear that could give her any idea of evil; let no worldly song pass her lips. As soon as she speaks intelligibly, impress something from the psalms upon her memory. Let no servant approach her who is worldly-minded, nor any child that could set her a bad example. Let her never learn what she could afterwards wish not to know. Procure her an alphabet of letters made of wood or ivory that she may learn them in her p . Teach her afterwards, by guiding her hand, to model each letter in wax, and then make her write the names of the patriarchs from Adam downwards. Be careful not to excite in her any distaste for learning, that she may keep the inclination to it in after life. Choose for her teacher a learned and virtuous man, who will not think it beneath him to instruct her in elementary things. Even Aristotle fulfilled this office to Alexander the Great. She must see nothing in her parents that she may not imitate. Let her be loving to all, and especially affectionate to her Pagan grandfather. Let her early know that she is to be the bride of Christ. When thy daughter is grown older, let her never go out without her parents, avoiding frivolous diversions and great entertainments. Let her model be the most holy Virgin Mary who trembled at the sight of an angel, because he appeared to her under the form of a man. Let her go nowhere but to church, and to the tombs of the martyrs; and let her chiefly remain in her own room, alternately occupied in prayer, reading, and working. In what regards work, she must know how to spin and to make her own clothes. She must read Greek and Latin fluently, and speak and write both languages in the greatest purity. This must be the order in which she must learn to know the Holy Scriptures. She must begin with the Psalter, and exercise herself at the same time in singing the psalms. Then she must read Proverbs, that she may learn to know the moral precepts. Let these be followed by the Book of Ecclesiastes, which is so well calculated to inspire contempt of the world.

Then give her the Gospels, which she should have ever in her hands. Afterwards, let her read the Acts of the Apostles, and their Epistles, and learn the Prophets and the historical books by heart. Then she may read the Canticle of Canticles, because she will be prepared to understand it in a spiritual sense. She may read, besides, without danger, the works of St. Cyprian, the letters of St. Athanasius, and the writings of St. Hilary. With regard to prayer, let her arise at midnight, and punctually observe the hours of prayer during the day, applying herself to the singing of psalms at Matins, Tierce, Sext, None, and Vespers. I disapprove of immoderate fasting. On a long journey we must spare our strength, because we should succumb half way if we ran too quickly at the outset. The penitential practice of fasting should, indeed, be strict; but rather for pampered worldlings, than for those whose life is a continual fast. Thy daughter's ordinary food should be vegetables, with meat sometimes; and each meal should be so moderate, that she should be able to read or sing psalms immediately after it. She need never drink wine. If the instructions I give thee cannot be carried out at Rome, send thy daughter to Bethlehem, that she may be brought up under the eyes of her grandmother. I will then, myself, be her teacher and guardian; and I should think myself honoured by instructing a bride of Christ, who is destined one day to reign with Him in heaven."

Læta carefully weighed St. Jerome's advice. And when she found that it was not possible to bring up her daughter at Rome, "as though it were in the temple and the desert," and that this kind of education must be the groundwork of her child's salvation, and the condition of her happiness, she took no counsel of flesh and blood, completely subduing the feelings of nature, which often seeks to satisfy self-love under the pretext of fulfilling a duty. She parted from her only child; the child of her prayers, in whom all the recollections of her happiness were bound up; and as soon as she was a few years old, she sent her to her grandmother at Bethlehem. She herself remained in Rome and sanctified herself by a vow of perpetual chastity, and by works of mercy. Paula received with nuspeakable joy the jewel, the tender soul that she was to fashion into a perfect victim, a spotless spouse of Christ. The little one grew up, truly as it were " in the temple and in the desert," under the influence of Paula's piety, and with the example of her abnegation before her eyes, surrounded by pure souls who emulated her.

But Paula's life was drawing to a close. Her ardent desire " to be dissolved and to be with Christ," was near its fulfilment; she fell grievously ill and suffered very much. Eustochium was indefatigable in the care of her beloved mother, and inseparable from her sick-bed, except when she took refuge in the holy Cave of the Nativity in prayer and tears, and there implored God not to deprive her of her mother, or to grant that they might both die at the same hour. But neither prayers nor tending could retain Paula now. She felt death approaching, and her limbs growing cold. Her heart alone, her great and loving heart, was still warm and retained its hold on life, and with gentle voice she spoke of God in the words of the Psalmist: " I have loved, O Lord, the place where Thy glory dwelleth;" "How lovely are Thy tabernacles, O Lord of hosts!" " Our feet were standing in Thy courts, O Jerusalem." But she never spoke again to men, although Eustochium and St. Jerome, and many bishops and priests were always by her side. The monastery was, as it were, besieged by ecclesiastics and seculars, who wished to hear of her, or if possible, to see her. Jerome asked her, "Wherefore dost thou not speak with us? Art thou troubled, or hast thou any burden?" Paula answered in Greek, "By no means, all within me is peaceful." And in total oblivion of the world and all earthly things, she shut her eyes, that the peace of her last hour might not be disturbed, and until it arrived she spoke in a low voice to God alone. Then she raised her hand and made the sign of the holy Cross, and saying with the spouse of the Canticles, "The winter is past, the flowers have appeared in our land," her soul took flight into the kingdom of everlasting love. No weeping, no mourning was heard; no inconsolable bitterness was felt. Psalms full of hope, of solemn joy, of sublime love, were sung. Wherefore should tears flow beside this corpse? Priests took lighted candles in their hands, bishops lifted the bier on their own shoulders, a long procession of the faithful joined them praying, and thus the pilgrimage proceeded to the church above the grotto of the Nativity. There the holy corpse was publicly exposed. She lay like one asleep, the beautiful countenance being entirely unaltered. The devout flocked thither from far and near. No monk or solitary was absent, however dear their cell and solitude might be to them. Even the nuns received permission to leave their enclosure. It would have been thought a kind of sacrilege not to pa the last honours to this truly blessed one. Theybeggars and cripples, the widows and orphans mingled their thanksgivings and praises with the singing of psalms, which for a whole week continued without intermission to resound over her grave in the Greek, Syriac, Latin, and Hebrew languages.

Paula died on the 26th of January 404, in the evening after sunset, being in her fifty-seventh year. She died poorer than the poorest person she had ever relieved. The entire charge of her two monastic foundations, containing a considerable number of monks and nuns, was the earthly inheritance that she left to her beloved Eustochium, who accepted it with a magnanimity equal to hers. "The Lord ruleth me, and I shall want nothing."[1] This was her support in continuing her mother's work. "Be comforted, my Eustochium," says St. Jerome in his life of Paula, "a large inheritance has fallen to thy lot, for God the Lord is thy portion. And that thou mayest rejoice the more, know that thy mother has won her crown by a long martyrdom. For martyrdom does not consist only in the shedding of blood, but it is a daily and wearisome martyrdom to serve God the Lord with an irreproachable and fervent spirit. The former martyrdom merits a blood-red wreath, but the latter a white garland of lilies. Therefore, red and white colours are ascribed to the Bridegroom in the Canticle of Canticles, because He distributes these victorious crowns to the conquerors, whether their martyrdom has been in the body or in the spirit. Thy mother, my Eustochium, obeyed the command of the Lord in Jeremias, where he says: "Flee ye from the midst of Babylon, and let every one save his own life."[2] This she did, for she left her own country, and remained in Chaldea, never looking back with desire to the fleshpots of Egypt. She has become one of the companions of our Blessed Lord in the company of virgins, and she has ascended to Him in the heavenly Jerusalem from the poor little city of Bethlehem. Now she says to Him, as Ruth did formerly to Noemi, Where thou shalt dwell, I also will dwell. Thy people shall be my people, and thy God my God." And the saint ends with this address to her: "Fare thee well for ever, thou blessed Paula, and do thou help, by thy intercession, the old age of him who ever esteemed and loved thee. Thy faith and thy

[1] Psalms xxii. 1.   [2] Jeremias li. 6.

works have united thee to Christ, and thy prayers will find favour in His sight."

Eustochium was chosen superioress of the monastery at Bethlehem, and lived there several years dead to this world, and with her gaze fixed upon eternity. But the world did not forget her, for misery and poverty blessed her, and the wicked hated her. The heresiarch Pelagius, who disbelieved in the action of divine grace on the soul, of necessity trampled on the tenderest and brightest blossom which the ray of grace unfolds, a life of virginity consecrated to God. There is one impulse which characterises all heresies as children of one stock, and it is this, they are all opponents of holy asceticism and of the cloister; in other words, of Christian perfection. And it must be so, for they have separated themselves from the Catholic Church in which alone perfection is cherished and cultivated. Pelagius was protected by the Archbishop John of Jerusalem. He well knew what sworn enemies to his doctrine were contained in the peaceful cloisters of Bethlehem under the guidance of the aged Jerome. He sent a band of ruffians thither to take vengeance upon him and upon them. Paula's monastery was laid in ashes, the monks and nuns chastised and illtreated, and a deacon slain. Jerome retreated into a strong tower, while Eustochium and her niece Paula escaped with difficulty from fire and sword, and wrote to Pope Innocent I. to complain of such violence and cruelty. The Pope took the injured ones under his protection; but Eustochium died soon after in the year 419, and was buried near her mother. Jerome had a high opinion of her strong and clear mind, and asked her opinion upon all that he wrote. Yet she was so immersed in Christ that all her learned studies were unable to disturb her interior recollection and union with God. Her niece, Paula the younger, died as she had lived, "in the temple and in the desert" of the cloister. She was the last of the house that had now sent three generations of saints to heaven. It had rightly understood its destiny, and had buried its former greatness in sanctity. With Christ the world vanishes. The last daughter of the Æmilii and Julii died peacefully and unknown in the Cave of the Hidden God.

THE TWO MELANIAS.

"Go forth out of thy country, and from thy kindred, and out of thy father's house, and come into the land which I shall show thee."—GENESIS xii. 1.

THE elder Melania was one of those holy and eager souls, who counted all things to be but loss for Christ; she was also one of those instruments of God, who gave to their age a great example of abnegation, and through whom Christian Rome regained what heathen Rome had lost. Her name became so celebrated, that by its side those of her husband and her race have been eclipsed. Her father was called Marcellinus, and was Consul in the year 341. Melania was of a rich and ancient Roman family, but she was born in Spain, where she had great possessions. She was related to the holy priest Felix, who had suffered a painful martyrdom at Nola in Campania a hundred years before. She married very early, but the cares and joys of marriage did not suffocate the great desire of perfection which she cherished in her heart. This desire was so eager and sincere that it kept her heart free from all inordinate attachment to her husband and children. She lost her husband and two sons in the same year. She worshipped the will of God, which, by means of these trials, led her into other paths, and she said, without tears or lamentations, "O Lord, it is now permitted me to serve Thee without distraction and without reserve." Melania was then twenty-two years old. One son yet remained to her, in remembrance of former happiness. The boy was called Publicola; he was endowed by nature with the noblest qualities of mind and body. She entrusted him for education to her relation the Prefect of Rome, and she chose also other learned and holy men to superintend his studies. She arranged all the affairs of her estates with the greatest minuteness. She destined all her property eventually for her son, who was also immensely rich through his father's possessions; but she retained her own income, which was very large, and took to herself, in the place of children, all suffering Christianity to profit by it. As Marcella had been the first noble Roman lady who professed the monastic life, so Melania was the first noble lady who made a pilgrimage to the East in order to see practised in perfection the Evangelical counsels which she desired to embrace. She travelled first to Egypt, the great school of holy asceticism, in order to visit the ancient masters of the interior life. The learned Rufinus, priest of Aquileia, who was then in Rome, became Melania's travelling companion, and his piety and wisdom made him worthy to accompany her. In the year 372 Melania left Rome, where all were astonished at her courageous enterprise, and rather blamed than praised it. She had had as yet no predecessor, none could tell how the affair would end, and they mistrusted the constancy of youth, and above all were unwilling to behold in this woman a living example of abnegation. The world is the same at all times and in all places. St. Jerome afterwards compared Paula and Melania together, and said: "If Jews and Pagans blamed such lives, it would be tolerable. Yea more, it would be a consolation to displease those whom Christ Himself did not please. But alas! Christians blame this, Catholic Christians seek the mote that is in their neighbour's eye. By their disapproval of the ascetic life, it seems as though they would hope for lighter punishment if whole multitudes were lost with them. If Melania and Paula had wasted their time in visits to the baths, and dissipated their possessions in costly essences and perfumes, and abused their widowhood by unlawful liberties, who knows whether they would not have been called holy women! But now that they desire to serve their God in sackcloth and ashes, in fasting and weeping, in poverty and prayer, they are accused of pride." From these expressions we may conclude that the city of Rome, even the Christian city, was not peopled entirely with Melanias and Paulas. However that may be, and whatever scorn and blame may have been heaped upon Melania, she received brilliant compensation for it fifty years later, when she returned to Rome in a triumphal procession. There is something very glorious about every portion of her life, and it is in this very distinct from the lives of her holy contemporaries, but not the less instructive and edifying. For how perfect must she have been, who, being as it were the cynosure of the Christian world, the woman most renowned for talents and virtue of the fourth century, honoured and admired by a St. Jerome, a St. Augustine, a St. Paulinus of Nola, yet raised herself to that marvellous detachment from every earthly and created thing which the holy abbot Ammois recommends to his monks in the following words: "If a man does not say to himself in his innermost heart, God and I—we are alone in the world; he will never find rest." Perchance Melania had learnt this doctrine from Ammois himself; for she spent nearly a year in Egypt amongst the masters and disciples of asceticism. On first leaving Rome she embarked with Rufinus for Alexandria, where she immediately sought out the holiest men, amongst whom St. Isidore was distinguished, who was superintendent of the large hospital in that place. From his early youth he had led a very penitential and humble life in the desert, and had so completely mortified sinful nature that he resembled an angel more than a man. St. Athanasius took Isidore with him to Rome, where he filled the voluptuous and worldly city with enthusiasm for the ascetic life, and fascinated every one by his winning manners, his explanations of the Holy Scriptures, and his knowledge of divine things. Such a charm of gentleness, goodness, and peace, was imprinted by his faith and devotion on his whole being, that the Pagans honoured not only himself, but even his very shadow. His spirit was often rapt in extatic contemplation, and that not only at prayer or during the Offices of the Church, but in the midst of the brethren at meal times, he would forget his earthly food, letting it fall from his hands whilst holy tears streamed from his eyes, and he sat as it were entranced. If he was asked wherefore he wept in the midst of the joyful contemplation of heavenly mysteries, he answered, "Because I must still live upon earthly food, instead of upon the joys of Paradise." Didymus, the celebrated blind teacher, also lived at Alexandria at that time. He lost his eyesight in his fourth year, and was thereby prevented from learning to read. Nevertheless he attained to such eminence by continual recollection of spirit before God, and uninterrupted attention to the contemplation of divine things, that he became a great interpreter of the Holy Scriptures. He knew by heart, and translated and explained the Old and New Testaments word for word. Once when the Arian disputes brought the great St. Antony to Alexandria, he visited the blind ascetic, and asked him, amongst other things, if he was sorry to be blind. Didymus was confused and silent. But Antony repeated the question, and then he frankly confessed that his blindness was certainly a great grief to him. "O my brother," said Antony, "grieve not that thou art without what even flies and gnats possess. Rejoice rather that the interior sun of knowledge has, by thy exterior blindness, risen so brightly upon thee." Melania frequently visited the holy and learned blind man, in order to profit by his knowledge of the Scriptures. She also went often to a servant of God called Alexandra, who had shut herself up in a sepulchral cavern not far from the city, and had led so solitary a life that for ten years no man or woman had seen her face. Melania says of her: "I have never been able to see the blessed Alexandra. I have spoken with her through the small opening by which a little food is passed into her tomb. I once asked her how she could find it possible to withdraw herself so completely from all human conversation, and to fight boldly against sloth, disgust, and discouragement of mind in such complete seclusion, and without any exterior help." She simply answered: "I cannot explain it any more than thou canst. I only know that I pray and sing Psalms from morning till None, and sew a little linen in the intervals. I spend the remainder of the day in contemplation of the lives of the Patriarchs and Prophets, of the Apostles and Martyrs of Christ. In the evening I eat my bread, and most of the hours of the night pass in reciting Psalms. Thus time flies, and full of confidence I await my last hour that will deliver me, and present me before my Saviour's Face." I asked further: "But what inspired thee, O thou holy servant of God, to withdraw from amongst men, and to retire into this sepulchral cavern?" The blessed Alexandra replied: "A young man loved me with an inordinate affection. I chose therefore to shut myself up alive in the grave rather than to afflict and disturb a soul that was created after the image of God." After ten years Alexandra felt, as so many of the saints have done, that her last hour was approaching. She lay down peacefully and modestly in the posture in which corpses are buried, and thus waited for the desired moment. When the person who brought her food received no answer from her, she was afflicted, and hastened back to the city with the news. People came from thence and broke open the door of the sepulchre. Then the holy and pure maiden was found asleep in the peace of the Lord.

It is, however, obvious from an example which occurred about the same time in the same city of Alexandria, that the outward appearance of holiness often resulted from very opposite qualities. Palladius, Bishop of Helenopolis, who also wrote Melania's life, relates it to the praise of the truly pious, and as a warning to others. An ancient father says, "From the least work that a man does up to his greatest, there is danger of pride in all, both works and thoughts." And pride which turns the soul from God and inclines it towards self is the root of all evil. A virgin of Alexandria had betrothed herself to Christ. She lived quietly and peacefully in her own house, as was often done at that time. She was rich, but instead of thanking the good God for vouchsafing to let her become the poor spouse of the Son of God, pride took possession of her heart, and suggested to her that she was doing a great thing and offering an admirable sacrifice. She listened to these suggestions of the evil one, and regarded herself and her resolution with complacency. This self-complacency brought her by degrees so low that at length she lost her purity of intention and fell a victim to avarice, under the disguise of virtue, that most fearful of all vices, which withers every germ of holiness. She had taken a little niece to live with her, and this child became her idol. She lived very quietly and economically; but neither the afflicted nor the oppressed, neither the poor churches nor the monasteries, ever received the least portion of her money; she hoarded up everything for her niece, and sought to persuade herself that this was virtuous and pleasing to God. St. Isidore grieved to see this unfortunate person departing so widely from her true end, and he attempted to give her a lesson. He went to her and said: "I know of a veritable treasure of jewels that is to be sold, jacinths and emeralds, a splendid bridal adornment for thy niece; and only five hundred gold pieces are asked for it now. Wilt thou pay them? I assure thee that each separate stone is worth much more than that." "I beg of thee to buy them for me," she eagerly said. "Wilt thou not first go with me to see them?" asked Isidore. "Oh no," replied the hypocrite, "thou knowest that I never go into the world." Her heart was longing for the jewels, and she pressed the five hundred gold pieces upon Isidore. Delighted with this sum of money, he left her, and entering his hospital he spent it all on his poor, his cripples, his sick, and his pilgrims. In the meantime the covetous woman waited anxiously for her jewels. But none came, and Isidore never returned. She was filled with uneasiness and fear, and yet she dared not remind the holy man of the affair. At last she could no longer restrain her impatience. She met him in a church and asked him what had become of the emeralds and jacinths. He answered, "I spent thy money upon them immediately; come into my house, I will show them to thee, and if they do not please thee, I will pay thee the five hundred gold pieces back again." This time she did not wait to be pressed, but went with Isidore to the hospital. The men were all together in the lower rooms, and the women above. "Behold!" said he, "how do these jewels of the Church please thee? Are they not worth thy money? Hast thou ever seen emeralds or jacinths costlier than these?" She left the hospital in much confusion, grieving in her heart that she had not given him the five hundred pieces of gold for the poor of Christ voluntarily, but only because she had been compelled to it by his pious stratagem. Her niece married shortly, and died soon after. For whom, therefore, had she laid up her treasures? She entered into herself, and gave herself wholly to God, as she had purposed in the days of her youth, and she blessed the holy Isidore who had given her so salutary a lesson.[1]

Isidore found in Melania a soul so desirous of holiness that he interested himself very much in her, and accompanied her himself to the Desert of Nitria. She remained for six months in the house of the pilgrims, where she was happy in seeing those men who had so mortified their bodies and their passions that the Holy Ghost made them worthy to become His living temples. One of these was Hor, an old man of ninety, with snow-white hair, and an innocent and joyful child-like countenance. In the solitude of the desert he had exercised himself for many years in the combats of a soul which strives after union with God, and clears away from before it every obstacle that it finds between itself and the object of its desires. By means of this spiritual combat, in which victory can be attained only by extreme humility and invincible patience, and in which the most bril-

[1] This master of the hospital is called Macarius by another author.

liant qualities are pitifully worsted without the aid of these two virtues, the aged Hor had risen to so great a height in the interior life that God wished him to become the master and teacher of other souls. For he alone can become a master in any matter who has been himself a disciple and learner. If this is necessary in the simplest trades, how much more so in the most difficult and important of all arts, that of forming souls, and often rebellious and disobedient souls, into the images of God. Thus Hor had come to Nitria, where five thousand brethren looked up to him with love and reverence, for he walked in the light of faith.

A strange brother once appeared before Hor half-naked, and begged for clothes. "Give him none," said Hor to his monks, "but fetch him his own again, for he has hidden them in divers places in order to receive better ones from us." After this no one dared to utter an untrue word. He never spoke but of spiritual things, and he never suffered a syllable to be said about worldly things in his presence. He imparted to others his own experience in the interior life, as a warning and instruction, but always as though he spoke of another. In this way he said in Melania's presence, A solitary was once severely tempted to pride, imagining that God must take great pleasure in his virtue. Then a brilliantly resplendent figure appeared to him and said: "I am contented with thee, O child of man therefore I will raise thee on high before the eyes of all, and take thee to heaven in the body like the prophet Elias; but first adore me." The heart of the foolish monk had rejoiced at first on hearing this speech, but the conclusion puzzled him. He thought to himself, I worship my God and Saviour every day, if this were He, He would surely know it. In silence he made the sign of the Cross and the apparition vanished in smoke. Thus is the ancient serpent ever near to the proud, and he loves to whisper to them: " Ye shall be as gods." Another solitary, said Hor, so loved his seclusion that he could not resolve to follow the call of God, Who had destined him to guide other souls on their road to perfection. He was troubled, and feared to endanger his own salvation by doing so. Then God sent an angel to console him, who said: " Be comforted, it is the Lord who lays this arduous duty upon thee, and who will reward thee more than royally; for the more souls thou dost gain to Him the more degrees wilt thou be nearer to Him in bliss. But beware of self-complacency." Thus did the holy old man relate much that was edifying and instructive, which, as the monks asserted, was his own experience. Melania says of him that no untruth, or oath, or detraction, or even superfluous word, ever passed his lips.

Melania had already imbibed from St. Isidore a high opinion of the ancient father Pambo, and it was changed to the deepest veneration when she came to know him in Nitria. The old man was ever mindful of the advice of his great master, St. Antony: " Trust not thine own justice, and restrain thy tongue." Interior humility and exterior silence are two watchful sentinels before the portals of the heart. Melania relates, with amiable candour, what happened to her in her first visit. "Isidore, the priest of God, led me to the blessed Pambo, who sat diligently at work, weaving palm-branches into mats. I caused three hundred pounds' weight of the silver vessels that I had brought with me from Rome to be placed before him, and begged him graciously to accept this gift, and to use it for the necessities of the monasteries. ' May God reward thy charity,' said Pambo to me; and he added to one of his disciples, ' Take this and see that it is assigned to our brethren in Lybia, and in the islands,[1] for they are often in great need. But

[1] The ancients called the oases islands, because they lie in

give nothing to the Egyptian monasteries, for in this fertile land they suffer no want.' In the meantime I stood there waiting to see if the holy old man would give me his blessing, or at least say a friendly word. But he was silent, and the silver was carried away without his vouchsafing it a single look. Then I said, 'My lord and father, that thou mayest know what I have brought thee, let me tell thee, it is three hundred pounds' weight of silver.' I spoke in vain, however, for without turning his eyes upon me, the servant of God replied: 'My daughter, He on Whom thou hast bestowed this gift has no need to learn from thee how many pounds it weighs. The mountains and the hills lie in His balance; He therefore knows already the weight of thy silver. If thou hadst given it to me, it would have been well to draw my attention to it. But as thou didst give it to God, Who counted and praised the widow's mite, it would have been better for thee to be silent.'" The servant of God died soon after, gently and painlessly, without any disease. He was plaiting a basket when his last moment arrived. He sent for Melania, and said to her: "I have nothing to give thee, save this basket; take it, and remember me." But to the brethren he said: "Since I built and inhabited my cell in the desert, I have never eaten a piece of bread that I had not earned by the work of my hands, nor poken a single word that I have repented of; butsI now perceive, my brethren, that I have not yet begun to lead a pious life." Melania gave away gold and silver with lavish hands, but she would not part with the basket and the sheepskin that Pambo and Macarius had given her.

the desert like islands in the sea. The great Lybian oasis was called by the Greeks the island of bliss, on account of its fruitfulness.

She once heard the instruction which the aged monk, Pinuphius, addressed to a young novice on his reception, and to some others. "From this day forth the world must be crucified to thee, and thou to the world, according to the teaching of the Apostle Paul.[1] And if thou wouldst know how that can be accomplished in this life, I tell thee that our cross is the fear of God. He who hangs on the cross cannot move his members as he wills; in like manner we must make our wills and wishes entirely dependent on the commands of God. He who hangs upon the cross is dead to the world, and to creatures, even though his heart may still beat; so must we be dead to earthly joys, and our mind must be fixed solely upon eternity, into which we may be called at any moment. He who hangs upon the cross no longer desires the earthly things that he has left; we also must let our whole soul be so penetrated with the fear of God, that we may feel a sincere contempt for the world and temporal things. And this contempt is the true mother of humility. For if we set no value upon anything earthly, we despise our own will, our comfort, and our works; and if we do this, not with our lips alone, but with our whole hearts, we are humble. The signs of humility are these; when a man denies his own will with complete abnegation, when he manifests his thoughts and deeds to his spiritual father in childlike simplicity, and submits them to his judgment; when he practises obedience with patience and meekness in everything that is commanded him; and when he does no one any injury, but bears those he receives with equanimity; when he bridles his tongue, and considers himself the least of men. Humility is the beginning of our salvation, for it fills the heart with contrition, which destroys our selfwill. The abnegation of our selfwill roots out vices, and

[1] Gal. vi. 14.

upon their extirpation follow the fruits of virtue. Virtue gives purity of heart, and the pure heart attains to perfect love."

She heard many more instructions from the holy and wise fathers of the desert, which were indeed chiefly intended for monks, but which are well worth being laid to heart by all men. For example:

"Beware of despising thy neighbour, for thou knowest not whether the Spirit of God is in him or in thee."

"Selfwill is a wall of metal betwixt God and man."

"There is no greater virtue amongst men than to despise nobody except yourself."

"How can a Christian attain to true humility?" asked a young monk. "By continually pondering over his own sins," replied an old man.

"If," said Macarius, "a monk is indifferent to blame or praise, riches or poverty, eating or fasting, he will not have a bad death."

"Alas!" said he, "if our distractions in prayer and our negligence in psalm-singing were all laid to our account, we could hardly be saved."

"Poverty, humility, and patience in tribulation are the best tools of the monk," said the abbot Moses.

The abbot Fœmen was told of a brother who fasted six days in the week, but who was nevertheless much given to anger. Pœmen exclaimed, "Oh! if he would only think more of overcoming his anger than of practising himself in fasting."

"He who lives amongst other men should be like a statue that is not elated when it is praised, nor angry when it is despised."

"If our works do not correspond with our fervour in prayer, all our labour is in vain."

"Flies and insects do not settle on a dish that is boiling, but only on one that is cool; so the temptations of the devil do not venture to attack a monk who is burning with the fire of divine love, but only those who are lukewarm and slothful."

"If a man fights bravely he will gain many a victory."

"He who would be saved must be of good heart on every occasion."

But Melania heard also of the fruit which these doctrines produced, the marvellous obedience, which was practised to a supernatural degree of self-denial. Two young novices were sent through the desert with a basketful of figs to a solitary who was ill. They lost their way and were starved to death. They were afterwards found dead in the position of prayer, and in the basket beside them not one fig was wanting.

The disciples of the abbot Sylvanus reproached him for loving Brother Mark more than all the eleven others. This complaint reached the ears of the other ancient fathers, and they went to Sylvanus in order to call him to account. Instead of defending himself he led them to the door of each cell, at which he knocked, and called the brother by name. But none of them came out at the first call. Mark's cell was the last, and Sylvanus had hardly knocked there before Mark stood on the threshold and asked his commands. Sylvanus sent him on some message, and then entered the cell with the other fathers and showed them how punctual Mark's obedience was, for he had been engaged in copying, and he had left the letter O without finishing it. The fathers were amazed and said, "Thou art indeed right in loving Mark, and we will also love him in future, for there is no doubt that he is very much beloved by God."

The abbot once said to John the Dwarf, "Catch for us the lioness that makes the road to church so unsafe for the solitaries." John took a rope and went towards the lonely little church. He had not long to wait for the lioness, but instead of attacking the holy man she fled before him. John ran after her calling out, "Stand still, my father has commanded me to catch thee." And the savage beast stood still, and let itself be bound. Late in the evening the abbot, to his great amazement, saw John coming, quietly leading the lioness by a rope. To preserve his humility, he hastened to meet him, and giving him a few blows on the shoulder he said, "Foolish man! how canst thou bring the wild beast hither?" John then gently released the lioness from the rope, and she fled back to her wilderness.

Rufinus, who accompanied Melania everywhere, and who lived even longer than she did amongst the ascetics, expressly says: "In all the monasteries the first and most distinguished virtue is obedience. The abbot will receive no monk who has not been much tried during his time of probation, and proved that he will not refuse to obey any command of the abbot's, however difficult or unjust it may be. For this reason the brethren who live in community are no less perfect than the solitaries." Rufinus also testifies that he saw with his own eyes, in the court of one of the monasteries, the little tree which was the proof of the perfect obedience of John the Dwarf, during the three years that he did nothing but water a dry stick at the command of his abbot, Pachomius. At the end of that time the little tree blossomed and bore fruit, which the holy abbot brought to the assembly of the brethren, saying: "Taste the sweet fruit of holy obedience." All the fathers agreed in the opinion that God required nothing more from those who devote themselves to the spiritual life than the laborious practice of holy obedience, but an obedience so perfect as to obey not only the abbot and other superiors, but even the least of the brethren for God's sake. It was related that a monk out of envy once said to his holy companion: "Go down into the Nile to the crocodiles." The obedient brother did so willingly, and the crocodiles came and licked his feet. For "the creature waiteth for the revelation of the sons of God."[1] That man who is crucified by holy obedience is a child of God, and a brother of the Son of God who made the Cross His sceptre. Abbot Hyperichion therefore said: "He who possesses this virtue will obtain all that he desires, and will appear without fear before the Face of our Lord Jesus Christ. For he follows to the Cross our Lord and Saviour who was obedient even unto death." Melania also heard much that was beautiful of the peacefulness and childlike simplicity of the anchorites. The following story, amongst others, pleased her particularly:—Two aged fathers had inhabited the same cavern in the desert for very many years. They had always lived in perfect concord, because they vied with each other in wishing and in doing nothing but the will of God, so that there had never been the smallest difference of opinion between them, still less any dispute. Their meekness was so great that they could not conceive how it came to pass that people could quarrel. Then one of the holy old men said to the other: "My brother, we serve God so easily and joyfully that we have no merit in our concord. Let us try to create a little disturbance between ourselves. That often happens in the world." "As thou pleasest, my brother," replied the other: "only I do not know whence discord should come." "Strife and quarrels in the world generally arise from the assertion and defence of mine and thine," answered the first. "Very well," said the other; "then each of us shall assert that this stone which I place between us belongs to

[1] Rom. viii, 19.

himself, and so we shall quarrel." The holy old man laid his hand on the stone and said, "This stone, therefore, belongs to me." "No, to me," said the other, stretching forth his hand also. "I declare that it is mine," affirmed the first one. "Then keep it, my brother!" gently replied the second, and the dissension never came to pass.

The Emperor Valens, who favoured the Arians, waged a fierce persecution against these defenceless lambs of Christ, during the time that Melania was in Egypt. Then she blessed God the Lord for her riches, for she supported five thousand monks who had been driven from their peaceful cells, and she also assisted the persecuted bishops and priests; thus making an heroic confession of the Catholic faith. Rufinus was also involved in the persecution, but Melania escaped by the special Providence of God, who wished to make use of her for the benefit of his servants in exile and poverty. The Arian governor of Alexandria sent, at the command of the Emperor, eleven Egyptian bishops, the abbot Paphnutius of Scete, the abbot Isidore of Hermopolis, and many priests and solitaries—in all 126 persons—to Diocesarea in Palestine, and Melania courageously followed these confessors of Christ, and provided them with all the necessaries of life like a faithful daughter and sister. The governor of Syria had forbidden any assistance whatever to be given to these confessors. He would willingly have put them secretly to death, but was afraid to do so publicly, and therefore let them succumb under privations and misery. But Melania took care that this should not happen, and however strictly she was watched, she found means to corrupt the guards, and to convey food to the prisoners. In order to be unobserved she put on the dress of a slave, and crept by night to the holy confessors. The governor of Palestine heard of the large sums that she distributed with unbounded generosity amongst the prisoners, and hoping to extort a ransom from her he cast her into prison. Then with calm dignity she sent to say to him, "My name is Melania, I was the daughter of a Roman Consul, the wife of a Roman Senator, but now I am the handmaid of Christ, and for this reason, and not from fear nor to conceal myself, do I bear the garb of poverty. Dream not, therefore, that thou canst terrify me. I make this communication to thee that thou mayest know with whom thou hast to deal." On hearing this the governor immediately altered his demeanour and released her, treating her with great respect, and allowing her thenceforward free access to the confessors. After their banishment was at an end Melania went to Jerusalem, and there built a monastery, into which she withdrew with fifty pious widows and virgins, in order to serve God with prayer and labour, in poverty and seclusion. Whilst this rich and noble woman lived in the utmost poverty and lowliness for more than twenty years, she accomplished immense works of mercy, both corporal and spiritual. Her royal income flowed in unceasingly from Rome as though it were oil for the ever-burning lamps, and it as unceasingly flowed out of her hands again over the whole Christian world. If any church, monastery, hospital, or prison was in suffering or need in the South or the North, from Persia to England, Melania came to their assistance, and found means of succouring them. She was a "Consolatrix afflictorum" of all the Christians throughout the Roman empire. In Jerusalem she founded a refuge wherein she received pilgrims, strangers and travellers, poor and rich, sick and healthy, seculars and ecclesiastics, and provided for all according to their necessities. When these people from all lands and nations returned to their own homes and spoke of the glories of the Holy Land, they reckoned amongst them this blessed Melania and her works of charity, and thus even in her lifetime she was called blessed among strange peoples in distant lands.

St. Jerome reverenced Melania so much that he called her a second St. Thecla. He could give her no better name than that of the spiritual daughter of the Apostle St. Paul, the first Christian woman that was martyred, whilst Melania was also the first woman in her time and of her rank who crossed the sea to serve God in that place, in which He Himself had taken the form of a servant. Like a second Mary the prophetess, she led the daughters of Israel through the desert, singing hymns of penance, and she drew them after her in crowds into the heavenly Chanaan. Palladins says of Melania, "She lived so as to injure no one, but to benefit nearly the whole world. For her gentleness and love opened all hearts to her, and her piety led her to use this salutary influence to work upon souls and win them to heavenly things." A monastery in Jerusalem was infected by the heresy of Macedonius, who denied the Holy Ghost to be the Third Person of the Godhead. Four hundred monks were involved in this error. As they suffered in temporal things also, and sickness and much tribulation visited them, Melania took advantage of the occasion of affording them assistance in external things. Thus she became acquainted with the most influential amongst them, and by degrees she turned her sympathy towards their spiritual necessities, and by her gentle wisdom became the instrument of God to bring back these wandering sheep to the right path, and to reconcile them to the Church.

A youth of the name of Evagrius once came from Constantinople to Jerusalem, and took shelter in Melania's Refuge for pilgrims. He was ill, and he continued so in spite of medical treatment and careful attendance, for an internal fever wasted him and withstood all remedies, having its seat in a diseased soul and fevered heart. Melania perceived this, and therefore bestowed especial sympathy on the unfortunate youth. She gained his confidence so far that she ventured one day to say to him: "My son, thy sickness has no natural cause. Thou wilt never recover so long as thy spirit suffers. What is it, then, that tortures thy mind? Tell me, my son; perhaps by God's grace we can help thee by other means than medicine." Then Evagrius answered: "Thou art right, my mother! no doctor in the world can help me; only the grace of God and the prayers of souls that love Him." And he shed floods of tears. Melania said lovingly: "God's grace is boundless, and here in the monasteries we have holy souls who will willingly storm Heaven day and night on thy behalf; wherefore confide to me thy distress." Then Evagrius said: "I was born in Pontus; the kind and learned Bishop Gregory of Nyssa perceived good qualities in me, and ordained me first lector, and then deacon. When he travelled to Constantinople for the affairs of the Church, he took me with him, and Nectarius, the Archbishop of that place, thought that I should make a good combatant against the manifold monstrous heresies which prevailed there, and would not hear of my leaving him. I wrote and preached against every kind of heresy, having large audiences, and gaining much praise; but, alas! my heart became inflamed with sinful love for the wife of a nobleman, who on her side had a guilty attachment to me. I feared God, and earnestly implored him to save me from the terrible temptation; but I would not do what could have saved me. I did not fly, and the longer I remained, the more powerless I became against the evil passion. Then I cried out to God for help in my distress, and He sent me a vision in sleep. I was thrown into a dark prison, and an angel appeared to me and said: 'Thou wilt perish here unless thou dost flee at once. Swear to me upon this book of the Gospels to leave the city to-morrow, and I will aid thy flight.' Rejoicing in the hoped-for deliverance, I took the oath and awoke. But the voice of the angel sounded ever in my ears, and I seemed constantly to hear the words—'Here thou wilt perish.' The prison that held me was Constantinople, and the chain that bound me was sinful love. I gathered up all my strength, and taking my goods on board a ship I fled to the Holy Land. But alas! the wicked enemy has not left me, he is always tormenting me with the terrible temptation to throw off my ecclesiastical habit and return to the world, there to live as worldlings live." When Evagrius had thus manifested his inconsolable grief, Melania lovingly said: "Certainly, my son, thou art in great need of the assistance of prayer, and we will earnestly implore Almighty God to restore strength to thy body and soul; but thou must first promise Him to do sincere penance if it pleases Him to lengthen thy days." Evagrius promised, and Melania and all the holy souls who lived with her ceased not to implore God's mercy upon the severely tried youth until He sent His heavenly legions to combat for him, and help him to overcome the ancient enemy of our salvation. He recovered, and found peace and strength once more in his resolution of doing penance. Melania brought him his ecclesiastical dress, and when he had put it on, he set out for Egypt and Nitria, where he first began the practices of the ascetic life, which he afterwards followed in the desert called Cellia, or of the cells. He spent fifteen years in these deserts fighting with his nature and his evil passions. He never touched any other food but raw herbs and water; and if fasting and prayer did not succeed in putting to flight the enemies of salvation, he used heroic means, as on one occasion, when being violently assailed by temptations to infidelity and blasphemy, he spent a fortnight under the open sky during the fierce heat of an African summer. He underwent this foretaste of the punishment of the damned in order to preserve himself from everlasting fire. Another time he was attacked by the impure spirit: then he descended into an icy cold river full of poisonous reptiles, and remained therein until he was half-frozen by the coldness of the water. But the reptiles did not bite him, and the unclean spirit departed from him, seeing that he dreaded the death of the body less than the death of the soul, and that he overcame the temptation by the holy fear of God. In this manner Evagrius consumed his body and his life; but God's grace so filled his soul with the Holy Ghost that he was celebrated far and near for wisdom, knowledge, and discernment. He was so dead to flesh and blood, that when the news of his father's death was brought to him, he smilingly said to the messenger: "It is well for me that I have an immortal Father in Heaven, Almighty God.'

It is very instructive to human infirmity to hear that this holy and prudent Melania once stood on the brink of a dangerous precipice. Rufinus, whom Palladins calls the gentlest and most learned of men, lived in a monastery upon Mount Olivet, at Jerusalem, and from thence he made frequent journeys into Egypt and to Sinai, to visit the monks. It was probably in Alexandria, where Origen had taught in the catechetical schools at the beginning of the century, and where his memory was held in the greatest veneration, that Rufinus was inspired with so great an admiration for that noble mind, that he embraced, without examination and without exception, all the opinions and doctrines taught by him; and even translated his Periarchon, a work that had been published anonymously in Rome, and had done much harm there, as has been related in the life of St. Marcella. This caused the abrupt cessation of the friendship that had existed for so many years between Rufinus and Jerome. The opponents of Rufinus reproached Melania for having been, as they declared, captivated by the errors of Origen, and for having zealously defended and propagated them. Perchance God let her fall into this spiritual danger in order to try her, and to prove whether humble submission to the authority and decisions of the Church in matters of faith was one of her many virtues. If possibly she had valued too highly in Jerusalem the opinions of Origen, yet when she learnt in Rome that the Church had condemned them, she proved herself to be so perfect a Catholic that she edified even the saints.

It was some important family business that led Melania to Rome in the year 397. Her son Publicola was worthy of his mother. Having married Albina, a noble Roman lady, he lived with her in a happy and holy marriage. He now sought a brilliant alliance for his highly-gifted daughter Melania, who with the name had also inherited the character and disposition of her grandmother; and he betrothed her at the age of thirteen to Pinian, a noble young Roman, then seventeen years old, the son of Severus, who had been prefect of Rome. The marriage was a happy one, for both husband and wife had been brought up in the purest principles of Christianity, and lived in accordance with them. In their hospitable house they joyfully and generously received strangers that came to Rome; but they preferred ecclesiastics, and above all, those who had suffered for the faith. Palladius lodged in this house when he came to Rome, in company with the great and persecuted Patriarch of Constantinople, St. John Chrysostom. He had formerly known the elder Melania in Jerusalem, and all that he related of her filled the heart of her granddaughter with such veneration for her, that she made her grandmother her highest model of genuine Christian perfection. She had borne her husband two children, who both died in infancy. She considered this loss as a sign from God that He desired to detach her from earthly joys, and draw her closer to Himself, and with a pure mind and glowing heart she sought to induce her husband to consent to her wish of living henceforward in sisterly friendship with him. She said to him: " God would not have required our children of us if He had wished us to occupy ourselves with earthly things." And her supernatural desires won from Heaven the grace that her husband should take the same resolution. He was then twenty-four, and she was twenty years old. She began at once to lead an ascetic life, eating only every other day, and serving her own servants. She dressed with extreme simplicity, and made her costly garments into ecclesiastical vestments. She sold all her diamonds and other valuables, and sent the proceeds to the monasteries and hermits of the East by the hands of the holy priest Paul. Paul went, amongst the rest, to Dorotheus, a solitary in Egypt, and gave him five hundred gold pieces, begging him, in Melania's name, to spend it in alms in a manner pleasing to God. Dorotheus answered: " I do not understand how to deal with these treasures. Take them to a brother who knows more than I do about such matters. I will keep three pieces, in gratitude for the good-will of the donor."

Melania the elder heard with great interest of the determination of the youthful pair, although it was not approved by the rest of the family. She thought it her duty to support her granddaughter in her difficult position, and to encourage her and Pinian to persevere in following the call of God. She had then just succeeded in effecting the reconciliation of Rufinus and Jerome. They had heard mass together in the Church of the Resurrection at Jerusalem, and had joined hands publicly. Melania passed indefatigably from one good work to another; and leaving Jerusalem she embarked at Cesarea, accompanied by various holy men and women, and landed safely at Naples. Her whole family had journeyed thither from Rome to meet her, not only Publicola and Albina, with Melania and Pinian, but also all those of her relatives who were Christians. Amongst them were several Roman senators, who travelled with all the pomp of their condition, and received the poor servant of Christ in golden chariots, drawn by splendid horses in sumptuous harness, and surrounded by numerous and magnificently dressed attendants.

The apostolic life of the early Christians, who had "one heart and one soul," flourished at that time all over the world, even to a greater degree than in the times of the Apostles. There were, it is true, divisions and heresies, and as a necessary consequence of these, dissensions, enmities, and apostasy; but those who remained firm in the faith, the true Catholics, were intimately united and held intercourse with each other from East to West. St Paulinus of Nola gives a very pleasing picture of this friendly meeting, and of the refinement of life prevailing amongst persons of the highest ranks. He himself was descended from a noble Roman family, which possessed large estates in France, and he was born at Bordeaux in the middle of the fourth century, his father being prefect of Gaul. He was brought up and instructed by the celebrated and learned poet Ausonius, who was a Christian only in name. At the early age of twenty-five Paulinus received the consular dignity at Rome. He was blameless in his morals, generous to the poor, and upright in the duties of his office, and he was encouraged in all his virtues by his noble wife Teresa, a rich and well-born Spaniard, whose heart was inflamed with a desire for greater perfection. In a journey to Bordeaux, Paulinus made the acquaintance of St. Ambrose, Archbishop of Milan, and St. Martin, Bishop of Tours, and his conversations with these holy men taught him that there was greater happiness in intimate intercourse with God than he had heretofore tasted, although his life had been so prosperous and blameless. According to the custom of those times, Paulinus was still a catechumen, although he was thirty-six years old. He now caused himself to be baptized by St. Delphinus, Bishop of Bordeaux, and the grace of the sacrament so enlightened him that his past now appeared to him full of faults and infirmities. In order to withdraw himself from the dangers of the world, and to labour more effectually for the sanctification of his soul, he gave up his offices and dignities and retired to one of his estates in Spain. Teresa joyfully followed him into solitude. His marriage had hitherto been childless; he was now gladdened by the birth of a son; but it was only to impress the more strongly upon him the fleetingness of all earthly happiness, for the child died when it was only a week old. Paulinus and Teresa lived together henceforward as brother and sister in the observance of the evangelical counsels of chastity and poverty, and devoted themselves to works of heavenly love, which increases in proportion as earthly loves die away. They both intended to go to the deserts of the East and dedicate themselves to a life of the severest asceticism. They sold all their possessions in Spain and Gaul, and spent the price of them in munificent almsgiving. They freed captives, paid the debts of the poor, and gathering all the needy around them, they clothed.

fed, and lodged them. This new course of life was thought by some to be madness, and by others injustice; but the great saints, who were so plentiful in that age, rejoiced over these holy deeds. Paulinus never suffered himself to be moved by blame or calumny, but always answered: " Oh blessed scorn that is shared with Jesus!" Things went so far that even his own slaves, whom he treated as brothers, refused to perform the slightest service for him, because they thought his humility and poverty unworthy of his position. He bore the trial with invincible constancy, and his most violent censors became suddenly changed into panegyrists.

At Christmas of the year 393, all the people of Barcelona desired to have him for their priest, and although he himself opposed it to the uttermost, the Bishop was constrained to bestow holy orders upon him, without observing the customary intervals of time between the different ones. Paulinus consented under the condition that he should not be bound to stay at Barcelona; and after Easter, in 394, he gave all that remained to him in Spain to the poor; and, after relieving innumerable wants, he went to Nola, in the south of Italy, where he possessed a small estate, the last that was left of his immense possessions. Nola is situated not far from Naples, in Campania, which was the favourite resort of the Roman nobility, on account of the sea-bathing and the beautiful scenery and climate. The most lovely and luxurious villas were scattered over the land; but, in the course of time, when their owners were converted to Christianity, these became the abodes of asceticism and penance. The country house of Paulinus was spacious, but very simple, and it lay close to the church which was built over the tomb of the holy martyr St. Felix. It was this situation that attracted Paulinus. He renounced all the offices, dignities, and privileges that his rank or his riches secured to him, and from being a Roman consul and senator, he became a poor monk, a watcher and door-keeper at the tomb of a holy martyr. Some like-minded men soon joined him, with whom he formed a monastic community. They lived, worked, and prayed together. One wing of the building was divided into cells, and the other into larger rooms. The former was destined to the reception of ecclesiastics, and the latter to that of seculars. Teresa took loving charge of the household.

Melania came hither with her companions. We do not learn whether she was related to Paulinus or was his friend, or whether they only knew each other in God as belonging to the same supernatural family of God's children. Paulinus himself describes the visit that Melania made to him. He had a friend in Aquitania, Sulpicius Severus, whom he had induced to follow his example in leaving the world, and embracing the ascetic life just at the time when he was the object of the greatest reproach. Severus lived in a village near Toulouse, with his former servants and slaves who had become his spiritual brethren, in the same manner as Paulinus at Nola, and their friendship was not diminished but heightened by their mutual love of asceticism. Paulinus wrote thus to Severus:—

"We have received that holy woman, who has returned from Jerusalem after twenty-five years of absence. What a wonderful woman she is! The strength of God is immeasurable in her. She was received at Naples by her children and grandchildren, and she came to our poor little dwelling at Nola with a numerous retinue. The pomp and magnificence of the world with which her relatives had filled the Appian Way encompassed her with gold and purple, whilst she herself wore a coarse black dress, and sat contentedly upon a mean little horse.

Her simple humility outshone all their splendour, and the rich were struck by her poverty, the worldly by her sanctity, while in her heart she smiled at their amazement. It was a beautiful sight, and redounded to the g of God, showing how the pomps and superfluities that she had despised now spread themselves at her feet, as though inviting her to rejoice in the victory she had gained over such vanity. But it was also beautiful to see how those rich people, her children, who had inherited poverty of spirit from their mother, rejoiced far more in her poverty than in their own riches, and thought it a great honour to touch her poor mantle or the hem of her black dress. We praised God from our hearts, who exalts the humble and fills the hungry with good things. Although our dwelling has only one story above the ground it took in all these guests, because it is a long building, and divided into many cells, so that we received Melania's pious companions from Jerusalem, as well as all her noble relatives. The peace of our house was not disturbed thereby, for whilst we with Melania and her women sang psalms to the praise of God in the neighbouring church of St. Felix at the appointed hours of the day and night, and fulfilled our spiritual exercises, the remaining guests lived very quietly, and showed by their silence their respect for the saints; thus joining in their fashion in the praises of God. If thou wouldst hear more about this chosen dove Melania, know that fasting is her refreshment, prayer her rest, and the Word of God her food. I read aloud to her the little book of the life and deeds of St. Martin of Tours, which thou didst send me about that time, as she takes great delight in such histories. She has brought me a little particle of the Holy Cross from the Bishop of Jerusalem, and the accompanying small piece of the Holy Wood is for thy worthy mother Bassula from her servant, my sister, Teresa. But you are both of one heart, one mind, and one faith, and therefore it will belong to you both. In remembrance of the King of Glory having hung upon this Wood, and the rocks having been rent for love of Him, we will rival the hard stones and bruise our hearts with the salutary fear of God."

The bond of intimate confidence which united these holy persons was very beautiful. They were all not only baptized Christians, but sincere followers of the Cross, and as that particle of the Cross had come from pious hands in Jerusalem, and passed to Campania and the distant Aquitania, so the spirit of sanctity that united them had descended also from the Cross. In those days holiness was not looked upon as something half impossible and half unnatural, something to be afraid of; but was simply held to be something supernatural, a grace which must be believed in and loved, a working of the power of God in loving souls. And hence sprang those beautiful and blessed families, those groups of saints which grew up around chosen souls, and which impart something so fascinating and attractive to life in the Church; just as the starry groups seem to make the nightly heavens more near and familiar to man.

Melania the elder went afterwards with her whole family to Rome, where she joined a glorious company of holy women. Marcella, the aged widow, lived with her adopted daughter Principia upon the Aventine; Fabiola lived in her hospital; Asella was superioress of a monastic community; Paulina, daughter of St. Paula, by the side of her noble husband Pammachius, vied with him in works of mercy; and Læta, the holy widow of Toxotius, in the place of her only daughter Paula the younger, whom she had sent to the monastery at Bethlehem, had adopted all the poor as her children. Melania's daughter-in-law Albina, and her granddaughter now took their places amongst these numerous holy women, and, whilst she encouraged them along the paths of perfection, she succeeded in effecting a brilliant conversion. Her niece, Avita, was married to a rich nobleman called Apronianus, who was learned and distinguished, but bitterly opposed to Christianity. Melania so won Apronianus by her talents, and edified him by her virtues, that he consented to receive from her instruction in the Christian faith. And as he persevered in this resolution, and opened his noble mind to eternal truth, a flood of light penetrated, as it were, into his heart, and took such complete possession of it for God, that henceforward there was room in it for nothing save God alone, nothing, that is, in the order of nature, but everything through God, with Him and in Him. Man can embrace the whole world in his desires and passions, but he cannot possess God and the world together. In proportion as he sacrifices the world, and seeks to mortify and overcome himself, and to place his desires firmly and solely upon God as the supreme Good, in like proportion does he enter into the order of grace, which, by another process, helps him to obtain once more all things in Him. In this new order of things he will find first God; in God the Incarnate God Christ; in Christ the whole of humanity which is indissolubly bound up with the Godhead by the gracious mystery of the Incarnation. Very many of the new converts in the first centuries went through this process in marvellous perfection. They embraced eternal truth so strongly and deeply in their purified hearts, that there was no room left in them to harbour anything that was transitory. The simple and reasonable conclusion at which they arrived was to gi their one heart to the one God, the flower of their love to the King of love, the fulness of life to the Lord of life. And this was done not once or twice only, but name after name of those who did so succeed each other on every page of the history of those early Christian days. Apronianus became one of these. By his baptism in Christ he felt himself to be "buried together with Him," and he entered upon the paths of the highest perfection, in which his happy wife accompanied him, more joyfully than she had ever done along the deceitful rose-strewn paths of the world. And this was not enough. Even his children, Eunomia and Asterius, followed the evangelical counsels after the example of their parents, and lived in abnegation, virginity, and helpspoverty, and that most beautiful of all things upon earth, the holy penance of a pure heart.

Melania, the widow, would gladly have seen her son Publicola in the ascetic company of her family rather than in the Roman senate, rather in the garb of penance than in splendid clothing, because her maternal affection feared the least shadow that ambition and vanity might cast upon him. But Publicola was one of those few men who can take part in all the affairs of the world without letting himself be ensnared by them. The fear of God and the humility of his mother had entered into his soul, and kept him free from self-complacency and pride in the midst of all seductions. He was very intimate with St. Augustine and St. Paulinus; and kept up a confidential correspondence with them; and Paulinus speaks of him as "the man in a high place, who does not think highly of himself, but who, on the contrary, puts himself on a level with the lowest, after the example of our Blessed Lord; and who takes pity upon the poor." But the day came at last on which he followed his mother's advice in part at least, and withdrawing from the capital of the world, retired into the tranquillity of private life.

Paganism was so firmly rooted in Rome, the queen of the heathen world, by the immense power of a tradition which had all that is pleasant and welcome to the senses on its side, that in the beginning of the fifth century the Christians were hidden amongst the heathen, like veins of gold amongst masses of baser metals. This gold had to be extracted from the mine, and freed from dross, which was not feasible by other than violent means. The emperor Theodosius published an edict in 392, which forbade idolatry and all its customs, under severe penalties. In 399 the Emperor Honorius commanded all the temples in the country to be destroyed, but those in towns to be preserved as works of art and ornamental public buildings. But there remained other temples which no edict could demolish—the hearts of men who cherished their own idols, and the universal manners and customs of public life. The Emperor Constantine had indeed prohibited the games of the gladiators, and yet they were continued in this way—that although there were no gladiators, criminals condemned to death were made to contend with the wild beasts. One of these feasts was given in the year 395, by the Emperor Honorius, at Milan, where he then resided. They did not cease in Rome till the year 404, when the holy hermit Telemachus precipitated himself into the bloody arena to stop the combat, and thereby lost his life. This sacrifice of Christian love triumphed over the heathen abomination. But the Roman people were unnerved, and averse to labour, loving nothing save gambling, the theatres, and dissolute revelry. Their temple and favourite abode was the circus, which they much preferred to their own homes, and where the chariot races were held, in which they took the most passionate delight. The Roman was excessive in his pursuit of pleasure on the one hand, whilst on the other he was oppressed and miserable, tyrannised over by the rich, and unjustly treated by the judges; so that if a person fell into poverty, he became the slave of any one who gave him relief with the object of bringing him into servitude. The noble descendants of the ancient senatorial families, lived as indolently as the populace, and as dissolutely, the only distinction between them being that made by riches. Surrounded by their slaves and flatterers, they had no taste left for anything but the joys of the table, the baths, and the theatres, or perchance for the chase or for play. With many it was thought fashionable to disbelieve in their gods, and to practise astrology, and arrange their hunting or pleasure parties and other affairs according to the favourable or unfavourable position of the stars. Christianity and holy asceticism grappled indefatigably with this unnerved and demoralised populace, now winning more and now less important victories, until at length Divine Providence sent them auxiliaries, who first changed the whole city into a fiery crucible, in which the pure gold of Christian Rome was purged from the dross of the heathen city, and she then became, for the first time, the capital of the Christian world. Hitherto Rome had been a Babylon; and until this state of things was changed, she could not fulfil her destiny and become the centre of a spiritual kingdom. Divine Providence placed this necessary cleansing and winnowing in rough hands, namely those of the barbarians. The whole epoch is full of their campaigns, their undertakings, their audacity, and their victories.

The elder Melania judged rightly of the times, and it was no selfish desire to regain the peace of her cloister, that urged her to say to her people:

" My children, remember that it is written: 'It is the last hour.'[1] Who knows whether the days of tribulation are not at the door ? Let us abandon the vanities of the world, and in the stillness of the cloister let us serve God, and do penance for all those who do none." Her warnings were so urgent and so strongly confirmed by what was going on in the world, that Publicola and Pinian, with their wives, determined to seek a new home. It cost them much pain to sell their palaces, for the Roman senate disapproved of the measure, and many of their relations were strenuously opposed to it. But they were not to be turned aside, and on this occasion Pinian and Melania the younger set free eight thousand of their slaves. They left to Pinian's brother some others who would not have been able to make any use of their liberty, and they only kept for themselves as voluntary servants fifteen, who would not hear of living separate from their beloved masters. They sold their possessions in Spain, France, and England, and gave the price of them to the poor, even to the last farthing. They kept their estates in Campania, Sicily, and Africa, to have the means of giving further alms; and as the swallow abandons her nest when the house is falling into decay, so did they now abandon the palace and the city of their fathers, and go at first to Sicily. They were hardly gone before Alaric and his Goths began the first siege of Rome, which he only raised temporarily for a heavy ransom, and which he renewed successfully two years later. It is characteristic of the decay of the Roman power, that when Alaric departed and pitched his tents in Etruria, forty thousand slaves ran away from Rome, and followed him. Melania the elder praised God that her family had escaped the fearful tribulation that seemed to be pouring itself upon

[1] I John ii. 18.

Rome out of the vial of the destroying angel of the Apocalypse. Plague and famine, fire and sword, raged in turn, and the noble Christian women alone were faithful to the practice of neighbourly love during this time of terror.

Melania and all her companions crossed the seas to Africa, whither Publicola and Pinian were attracted by their friendship for the Bishops of Hippo and Tagaste. These two bishops were St. Augustine and his friend St. Alypins, who had been converted with him. The saintly family settled in Tagaste, and lived there in the manner they had already practised for many years, both in Rome and at their country house in Campania. Every hour of the day had its appointed holy occupation: prayer, psalmody, reading, and contemplation of the Holy Scriptures, visits to the poor, and the care of the sick alternated with each other. A part of the night was also dedicated to the praise of God in solemn Matins. Earthly things received but little attention, and food and sleep were reduced to the lowest possible measure. Their estates in Campania and Sicily were sold for the sake of the needy, and they lived scantily and poorly on the proceeds of their Numidian lands, in order to give away more and more. This happy and holy family lived as if they were a choir of angels come down from heaven to show men how to love and worship God. Publicola died soon after their arrival in Tagaste. His holy mother wept for him in silent grief. St. Paulinus of Nola thus writes about his death to St. Augustine. "He was so meek and humble of heart, according to the teaching of Christ, that we can have no doubt of his salvation, for the meek shall possess the land, and shall please Almighty God in the land of the living. Therefore his descendants have already become powerful in this world, and exalted among the great ones of the earth, and the blessing of grace rests upon his house and race. But I, a poor sinner, cannot speak worthily of this holy man, my dearest friend, nor of his saintly mother, because I am too far below them in virtue Thou who by thy holiness dost shine in the Church of God as a bright light and a teacher of the truth, wilt know better than I do how to praise duly these courageous souls."

The task of the elder Melania was now fulfilled · her relations on earth, as well as those in heaven, were united to God. She was free to follow the attraction which had separated her so early from the world and led her into solitude. She longed for perfect seclusion from all that was not God, and what she had done in her youth, she did once more in her old age; she took ship for the Holy Land and returned with peaceful joy to her widowed monastery. But the earthly Sion could no longer retain Melania, who was ripe for the heavenly Jerusalem. On her arrival she distributed the small residue of her immense fortune to the poor, and after she had spent forty days in complete denudation with her Saviour in the desert, He called her into His heavenly kingdom by a peaceful death in the year 410.

The holy bishop Alypius blessed God for sending his friend Pinian to Tagaste, and thus placing an example so worthy of imitation before the eyes of his flock. The monster of heresy, which ever goes hand in hand with political and social disturbances, had made great inroads in Africa, and had introduced poverty and confusion into the Catholic churches. This made such examples of humble submission and Christian charity doubly necessary. Pinian and his family lived entirely for the interests of the Church. They were not contented with helping the oppressed, but they also assisted those souls that felt themselves called to a higher perfection, by building two monasteries, and endowing them with sufficient revenues. In one of them eighty monks, and in the other one hundred and thirty virgins, served God night and day. The church at Tagaste was beautiful and spacious, but very poor. Pinian supplied it with altar vessels and decorations, and furnished it worthily for the celebration of the most Holy Mysteries. The holy vessels that held the worshipful Body and Precious Blood of our Divine Saviour; the candlesticks and lamps that burnt before His tabernacle, the thuribles from which fragrant incense arose to His honour, were all made of gold, and adorned with precious stones. Melania and Pinian would not think of withholding their diamonds when the King of the universe had not spared His own Blood. They also made over to the bishop sufficient estates to provide for the wants of the Church, and many a parish envied that of Tagaste its generous guests.

Pinian had wished for some time to visit St. Augustine at Hippo. He travelled thither with Melania and Albina, accompanied by St. Alypius. Here the Donatist heresy prevailed, and was opposed by St. Augustine with all his power, which caused a certain uneasiness of spirit amongst the congregation. They were so edified by Pinian's holiness, that one day an occurrence took place which was not rare in the early Church; at the beginning of the holy sacrifice of the Mass, the faithful surrounded Pinian so closely that he could not escape from them, and implored St. Augustine to ordain him priest. St. Paulinus had been thus ordained at Barcelona, and St. Augustine himself at Hippo. Both thought themselves entirely unworthy to execute the duties of a priest, and refused to receive holy orders, as so many holy men both before and after them have done, who either perceiving it to be the holy will of God finally submitted, or withstood even to the end. Pinian did the latter, and fled back to Tagaste with his family, whereupon a general tumult arose in Hippo. Nevertheless, he was completely determined to lead a spiritual life without embracing the ecclesiastical state. He remained seven years more with his family in Tagaste. The favourite occupation and sweetest recreation of them all, was reading and copying together the works of the great Fathers of the Church.

If grace were not God's free gift, we might reasonably be surprised to find that there was still a heathen in this family, namely Volusian, Albina's brother, a very intellectual man, learned in science and in Pagan philosophy, who became afterwards Prefect of Rome and Proconsul of Africa. About this time he wrote to St. Augustine laying before him some questions about the Incarnation of God, and the miracles of Jesus. At the end of the letter he said, "It is not surprising that every priest cannot answer these questions satisfactorily. But if recourse be had to Augustine, and he cannot answer them, it will convince me that there is some imperfection in the Christian faith." The saint replied to Volusian: "In all that concerns me, believe me and not others; give up the high estimate that you have formed of me. The science of Christian doctrine is so deep that if I had studied it, and it alone, from my earliest youth till the most advanced age with the utmost zeal and diligence, and with much more intellect than I possess, I should daily make new discoveries in it. I do not say that the things necessary to our salvation are so difficult to discover; but the more faithfully they are examined, the greater mysteries of Divine Wisdom unfold themselves. The most powerful mind, and most penetrating intellect, must confess what the Scripture says: 'When a man hath done, then shall he begin.'"[1] But in spite of his correspondence with the most enlightened and holy of bishops Volusian remained for the time unconverted.

[1] Eccl. xviii. 6.

In the year 417, Pinian undertook a pilgrimage to Jerusalem, and went thither with Melania and Albina through Alexandria, and across the desert. At Jerusalem they met Pelagius, whose heresy about grace and free will was so ardently combated by St. Augustine, and they had such lively controversies with him that he confessed himself overcome, and condemned his own heresy. They announced this joyfully to St. Augustine. But heresy has its seat more in the stubbornness of the will, than in want of understanding; and Pelagius, like many other heretics, might be convicted of heresy a hundred times without renouncing it. St. Jerome and the younger Paula received at Bethlehem with great joy and love these souls who were spiritually united to them. From thence, Pinian and Melania made a journey to the Syrian and Egyptian monks and solitaries to prepare themselves for a life similar to theirs. Albina now separated herself for the first time from her daughter, and settled in the convent at Jerusalem founded by her mother-in-law, the elder Melania, in which the spirit of that holy woman still reigned supreme. It was, however, not lukewarmness but great age that hindered Albina from accompanying her children upon their laborious journey. They returned from it still more inflamed with holy love, and Pinian founded at Jerusalem a community of thirty monks, in which he lived separated from Melania, and occupied in spiritual exercises and the cultivation of his garden. She, on her part, founded a convent, but she was not to be persuaded to undertake the superintendence and guidance of it. She sought out a solitary cell on Mount Olivet, where she might dedicate herself undisturbed to mortification and heavenly contemplation. This favoured soul spent the remaining fourteen years of her life in that complete abnegation which seems pitiable to the earthly mind, but which, on the other hand, is esteemed as a token of election by the saints and the angels in heaven. Melania's habit was of sackcloth, her bed a straw mat upon the bare ground, her table a block of stone, her furniture holy writings, her nourishment bread and water every fifth day. Of all the holy Roman women of that time, none practised such severe austerity as the younger Melania. Her fame spread from her retired cell over the whole world.

In the year 433, Albina died; she had loved her daughter with a twofold love, first as her dear child, and secondly as her model of Christian perfection. But she did not live to have the joy of seeing her brother Volusian won over to Christianity. He was ambassador to the Emperor Theodosius II. at Constantinople, and was held in great honour and consideration there when grace suddenly touched his heart. He wrote to his niece Melania, and expressed the wish to see her once more. She was very desirous to be of service to him, but so humble that she did not believe she could make any favourable impression upon him. The enlightened and holy men whom she consulted, urged her earnestly to make the sacrifice of undertaking this journey for her uncle's sake. She chose, therefore, a suitable escort, and set out upon her way. At all the places where she stopped, bishops and priests, monks and nuns, and also all the faithful of both sexes who lived piously in the world, received her with great honour and greeted her as an angel from heaven. She arrived safely at Chalcedon, a city of Bithynia, situated on the Asiatic shore of the Bosphorus, opposite Constantinople. There she suffered a moment's discouragement and fear. It was more than a quarter of a century since she had left Rome and kept apart from the world, and for the last nine years she had lived in extreme poverty and seclusion. And now she had left her narrow cell that was so peaceful, and was about to enter the great tumultuous and luxurious Byzantium, which lay outspread before her eyes, in its beauty and magnificence, divided from her only by a narrow arm of the sea. She feared the dangers that threaten every soul in the world, and the spiritual pride that might so easily tempt her through her circumstances and position. Then she turned away her eyes from the enchanting picture, as her Divine Saviour had done when the devil showed Him the kingdoms of this world from the high mountain, and she went to the hospice that belonged to the Church of St. Euphemia. This virgin martyr had laid down her life amid the flames for the Name of Jesus, in the year 307. A church had been built over her relics on the seashore, and also a house for pilgrims, into which Melania entered. She spent the night in prayer before the altar of the martyr of Christ, and there received such great consolation that the next day she joyfully entered the little ship which carried her to Constantinople. Melania and her companions found a habitation prepared for her in the house of Lausus, the chamberlain of the Emperor Theodosius, who was a very pious man. Volusian was ill and could not visit her, and Melania therefore hastened to him. When he saw her whom he had last seen in Rome in all the glory of her youth, beauty, and position, and whom he now found so poor, so meanly clad, and with that appearance and expression which makes men unsightly in earthly eyes, but beautiful in the sight of heaven, he exclaimed: "O Melania, how art thou changed!" She seized the opportunity of answering him thus: "This change proves to thee more forcibly than any words the power of the Christian faith. For what could have induced me to sacrifice all that on earth is called happiness, and to renounce every pleasure and joy, if I did not share with the Apostle St. Paul the belief that the sufferings of this time are not worthy of the glory to come, and that we enter into the kingdom of God by tribulation? But every tribulation is sweetened for me by faith in the promise of the Son of God, that those who renounce earthly happiness for His sake shall be rewarded a hundred fold in eternity." Thus Melania explained her life to Volusian by Holy Scripture, and rendered Holy Scripture intelligible to him by her life. The doctrines of the faith, and the life by faith, are necessary to each other, and explain each other. Melania went to Proclus, the holy Patriarch of Constantinople, and begged him to visit Volusian sometimes during his sickness, and to influence him favourably towards the Christian faith by his holy and spiritual conversation. Proclus promised to do so, and kept his word so faithfully that Volusian was accustomed afterwards to say of him, "If there were but three such men in Rome, Paganism would shortly be known there only in name." Volusian never recovered from his illness, but his soul received its health. He was converted with his whole heart to the Catholic faith, and received the Holy Sacrament of Baptism. Melania was attacked by a severe pain in her foot, which made her lame and confined her to her room, preventing her from visiting Volusian for some days. But the joyful news of his baptism cured her on the spot, for she then knew that he was saved for eternity. She would have been unspeakably grieved if he had died without baptism. She hastened to him and never left him again. Volusian died a blessed Christian death, filled with spiritual consolation, and nourished by the precious Viaticum of the true Flesh and Blood of Jesus Christ. God had willed to make use of Melania and not of St. Augustine, as the instrument of his conversion.

Melania's happy influence did not restrict itself to Volusian during her stay at Constantinople.

The Nestorian heresy of two persons in Christ, which infatuated so many in Constantinople, notwithstanding the condemnation of the Council of Ephesus, was as a sharp sword to the heart of the orthodox Melania. She indefatigably opposed the false doctrine by means of the Holy Scriptures, which she had imprinted in her memory by long study and by the explanations and illustrations she had gained from contemplation and the inspiration of the Holy Ghost. From morning to night she gave audience to all who sought from her instruction in the knowledge of the truth, or any other spiritual assistance. What she had formerly done corporally she now did spiritually, namely works of mercy. Her earthly goods had been all spent in almsgiving; therefore she was now allowed to dispense spiritual and imperishable goods. She led back many deluded souls to the true light, and she kept others firm in the right road. The Empress Eudocia, with her refined and educated intellect, knew how to prize rightly Melania's talents, and took pleasure in seeing her frequently. Melania took advantage of this affection to endeavour to detach the imperial pair, if possible, from their affection for worldly pleasures and glory, to which they were excessively devoted, like so many who are placed in a high position. Melania sought to rouse the yielding disposition of the emperor into a determined opposition to every heresy, but the excitable and imaginative empress she endeavoured to win to the seriousness of a life of faith by the consideration of heavenly things. The descriptions that Melania gave of the Promised Land, of the Holy Places of Jerusalem and Bethlehem, the asceticism of the solitaries and monks, the devotion of the pilgrims, and the graces they received, so impressed the empress that she persuaded her husband to give his consent to her making a pilgrimage to Palestine. The betrothal of her daughter Eudocia, with Valentinian, the emperor of Western Rome, was then going to take place, and Theodosius agreed to allow her departure as soon as the solemnities connected with it should be over. At length Melania escaped from the golden prison of Byzantium, which she willingly exchanged for her beloved freedom. Pinian died shortly after her return home. Supernaturally consoled, she saw him depart to take before the throne of the Lamb that place to which she had with holy love urged him forward. She had understood as referring to perfection, the question of the Apostle St. Paul in the First Epistle to the Corinthians: "How knowest thou, O wife, whether thou shalt save thy husband?"

In the meantime, Eudocia had set out upon her pilgrimage. She travelled through Asia Minor and Syria, lovingly bestowing large alms everywhere, and she was received in Jerusalem with respect and joy. Melania and many religious women went forth solemnly to meet her; but the empress showed still greater honour to the saint than the saint to the empress. Eudocia called Melania mother, and all the nuns of the convent founded by her, sisters, thanking God for two great graces; first, for having reached the Holy Land and Jerusalem; and secondly, for having there become, at least in spirit, the daughter of such a mother. Eudocia stood at that time upon the highest pinnacle of earthly grandeur, being empress of the Eastern Roman empire, and mother of the young empress of the West. She little thought that she should revisit Jerusalem after a few years more under very different circumstances. The Emperor Theodosius died before he was fifty years old. His sister, Pulcheria, mounted the throne, and Eudocia became empress-dowager instead of reigning empress. Neither was her daughter any longer empress, but the prisoner in Africa of the Vandal King Genseric, and her son-in-law, Valentinian III., had been murdered. In search of consolation, she fixed her habitation on the place sanctified by the bitter Passion of the Son of God, and she probably often thought of Melania, who by a voluntary sacrifice had placed herself beyond the reach of all temporal sorrows. In the year of Pinian's death Eudocia made her first pilgrimage. At Jerusalem she was present at the consecration of a new church. During the holy function she slipped and sprained her foot, which was cured by the power of Melania's prayers. The violent pain would have made it impossible for her to have assisted at the solemn ceremony, and her departure would have created a disturbance. Full of confidence, Melania made the sign of the Holy Cross upon the injured foot, and the token of salvation wrought a cure. Eudocia returned soon after to Byzantium.

Melania lived four years longer in increased penance and austerity. She spent the holy festival of Christmas in the year 439 at Bethlehem, and returning from thence to Jerusalem, she repaired to her convent with the sure foreknowledge of her approaching death. She informed her spiritual daughters with certainty that the hour of her departure had arrived. Loud lamentations were heard in Jerusalem. They did not grudge Heaven to the saint, but they were reluctant to spare her from the earth. She comforted all, both ecclesiastics and pious seculars, who with many tears visited her. She exhorted all to persevere in virtue, pointing out its heavenly rewards, and, on the 31st of December in the year 439, she died, full of holy confidence in God Whom she had so ardently loved.

ND - #0027 - 220822 - C0 - 229/152/17 [19] - CB - 9780267753529 - Gloss Lamination